THE SPORT HORSE PROBLEM SOLVER

What Works, What Doesn't, and How to Make It All Better

Eric Smiley, FBHS

TRAFALGAR SQUARE

North Pomfret, Vermont

First published in 2023 by
Trafalgar Square Books
North Pomfret, Vermont 05053

Disclaimer of Liability
The author and publisher shall have neither liability nor responsibility to any person or entity with respect to any loss or damage caused or alleged to be caused directly or indirectly by the information contained in this book. While the book is as accurate as the author can make it, there may be errors, omissions, and inaccuracies.

Trafalgar Square Books encourages the use of approved safety helmets in all equestrian sports and activities.

Library of Congress Cataloging-in-Publication Data
Names: Smiley, Eric, 1951- author.
Title: The sport horse problem solver : what works, what doesn't, and how to make it all better / Eric Smiley, FBHS.
Description: North Pomfret, Vermont : Trafalgar Square Books, 2022. | Includes index. | Summary: "Former international event rider Eric Smiley channels the immense knowledge he has gained starting his own horses for decades. Most horses, unfortunately, do not get "the right start," and the result is a mount with behavior or training problems that are difficult to pinpoint and solve for optimal performance. Smiley addresses the most common issues he sees in dressage, eventing, and show jumping circles today, including problems with head and neck position; connection issues; lack of understanding of forward, straight, and regular; factors that interfere with collection; and a lack of consistency. Smiley provides an easy-to-follow system to determining what's wrong and gives you sensible exercises and methods for fixing it"-- Provided by publisher.
Identifiers: LCCN 2022011178 (print) | LCCN 2022011179 (ebook) | ISBN 9781646011193 (paperback) | ISBN 9781646011209 (epub)
Subjects: LCSH: Horses--Training. | Horse sports.
Classification: LCC SF287 .S545 2022 (print) | LCC SF287 (ebook) | DDC 636.1/0835--dc23/eng/20220708
LC record available at https://lccn.loc.gov/2022011178
LC ebook record available at https://lccn.loc.gov/2022011179

Diagrams by Emily Secrett-Hill
Cartoons by Penelope Daukes

All photographs courtesy of Eric Smiley except: 1.1 (Chris Dundee); Maria Sage (figs. 3.5, 3.6, 4.2 A—D, 4.9, 4.10, 9.3, 9.4, 9.5 A & B, 9.14); Ami Clark (fig. 4.4); Megan Kelley (figs. 4.11, 4.14, 5.2 B); Lotte Koefoed (figs. 4.6, 4.7 A—C); Annie Penfield (fig. 5.3 A); *Horse & Hound Magazine* (figs. 8.2 A & B).

Book design by Maria Mann
Cover design by RM Didier
Index by Andrea Jones (JonesLiteraryServices.com)
Printed in China
10 9 8 7 6 5 4 3 2 1

To Sue, my soulmate and wife, who continues to make my journey with riding and coaching and our life together with horses, an absolute delight.

CONTENTS

Finding a Place to Start

WHEN I TEACH, PEOPLE SELDOM SAY TO ME, "I HAVE A LOVELY trot, can you help me make it better?" The focus is usually on their problems: "Why does my horse knock rails?" "Why is my horse's neck so short?" "Why can't I score higher than a '6' on my canter?" And on it goes.

The unfortunate fact is, solutions are not easy to come by. Why? In part, because everything having to do with horses and riding is so complex. Problems cannot be viewed in isolation—they are by nature inter-related, and thus, it's sometimes difficult to know where to start.

Some problems have physical origins. In order to develop a keen sense of what is "normal" and "abnormal" behavior from our horses (so we can pinpoint when injury or a conformational flaw may be in play), we must cultivate the crucial skills of looking at and watching our horses (the topic I cover in chapter 1—see p. 15).

More frequent, however—and sometimes trickier to solve—are problems originating from errors in training. In many of the cases I encounter in my teaching and training, the baggage that follows a horse on his journey through life isn't his fault through his breeding or nature; it is actually something he picked up along the way *in his training*. Often, these little problems that occupy much of our time have been there for a while and were never identified or resolved when a young horse was being started. Of course, sometimes we create our own problems, rather than inheriting them from others.

Either way, this book focuses on how to diagnose and address these types of training problems. But before we get into the business of solutions, I want to talk a little bit more about where problems come from and why they are often so difficult to fix. In my experience, it comes down to a lack of understanding—on the rider's part, the horse's, the coach's, or all of the above.

The Growing Divide Between Horses and Humans

The advent of the technological age has totally changed our lives. It has changed everything about us: the way we live, the way we think, how we interact with people and expect people to interact with us. There is nothing we do today that isn't affected by technology. And this includes when we go and visit our horse.

Because our way of thinking and doing has been so changed, it has become harder for us to understand horses and adapt ourselves to their way of receiving information and learning tasks. The gulf between us and them has been growing as technology has become more a part of our lives. This trend, coupled with the education system, has made people more dependent on being fed information than finding it out for themselves.

At the push of a button, we have easy access to information, but this can fool us into the belief that we know more than we do. Our perceived knowledge is way above our actual knowledge—we are instant experts. As a result, we have become less curious.

Yet the horse remains the same, largely unchanged by the evolution of the human species.

We have invented many methods of explanation to try and bridge the gap between horse and rider, including books, videos, articles, clinics, lessons, and technological gizmos. Each of these is used in an effort to make things more clear and to improve our understanding of what we should be doing to make our riding experience more rewarding. But if we don't grasp how learning happens, how to use these sources, and how the overall picture should look, we will never succeed in fixing what is wrong.

The Problem of Overfacing

The development of the mind and body, either human or equine, to perform at its optimum goes through many stages before it reaches its peak. Along the way, it encounters mental and physical barriers, which must be overcome if it is to be the best it can be. Some of these challenges improve the resolve to succeed, while others leave scars that impede progress or even threaten the realization of the ultimate goal. How do we keep our horses and our partnership with them on the right track?

Education should be an enlightening experience full of understanding, but the success of all forms of education depends on adhering to a progressive system: one step at a time, layer upon layer of information, you build a solid foundation, progress to the next level, and so on. This applies to both physical and psychological challenges, especially in the early years of development. To move from one stage to the next requires a confidence in where you are and a belief that where you are going is within your capabilities. Without this solid base, progress is uncertain. This is true of humans in their education but is even more true of horses whose education is guided by humans.

How often have we heard of parents entering their children for a competition that is above their level with reasoning such as, "It'll be good for them," "They will see what the standard is," "It will show them what to work on"…only for the child to be knocked out at the first metaphoric hurdle and come home deflated.

On the way home the parent then says, "Don't worry, it'll be better next time."

But the chances are that it won't be. A *marker of failure and for failure* has been put in place and that is very difficult to overcome.

Draw the same analogy with a young horse. Move him up in level to gain experience, only to find that he knocks fences or has run outs. The *marker of failure* has been laid down. Or he tries so hard to please and jumps clear, but the next time out he remembers the experience as being unpleasant and performs badly. Now that *marker of failure* has had a confirmation. Bad news.

This is what's known as *overfacing*, a term that is defined as: *to intimidate, especially by presenting too great a task or obstacle*. Although the word is typically associated with asking a horse to jump something beyond his ability, it can be equally useful when applied to other aspects of training, including groundwork and riding on the flat. It's crucial, in fact, that we embrace this broader understanding so we don't become the architects of our own problems by pushing a horse too far, too fast. For just one example of the perils of overfacing, consider Thoroughbreds that begin a racing career at age two—those that go on to retire sound in mind and body are in the minority.

Most horses come with "baggage."

Horses are generous animals, constantly curious, and willing to take an interest in most things that are asked of them. Very few are disingenuous, which makes them good students. The key is to stimulate their interest, understand their limitations, and be cautious not to take advantage of their desire to please. In stimulating their interest we must set achievable goals. This is how we create a pathway to learning: with clear, well-planned steps, direction, and plentiful rewards as we go. With *interest* and *achievement* much can be done.

These are the fundamentals of *Progressive Training*.

A Year-by-Year Breakdown

Ultimately, the goal of any horse's journey should be for longevity, in his sport or just in his life as a nice riding horse. Horses that are still competing at the highest level when they are well into their teens tend to have been brought up the correct way.

In simple terms:

- A four- to five-year-old is starting.
- A six- to seven-year-old is learning the mechanics and skills of his trade.
- An eight- to nine-year-old is developing and improving these skills.
- A ten- to fourteen-year-old is in his prime.
- Fifteen years old plus is bonus time.

The most critical years are between four and five and then again when a horse is seven. At seven there is a temptation to think of them as mature and adult. But that would be foolish. This time of life is fragile, as horses are beginning to show what they can do (their potential) but are not yet secure, either physically or mentally. To make a mistake in either physical or mental development can leave scars they may never recover from. However, using this time to consolidate experience, skill, and confidence at the appropriate level will allow horses to learn to believe in themselves and the future.

PROGRESSIVE TRAINING:
The Key to Avoiding Problems from the Start

In a world changed dramatically by technology, questions can be answered at the press of a button. But with everything and everyone moving so fast, we don't always have an understanding of the information we're consuming. However, when humans have to interact with and train horses there is a need for understanding how horses learn—we must slow down and make sure we are communicating clearly and that the message is getting through. Otherwise, there's a lot of room for misunderstanding.

We know horses learn from *repetition* and what's known as *conditioned responses*. The more often we repeat a task, the more they understand how to do that task. Little is learned from the kind of cognitive processing that takes place in the human brain—it's more about the creation of a habit.

It is our responsibility to not confuse the horse in the course of our training.

It is, therefore, our responsibility to ensure that each habit or piece of the jigsaw puzzle is taught correctly and in the correct order so that a correct picture emerges. We need to be patient and methodical. Only then can horses begin to understand what we are asking them to do.

In the beginning, we introduce horses to the concept of a relationship with humans by handling them, putting on tack and equipment, and generally getting them accustomed to people and some of our requests. We are careful not to ask too much and ensure that the horse understands each step along the pathway.

The more we do, the more we expect the horse to stay with us on the journey. But the more we must also be attentive to signs that he is struggling or finding things too difficult.

Horses will react to overfacing in their own characteristic ways. Some "down tools" (refuse to work), and say, "I don't understand. It's too difficult. I can't cope." Others run away (literally or metaphorically), avoiding the question that they can't find a solution to. Others will hurry through the question the best they can without any understanding.

We need to understand each horse's way of dealing with their concerns, learning to discern when a horse has a can-do attitude and tries to work out the solution but needs help.

What we do not want is the horse to be left with anxiety about the question, for anxiety creates a doubt in his mind each time the question appears. Think of a young horse being introduced to trot poles on the longe line for the first time. I had a three-year-old, for instance, who just stopped and said, "No!" Because I knew his character by that time, and that of his family members, I understood that he was really saying was, "This is new and I don't understand."

> *To become a 'really good horse trainer' takes an enormous tolerance for systematic schooling, day in, day out. There's not much in the way of drama, not much place for strong emotion, just that quiet perseverance that chips away, little by little, to create a calm, unworried, well-trained animal. Who has that much serenity, that much ability to avoid exasperation, that simple adherence to correct basics?*
>
> —Denny Emerson, Author of *Begin and Begin Again; Know Better to Do Better; and How Good Riders Get Good*

Some horses react to being overfaced by becoming resistant or aggressive.

When a horse has a can-do attitude, there is a chance you can work through any lack of understanding with good communication.

When we repeated the exercise, the young horse trotted through a few times but stood on every pole! Next, he hurried through and jumped the last two poles. What he was saying this time was, "I can't get my trot to fit into these distances," or, "Your distance is wrong!"

But we stuck with it and after two days of quiet explanation he got it and looked very pleased with himself as he adjusted his own stride and accurately measured the distance between each pole. He understood the question, and we were able to move on from a place of confidence and trust to new and harder skills.

The unsure horse is not likely hesitating for no reason. Seek to clarify what you are asking for, and you can go from "maybe not" to "maybe."

To Solve a Problem, Find a Start Point

As you might expect, it is easier to get things right from the start when training young horses—they're a clean slate. But training and retraining are not confined only to young and older horses respectively. Horses of all ages develop unwanted habits no matter how hard we try to avoid them. At all times we must be conscious of where things are correct and reproducible and mark that as a *start point*—a place of security and stability where the horse is confident that he knows the right thing to do. The goal is to build a series of these correct reference points in our training as we go along, painstakingly assembling one on top of another to establish a strong foundation that won't come apart when challenged. At any time, if something goes wrong, tension arises, or a misunderstanding occurs, it is possible to return to a start point—to go back in a horse's training to a place where we know the response is secure and correct, and to regroup and fill in any blanks in the horse's education before moving forward again.

Overfacing challenges a horse's (and sometimes the rider's) security, which is how many riding problems come about. A start point is a very important tool to help us with both the effective execution of progressive training and retraining plan. Returning to these places of security will be a key part of our approach to solving problems throughout this book. Finding this common ground is how I work in a clinic situation. Once found, it is easier to take the horse and rider in the desired direction.

WHEN EXPERTISE IS LOST IN TRANSLATION:
Another Barrier to Solving Problems

It is equally important to understand the stresses placed on riders—both young riders and adults—in their education. Expectations come from many sources: parents, siblings, fellow athletes, instructors, or the riders themselves. As a result, they, too, are often overfaced, pushed too far too fast without sufficient understanding of what is correct.

As coaches, we need to understand how humans learn at each stage of their development and meet them at their level. The trick is to use appropriate language to make sure that what we teach is understood by every student. Often people don't want to admit that they don't understand for fear of appearing stupid. I was certainly like this when I was younger. But this reticence leads to guesswork and further misunderstanding.

The responsibility for understanding falls mostly to the coach. Words matter (something I will talk about more in chapter 2—see p. 15). Experts should strive to explain complicated and weighty subjects in layman's terms so that the ordinary person can feel involved, engaged, and enthused. But all too often, they fail. The Expert is proud to be known as an Expert. It is an acknowledgment that the Expert has "made it" in a profession, received a certain status, and been rewarded for endeavors. They tend to mix easily with other Experts; it's a sort of members-only club. They talk a certain "knowing" language, that only those who have reached the dizzying heights of being an Expert can really understand.

When the public listens to Experts talk, there is an air of respect that pervades. We admire the confidence, the lofty language, and the grasp of the topic so eloquently explained. But underneath there is another thought that is far too embarrassing for most people to admit: *they haven't understood a single word!*

Oh, if only we had more experts who could make things clear and offer concrete, easy-to-understand solutions to our problems. Using words that are simple, explaining the rationale behind our instruction, and practicing within a rider's and a horse's capabilities should not be thought of as patronizing but as critical to the building of a solid foundation. Only with this beginning can the human understand how to guide the horse correctly. Again, the concept of finding a start point comes in handy.

When I was teaching some Pony Club members recently, a group of instructors was in attendance on a Progressive Development day. Between lessons, I was asked, "Why do you always return to basics to start each lesson?" My answer was that I returned to whatever point I found a common understanding between horse and rider because to continue without it would ultimately cause problems for both.

A Roadmap Through This Book

Let's step back now and look at the bigger picture. As important as the idea of a start point is to problem-solving, it's not where the process begins. There are many stages to this process.

In order to overcome challenges big and small, we need to develop a clear understanding of how things should be and then follow a clear, methodical approach to diagnosing and addressing a problem that is hindering our progress. Like most clinicians, my mind works its way through multiple steps when working with a horse and rider:

1 What is the problem?

2 How, when, and why did it arise?

3 Why does it need solving?

4 How can we formulate a plan, finding a start point?

5 What do the results of our experiment mean in the context of now and the future?

Throughout the book, we will cover a good deal of the most common issues encountered in riding, applying the above five-step process wherever possible. There will undoubtedly be cross-referencing going on throughout. As I've mentioned, most issues we encounter with horses are so complex and multilayered, they cannot be considered on their own, but must be seen as interrelated. That's real life and part of the development of *horsemanship.* It requires learning to break down the big picture into simple tasks and skills and put the pieces together again. I hope this book will help in that endeavor.

Here's what to expect in the pages to come.

Chapters 1 and 2 will further explain how we begin. The first chapter deals with what we see when we look at a horse, both with and without a rider. Learning to look at and watch our horses is really about developing greater awareness. We get to know horses, observing them in their natural state so we can detect anything out of the ordinary and rule out conformation, lack of soundness, or other health issues as the origin of our problems. It's also important to be able to accurately assess ourselves and our capabilities as a partnership. In chapter 2 (p. 34), I briefly cover the necessary qualities we must develop in our riding and why I've decided to focus on certain qualities over others. My goal is always to make things simple and understandable as clarity is too often absent from instruction. If you've read my other books, much of the discussion of riding qualities and the scales of training will be familiar to you, but please humor me and read them again.

Chapter 3 (p. 37) looks at the foundational qualities of *forward, straight,* and *regular* and their fundamental importance to all riding whether we're solving problems (retraining) or enjoying horses, riding correctly. We'll look at how things *should* be so we can pinpoint where things have gone awry, working through problems that commonly arise within each of the three qualities.

The next three chapters do the same for the qualities of *contact* (chapter 4—p. 69), *connection* (chapter 5—p. 113), and *consistency* (chapter 6—p. 147). Chapters 7 and 8 (pp. 161 and 193) turn to issues with jumping and in chapter 9 (p. 211) I talk about how to actually solve problems riders encounter (with position, coordination of the aids, and effective communication with their horses in general).

Seeking Moments of Illumination

Nothing much changes in the horse world, but everything is new to the newcomer.

I never mind covering the same ground year in year out and watching as this journey of discovery happens. The light bulb moments along the way ignite the inner glow of curiosity that becomes a burning ambition for more. These moments of illumination—reached only by grappling with our issues—are fun for both coach and pupil.

However problems materialize, we have to deal with them. We have to solve the puzzle that hinders us from achieving what we want with our partner. The quest for solutions and progress will occupy much time and thought, will cause much frustration, require many hours of help, and produce endless hours of happiness in the process. Our problems may never be totally resolved but the journey will ultimately make us better horsemen.

Although the focus of this book is on problems, I believe the journey must be a positive one. While we shouldn't ignore the fact that some things don't work as well as we want, our troubles will often diminish in their importance if we opt for positive actions.

I admit that I do not have a crystal ball. I do not have an answer for all problems and why they have appeared. Nor will my solutions be the only possible solutions out there. Where I have misgivings about methods, I will give my reasons why. The book is not meant to be an exercise in criticizing methods or practices, but rather a way to explain a possible reason for a problem and a route to a solution. My hope is to always leave people and horses with a positive journey to go on, with the prospect of "better to come."

CHAPTER 1

Developing Awareness of Our Horses and Ourselves

*The biggest communication problem is
we don't listen to understand, we listen to reply!*

THE SUBJECT OF THIS BOOK IS PROBLEM-SOLVING, AND IN ORDER to be a good problem-solver, you need to know right from wrong and good from bad. Understanding how you have arrived where you are may give you a route to a solution. You should also know what the ultimate goal looks like and how the journey to arrive might unfold.

Developing a keen awareness of your horse and yourself is essential work for every horseman. Doing this begins with learning to look at and watch your horse, paying attention to conformation, the function for which he was bred, and his way of going. Spending time getting to know your horse and what is normal and abnormal in terms of their behavior and movement will clue you in to issues with health and soundness. It will also help you map out your training or retraining plan for the particular challenges you're facing. You must be discerning in choosing which methods to follow. In making these judgments you need to think logically, with clear thoughts of the changes that need to be made. Know what is possible and what is not—this takes an awareness of your capabilities as a trainer and rider as well as the ability to accurately and fairly assess results.

Do not change everything at once, but allow the horse to assimilate each correction before moving on to the next. Understand how to execute the correction and the likely responses you will get from the horse as you go through the process. There will be times these corrections will only be partiality accepted and it is important to know that many partials can come together to make a complete picture. You need to know when to press the point and when to back off or to be creative in how you encourage the horse to "let you in" to join him on his journey. Always be watchful for signs of overfacing (see p. 3). Our horse's welfare is our top priority.

Learning to Look and Watch

Although we often use the verbs "looking" and "watching" interchangeably, they are actually two very different experiences.

To look means to direct your eyes in a particular direction.

To watch means to observe someone or something for an amount of time and pay attention to what is happening.

As horse enthusiasts, we spend a lot of time *looking* at horses. It is, indeed, a pleasure all in itself. They are the most wonderful animals to look at. But we must also become accomplished at *watching* if we are to increase our awareness of the animal and how we should approach our relationship to them and our work together.

Do we always know what we are looking at? What aspect of the horse draws our attention and why? What makes us like or dislike the way he does things? Why do we like this horse's jump or that horse's trot or canter?

How do external influences such as what we read, listen to, or see relate to what's in front of us? There is a skill to *horse watching*, a skill that only improves with practice and an informed awareness of what we are looking at. Improving our understanding of how the horse is put together, and how he moves, thinks, and reacts, helps our interactions with the horse when we ride, train, and compete. Watching improves our horsemanship.

What Are We Watching For?

When watching horses, we should be methodical, thinking in "compartments." It's a little like seeing a horse for the first time with a view to purchase.

- Look at the whole picture to form an initial opinion of the individual.
- Focus on the details of the horse's conformation.
- Study the paces when the horse is being led in-hand.
- Watch the horse under saddle.
- Assess the three paces.
- If required, watch the horse jump.

A dressage judge will assess a partnership based on many of the same factors, looking at the overall picture, then the correctness of the paces and the way of going, followed by the accuracy and quality of the movements in the test.

As part of your evaluation, ask yourself:
- Are the components in proportion?
- Does the picture look right?
- Does anything stand out and if so, why?

By standing back and looking at the whole, we will be able to answer these questions. I'm not suggesting that you should be put off a horse if the animal isn't perfect, just that you should be aware of any imperfections and how they might cause issues in the future.

In younger horses, there may be a "filling out" of the body in adulthood that will improve the proportions, for instance. Or an older horse may have a shortage of muscle bulk that needs addressing. Otherwise, the weakness may be reflected in the way he works.

In general, conformation is the structure and biomechanics of the horse and the gaits are the way the horse moves. My intention is not to write a book on conformation—there are many others out there on the topic if you want to learn more. I'm merely arguing that learning to look at and watch your horse, including how he is put together and how he moves in each gait is important to our training and our ability to solve problems. Let's briefly look at each in turn.

CONFORMATION

Conformation is the accepted shape and structure of the horse—the way he has been put together. It has been argued that the correct structural shape functions better and stays sounder. All showing classes are based on this premise. So we should have some knowledge of what the correct shape looks like.

To begin with, we should know what discipline we want the horse to do. Each equestrian discipline will have different priorities (fig. 1.1). For example, racehorses that sprint will need a strong, powerful hind end and can get away with a neck slightly lower on the shoulders. A dressage horse will need a neck built more uphill and to be less on the forehand. The horse has to have a form that functions in its chosen role. When choosing horses, we need to be aware of this, as there are implications to function if we ignore form, and vice versa. This is especially important for us to understand when we change the roles horses are used for. We must always strike a balance between function and form.

1.1 The horse should be built in a way that is appropriate for his discipline. This horse has a nice head-and-neck conformation and has Thoroughbred-type characteristics that can help him excel in the sport of eventing.

When looking at the conformation of a horse, do so with a plan. Looking at every horse with the same plan will ensure you become practiced at it. Eventually, the process becomes second nature and we miss less. Personally, I always start with the head and all its features, how it might look out of its bridle, and the ears, which I like to be big enough to denote positivity.

Here are some of the things I watch for when assessing conformation in general:

- **How the head and neck join.** The head is heavy, so a good join to the neck is important. It should not be too thick as this can interfere with breathing or flexion.

- **The neck length and shape,** which gives us the desired length of rein. It also plays a part in breathing and will determine the horse's likely shape under saddle.

- **The join of neck to the withers** and its shape: this will determine where the saddle fits.

- **The shape and angle of the shoulder** as they relate to the horse's movement.

- **The forearm to the knee** and then the lower limb. The strength, movement, and durability of the whole leg is SO important. The lower limbs do a lot of work throughout the horse's life.

- **The barrel and body** of the horse, which determines room for the lungs and heart and saddle position. This is also the site of the critical join between the back and the front end of the horse.

- **The loins** and the strength of the join between the part of the horse we sit on and the power of the hindquarters.

- **The shape of the hindquarters** and the angles of structure, which determine the hind end's strength and push, while the degree of muscle bulk determines the power. The shape of back leg indicates likely action and efficiency of power.

- **The way the tail sits;** this can indicate the freedom of the back.

As we look at the various aspects of a horse's conformation there are issues that will stand out. When you start training, or prepare for retraining, these issues need to be taken into consideration from the beginning. Variations from the "perfect picture" do not always mean that horses can't perform correctly or well, but an awareness of their

What Is a Good Neck Shape?

The neck and the way the neck is attached to the shoulder is one of the first areas of the horse that we look at. It may be something we have had a hand in shaping or something that has been created for us.

I like to see a nice arched neck coming out of the withers, one that will look natural when on the bit. The head should look as if it belongs to the neck and the rest of the horse. Remember, the head is very heavy for the neck to support. There must be enough at the top of the neck to carry the head, but not so much that the horse will find difficulty in flexing into an outline.

The spinal column is a comparatively rigid structure with little movement between vertebrae. There are seven vertebrae in the neck, known as C1 through C7 (fig. 1.2). The Atlas (C1) and Axis (C2) are very important parts of the connection to the skull as they allow for a degree of rotational movement, unlike the rest of the spine. *Please read that sentence again!* It is important to understand the physiological details as this is an integral part of how the horse comes into a shape, looks right and left, and carries himself, correctly or not. If this part of the neck does not offer relaxation, acceptance, and understanding then it will be impossible to achieve many of the other words we hear in our equestrian lives—"through," "soft," "straight," "round."

That is why I single out neck shape here, even though it may seem strange to deal with the conformation of the neck without also talking about the acceptance and influence of the bit. They are intimately related after all. I have separated the subjects for now, but will join them up later on in chapter 4 on the quality of contact (p. 69).

existence and implications will help us train the horse through these imperfections. For example, be aware if a horse appears naturally downhill or on the forehand. Don't complain later to your trainer that the horse has difficulty in rebalancing or becoming more collected as his conformation makes this harder to achieve.

Remember that history is full of misfit horse that shouldn't have achieved what they did. So conformation is something to be aware of when analyzing certain training problems or acquired ways of going, but it is not the sole consideration.

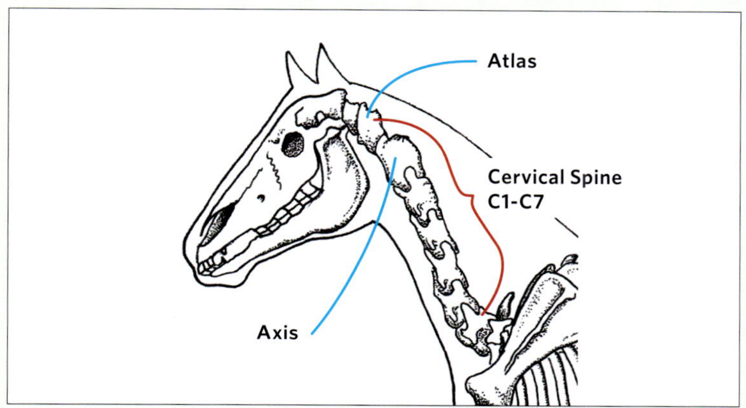

1.2 There are seven vertebrae in the horse's neck. The first two, the *atlas* and *axis* are important as they allow for rotational movement.

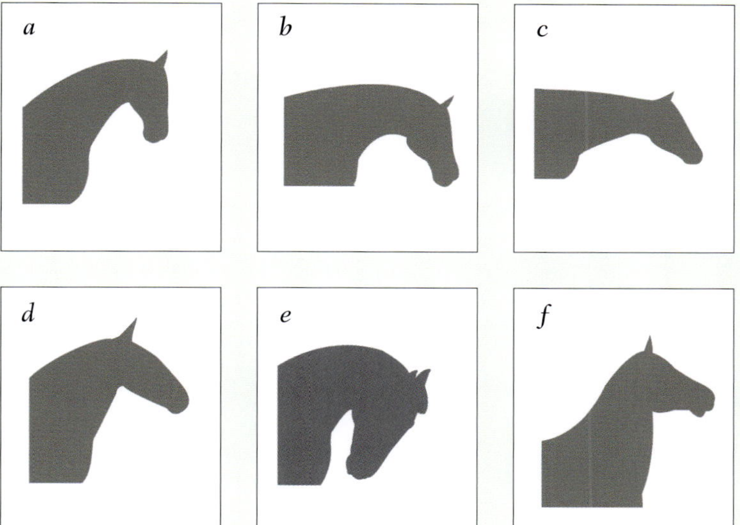

1.3 A–F Silhouettes A and B show nice neck shapes, while C and D show naturally low and high neck shapes, and E and F demonstrate overbent and upside-down necks.

THE GAITS

Looking at the gaits in the same way as we look at conformation is helpful. Most people are impressed by a big, fancy trot, and most horses are shown in trot to potential customers. However, we shouldn't be overly focused on this gait. The trot is only a small part of what we want.

Being shown a horse in trot can be helpful in other ways, though. A horse that has a naturally loose and free trot with a clearly defined two-beat rhythm is very appealing. This can be a naturally good trot to take with you into a dressage test as it fulfills some of the qualities the judge will be looking for.

Being straight of action is preferable but should not influence our schooling approach. Placing the foot squarely on the ground is more important, as this is more likely to remove excessive pressure and ensure long-term soundness. I also like to see a little knee action in the trot, which is likely to indicate a good jumper and the ability to produce extensions on the flat.

Bloodstock Agents will spend large sums of money on Thoroughbred horses having only seen the walk. So what are they looking at and watching for? Horses need to walk with a "swing" and track up. The ability to do this tells us so much about the other gaits. It gives us an indication of the likelihood of delivering what the dressage judge likes to see and how the horse might gallop or canter. A swing in the walk indicates a freedom of movement that also appears in canter and gallop. This relates to ground cover and the horse's ability to bring the hind legs underneath him.

Questions of form and function are also important to keep in mind when assessing the gaits. Dressage horses do not have to be straight of action, but show horses do. Show jumping horses do not need to show a good trot, but having a good canter is helpful.

A lot of work may be done in canter, so I believe we should look to the canter as the gait to impress. The canter must please the eye. Ideally, it should be easy to start and not require speed to maintain. A horse that is happier to show canter rather than trot is also a good thing. A natural desire to canter makes a horse easier to train. It should be correct in its rhythm and remain regular, with a pleasing balance.

You can see the train of thought here: While it is possible to correct a lot of things and to work with what nature has given us, flaws in conformation or the gaits should be viewed as *training challenges*. I always encourage you to take a positive approach to horse watching and look for the good attributes as well as the flaws. A good mind in a horse will be most helpful and is something to celebrate. A horse that is calm but attentive, one that is interested and forward-thinking, one that tries to please, these are qualities that are rewarding to work with.

Also remember that horses do not know what good conformation is. In spite of their conformation, they may well swing at the walk, show good regularity in the trot, and have lovely balance in the canter. The jumper doesn't have to have good technique but *must* have a conscience not to hit poles. So we shouldn't overlook what a horse does well and become too selective.

Which Would You Choose: The Natural Athlete or the Trainable One?

This is a subject that coaches in **all** sports around the world have great fun discussing. Which player would they rather have? The talented one who doesn't try or the less talented one who does?

The answer is almost always the less talented but trainable individual. If we are lucky enough to have a good mind and talent then success will be easier to come by.

Horses come with baggage—some that we gave them, and some that nature did. It's our job to make the most of it.

SOUNDNESS

Before we begin to address a problem through training or retraining, we should first make sure that the horse we are dealing with has no physical issues that might be causing the problem or hinder its correction.

Watch for Signs of Overfacing

Getting to know your horse and developing an awareness of what is unusual in his behavior or way of going will help to guard against overfacing. As I mentioned in the Introduction (p. 3), horses are generous animals, and we must be cautious not to take advantage of their nature.

Watch for signs that your horse is struggling or finding it too difficult to perform whatever task you're asking him to do. If he does any of the following, he likely doesn't understand and needs help, rather than frustration or anger:

- Refuses to continue.
- Runs away or otherwise tries to avoid the question.
- Hurries through the assignment.

We must become adept at recognizing signs of pain and discomfort. To be able to detect the signs of injury or health problems early and do something about them ensures that the horse will not go untreated and that the problem won't become a behavioral trait that we pass over, assuming, "Oh he's always like that!"

Knowing what "normal" looks like for our particular horse will make it a lot easier to determine when something is "abnormal." A change in character, response, or movement may indicate that something is not right. If we fail to develop this awareness, miss the signs of trouble, and carry on with our training or retraining work, we're unlikely to meet our goals—and may even create new problems that will need to be solved later. We also run the risk of our "social license" to ride and

Ask yourself:

What undesirable or negative attitudes and habits do I bring to my relationship with my horse? Can I see them reflected in my horse's behavior?

partner with our horses coming under increased scrutiny. It's important to understand the results of poor education and to always keep the physical and mental well-being of the horse at the front of our minds when we attempt to re-educate this delightful animal.

Luckily, getting to know your horse as an individual is an extremely pleasurable task, although doing this takes time. Time spent in his company—in the stall, the paddock, and when training, both under saddle and from the ground—will help us learn about the species and the individual. This will allow us to determine what is normal for an individual horse and what is abnormal, and will also help us learn how they interact with us, which will inform how we interact with them.

If there's any doubt whether pain or education is causing a horse to behave in an abnormal way, have the horse examined. If the horse is given the all-clear by the veterinarian, then you have a schooling issue to deal with. It is better to know this at the beginning of your interaction with the horse.

Go Ahead and Be Judged

A valuable tool for self-assessment is to use the same scale of "0" to "10" and the same words that are used in judging a dressage test. These words can also help you develop your own start points in your training or retraining.

Example: assessing a transition from walk to trot.

- If the horse falls to the left as he performs this task, you may give the horse a "5" for leaning, and yourself a "6" for the clarity of your aids in asking for the transition. ("The horse stayed in a good outline, responded reasonably well to the aid, which I applied correctly, but drifted left.")

- As you continue work, you might award a "6" when the horse stays straight, and improve your score as the elements for which you are responsible get better results.

- Award a "7" when the horse stays straight and responds even more quickly to the aid, and so on.

Know Thyself

Problem-solving with horses requires curiosity and patience, qualities we must know we possess before we tackle the project. This is where self-awareness comes into play. Being realistic about our own abilities can be difficult and sometimes painful, but it is important to foster this characteristic.

Looking at ourselves is sometimes uncomfortable, but we should do it because there is a certain truth to the idea that the horse is a reflection of his rider or handler. For example:

- If we are slow in how we do things...
- If we are casual in our attention to detail...
- If we accept casual attitudes in others...
- If we accept second best...

then we are likely to get the same from our horse.

Developing self-awareness isn't easy. If necessary, seek help and guidance from others. And I don't mean to suggest that we shouldn't have ambitions. But in all fairness to ourselves and our horses, we must err on the side of caution when it comes to deciding what is possible. We should set achievable goals and enjoy reaching them. Small changes should be our expectation.

It's also important to be realistic about the fact that everything having to do with horses is related in one way or another and that some problems will be more challenging than others. It simply isn't possible to fix most issues in total isolation. We need to be aware of how each issue relates to and influences other aspects of the horse to help us identify what needs fixing. It's also useful to consider how and why a particular issue arrived in the first place—this is all part of learning to look and watch and developing our awareness.

Each time we break things into smaller portions—like jigsaw pieces—it is our ultimate aim to reassemble them the way we want. It can be helpful to approach problem-solving as a "controlled experiment." A *controlled experiment* is a scientific test done under controlled conditions, meaning that just one factor is changed at a time, while all others are kept constant. This is done in order to relate the change to the constant. Make too many changes at the same time and there's no way of determining the effects of each variable. This is a key part of that five-step process we discussed earlier for solving problems (p. 11): try something, assess the results, and if it doesn't work, try something else.

Successful Training Requires Awareness

The ability to look at and watch horses and to hold a realistic vision of ourselves and our capabilities is a critical skillset—a prerequisite, you might say—to bring to our training. We must not lose sight of the fact that we are the only source of information and education that the horse has. This is a big responsibility, one that requires us to be clear in our knowledge of training and retraining methods along with their respective uses, merits, and pitfalls. In our awareness of current trends and fashions, we need to be able to sift through the sales pitch to get to the real value.

Any uncertainty, ambiguity, or unclear messaging on the part of the trainer cannot be good for the horse's education or his trust in us. **As you strive for clarity in your own work, be aware that you will come across a lot of mystique and lack of clarity in the equestrian world**. This must encourage us to carefully assess what we learn and make sure that it makes sense to us before we introduce it to the horse. In the next chapter, I'll talk more about the importance of striving for clarity and understanding in instruction and why I choose to use certain words and not others in this book and beyond.

Our aim is to produce a nice riding horse, with few issues, that has good manners and social skills. He should have an all-around education that makes him pleasant to be with. We should never underestimate the value of being "allowed in" by the horse as this is an indication of the horse investing in the partnership. Each time the horse "lets us in" and finds that the experience was a good one, he is more likely to let us in again.

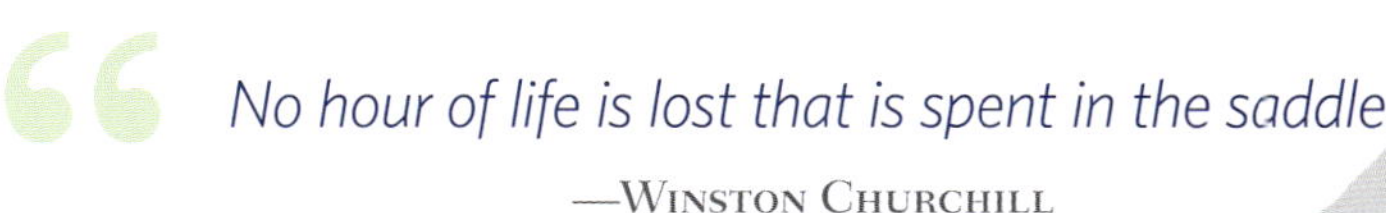

> *No hour of life is lost that is spent in the saddle.*
> —WINSTON CHURCHILL

CHAPTER 2

A Brief Thought on the Importance of Words

I HAVE SPENT MUCH OF MY COMPETITIVE LIFE WATCHING AND listening to coaches. I have been the recipient of much coaching and have delivered many thousands of hours of instruction myself. Over a lifetime of learning, I have come to some understanding of what separates the good and the bad. One of the best indications of the success of a lesson is revealed by watching the pupil as you listen to the coach. All too often, you'll find misunderstanding at best and discord between parties at worst. Why should this happen when both are enthusiastically trying to please?

There are a number of factors that can lead to this unsatisfactory situation:

- Poor lesson management, including words of command, school movements, and lack of a plan.
- Inappropriate content for horse or rider.
- Language choice.
- Manner and delivery of content.
- An unclear philosophy to start with.

I am lucky that my early training gave me the discipline of how to use words of command to move people around in a lesson to achieve results. I have also become thoroughly familiar with all sorts of school movements. These two skills have become instinctive, allowing me to focus solely on the content of the lesson.

Over the years, I have developed a vocabulary for all levels, from beginners to the most advanced horse-and-rider teams. The words we choose must be appropriate to the level of each lesson if they're to be understood and of value. If we fail to do this, we waste everybody's time and effort.

I have found that it also helps learning if we can think of as many senses as possible when we speak: hearing the words, being able to do what is being asked, seeing and feeling a change. Connecting to the senses comes from using verbs—"doing words." So my vocabulary has become focused on these.

You'll see that the next several chapters focus on solving problems within several riding qualities: chapter 3 (p. 37) focuses on the qualities of forward, straight, and regular; chapter 4 on contact (p. 61); chapter 5 on connection (p. 113); and chapter 6 on consistency (p. 147). In my teaching and training, these are the words that I have found to be clearest and most effective. Why? Because they apply to everyone no matter the discipline—riders of jumpers, racehorses, dressage horses, or ranch horses.

Why Not the Scales?

Some may wonder why I don't refer to the Scales of Training (or Training Scale or Training Pyramid) in this book. (If, on the other hand, you have read my previous work, you will already be familiar with my philosophy, in which case, I don't mind you skipping this piece, but I would really like you to read it again.)

Let me explain: Since its invention some 50 years ago by the German Equestrian Federation (FN), the Scales of Training have developed a popular following. In most countries that do dressage, the Scales are considered an important training sequence to follow. This may be due in part to the success Germany has had in this discipline over the last half-century. However, the majority of people who ride have never heard of the Scales. What's more, there are many people who are familiar with them, but who have little understanding of their meaning.

That might prompt you to say, "Shouldn't you teach them to understand?" I believe my most important role is to make riding easier to understand for the majority of people who enjoy horses. To fulfill this intention, I choose language that is used and easily understood by all. The fact of the matter is that the words and structure of the Scales are confusing. They do not follow a logic that is easy for most people to grasp. They miss out on the fundamental quality of "forward" entirely. This is something everyone is taught, but somehow got missed.

It is easy to see why people talk about "bending horses" when the word *suppleness* appears at the bottom of the Scales. To some people, the two concepts could be considered linked when, in fact, they are not. *Suppleness* is the demonstration of the horse accepting and understanding the rider's aids. The horse was born supple, so we are merely asking him to do what he does naturally. The qualities of "stiffness" and "resistance" are manmade. They are an indication that the horse doesn't understand what we are asking.

Impulsion is another case in point. *Impulsion* is an availability of energy, but if you haven't got it, you can't use it! Impulsion can only be created with a desire to go *forward* in answer to the request from the leg aids (which must, firstly, be understood). But once again, the Scales are silent on the subject of forward.

We can't and shouldn't ignore the quality of *straightness* as training in any discipline will require development of an athlete that performs equally well on both reins. From the very moment we begin training the young horse or retraining the older horse we must be conscious of the lack of straightness, which makes going for a ride or executing a school movement feel strange and incorrect.

The Scales of Training

A reminder: the Scales are traditionally made up of six elements:

- Rhythm
- Suppleness
- Contact
- Impulsion
- Straightness
- Collection

I continually have to remind people not to confuse the words *rhythm* and *regularity*. One describes the footfall of the pace, and the other describes how regular that rhythm remains. They are two totally different qualities and yet *rhythm* appears at the base of the Scales and *regularity* is nowhere to be seen.

The importance of being precise as a coach cannot be overemphasized. The words you choose stay with the rider as the rider performs. It would be a pity if the rider was trying to improve something that can't be changed! For example, a trot has a rhythm of two-time, which never changes (except when asked to *pace* in harness racing). So it is pointless for a coach to say, "You have to improve the rhythm," because it is not possible to do so. The rhythm of the gait simply is what it is: one-two, one-two, one-two, one-two.

But the gait can be *irregular.* When a horse is lame, he trots in an irregular way; when not connected or well "in-gear," he can be irregular. The instruction, "Ride to maintain the regularity," is a valid message as doing this will improve the quality of the gait.

Feeling confused? That's my point exactly. Let me be clear about this: I am not against the Scales of Training. I just happen to think that they are too often mis-taught and misunderstood. When I ask riders to explain what they are doing, their replies are very revealing. People often find it difficult to put into words or explain what they are trying to achieve, but if it is something they are asking their horse to do, then I feel strongly that they should understand it themselves. It is only fair to the horse.

For the purposes of clarity, I'm including definitions for the six riding qualities addressed in the following chapters: *forward, straight, regular, contact, connection,* and *consistency* (see below). With the training of a young horse, all six words are key, allowing us to enhance a horse's natural qualities as we transform him into a "well-schooled horse."

The same riding qualities are just as important to helping us remedy problems and restore the natural qualities that we are trying to demonstrate with the retraining of a horse, for our goal is the same: to make him a "well-schooled horse."

Why I Don't Like the Word Collection

I find the word *collection* difficult to deal with. In fact, I can't think when I last used it. Let me explain.

To me it is the one word that ruins more good riding than any other in our equestrian vocabulary. It's there to define a stage in a horse's schooling when the horse shows true engagement of the hindquarters and a lightening of the forehand, where the horse is light and responsive to the rider's aids, and at a mere thought, is able to do what is asked of him. This is a lot to ask of our education process and the horse's understanding of it.

Along the route to achieving collection, there are many difficulties to face, some educational and some physical. Each educational effort will produce some success in seeking a more collected horse. There is no destination, as collection is part of the journey. There are only degrees of collection dependent on the stage of training. These degrees are likely to be a compromise, which depend on a horse's physical and mental ability to cope with what is being asked.

In my experience as an FEI (Federation Equestre Internationale) judge, the introduction of the word at the lower levels of dressage was a grave mistake. It encouraged the training of horses to be pushed beyond their level of expertise with the result of schooling faults appearing, including short necks, four-beat canters, loss of impulsion, and horses not going forward. These are all faults that come from collection being asked for too soon or by the uninformed or both. They are all faults that can be difficult to correct once established in the horse's mind.

So, in general, I avoid using or talking about the word *collection*. Only when the partnership displays work in the correct direction is it worth talking about "A little more push from behind," "Readjust the balance," "Not so hurried," or "Encourage more cadence." These are expressions that retain *good* work on our way to a more collected gait.

It should be understood that a solid "7" in a dressage test for producing good work without asking for collection, even when it is indicated as part of the movement, is infinitely better than getting a "5" or less for losing forwardness and impulsion or a shortening of the neck.

Each horse will demonstrate a degree of collection in a different way. Do not lose the constant qualities in an effort to produce the *appearance* of collection.

Forwardness

This is the feeling of the horse *taking* the rider. It is a state of mind and a prerequisite to everything in riding.

Straightness

This is when the horse's hind legs follow the front legs, which follow the head and neck, on whatever line you ask for. The spine is on the line of motion.

Regular

Refers to the ability to keep the footfall the same. It is related to rhythm and tempo, but is not the same thing.

Contact

This is the mutual feel the horse has at the end of your rein. The horse must hold the bit in a non-resistant way. The lower jaw and the poll both have a role to play in this non-resistance. You must strive to be consistent with the contact so there is an appearance of harmony. To achieve this, there must be elasticity in both reins.

Connection

I like to include this quality in addition to contact. It is the feeling that what you are asking for with your legs has a direct link to what you receive in your hand. The horse feels connected from back to front.

Consistency

This is the ability to produce a predictable performance as a result of being rideable.

My Scales

The version of the Scales that I have developed in my work includes additional qualities, many of which are also found in the original version (see p. 31). However, I have found that *my* six words can be used to elicit understanding at any stage, even at the beginning of a rider's and a horse's journey. As each party grows more educated, there may become a need to expand on the basic vocabulary to include qualities such as suppleness, impulsion, "throughness," or collection. There are also nuances to the improvement of each quality that may require other words. But even as a horse and rider progress, learning more and more complex skills, these six basic qualities must not be lost.

I have watched and taken part in lessons where coaches' inability to express themselves made the lesson a complete waste of time and a waste of their knowledge and experience. I have also witnessed extremely good lessons given by coaches who used simple, accessible language with wonderful timing and tact to great effect—these experiences are worth a fortune.

It's a well known cliché: "Experts make their sport look easy." But, in reality, most people in the horse community are not experts, and unless we make what we teach user-friendly for the average person, who has little expertise or knowledge (or even worse, *thinks* they have more knowledge than they do) things fall apart quickly.

There is a big gap between the wild horse in the field and a safe riding horse. We must aim to teach the rider in a language that is understood clearly enough so that the horse

What About the Sequence of the Riding Qualities?

I prefer to think of the process of training as an "orbit" or a "spiral" rather than a pyramid or a linear progression or checklist. There is a belief held by many coaches and riders alike that you start at the bottom of the scale and work your way up, one quality at a time. I believe this is not the most accurate way of looking at things. In the orbit and the spiral analogies, the horse and rider dip into and out of various qualities. There are times when great forwardness and impulsion are achieved, then disappear. Occasionally, even a young or inexperienced horse will collect for a moment before the feeling is lost. Sometimes, all of the desired qualities appear together, and then desert you.

One quality should not be seen as following another, therefore, or as being firmly established once and for all before moving onto the next. Instead, the process is dynamic, constantly evolving. No matter how schooled a horse becomes, he will need to visit and revisit these qualities to reconfirm their availability and correctness. The more educated the horse becomes the more available each quality becomes.

gets the correct message and will perform all the things he does naturally on demand. This is quite a task. When we use language that confuses people and then, they try to explain something poorly grasped to their horses, we are asking of the horses an almost insurmountable task. Actually, I think horses do great "guess work." For all that they are "taught," they are remarkably obliging.

However, horses will sometimes make a guess, thinking only, "What's best for me?" We should anticipate that this is likely to happen and be prepared for it. But we can also use a best guess in our favor. We can be creative in positioning exercises to "help" the horse choose the correct answer. For example, asking a young horse to canter going into a corner of an arena will give a pretty clear indication of direction, and so, help the outcome. Doing a downward transition from trot to walk after a trot pole will help introduce the concept of the rebalance after a jump.

Remember that the horse is not familiar with the six riding qualities we will explore in the following chapters, nor with any others. So when applying these words as a coach or a rider, we should not assume equine intelligence, or the ability to reason. Being creative in our approach will help to bring the horse with us in our pursuit of these six qualities. It may take many repetitions for the young horse to understand and many more for the retrained horse to erase the bad reaction and adopt the correct one. But if we are clear in our own understanding (and instruction) of the concepts involved, we increase the odds that the horse will understand what is being asked and deliver the desired response.

To be a legend is easy. To become one is hard work.

—SIR AP MCCOY, 20 YEARS CONSECUTIVE NATIONAL HUNT CHAMPION JOCKEY

CHAPTER 3

The Foundational Qualities of Forward, Straight, and Regular

I BELIEVE ALL RIDERS AND TRAINERS SHOULD USE THE CORE QUALITIES of *forward, straight,* and *regular* as the beginning of their journey with horses. Even for very young riders, the words are easy to grasp and learn how to apply. They are sound principles that form a platform from which all riders can build a solid base, and there is plenty of scope for refining them along the way.

These may seem like simple words that need little explanation—after all they are similar to other words we use, so understanding may be assumed. They do, however, require some explanation and clarification (beyond the definitions provided in the previous chapter and repeated in this one as a reminder) so you can understand why they are so important to me. Please do not skip over this explanation believing that you understand their qualities. You may well understand, but there is no harm in *confirming* this understanding.

Clarifying the Core Qualities

FORWARD: This is "the horse taking you." This is a willingness on the horse's part to go in the desired direction, to be part of what we want to do, to be an enthusiastic partner. It should be offered freely and should not require pushing.

STRAIGHT: This is when the horse's hind legs follow the front legs, which follow the head and neck, on whatever line you ask for. The spine is on the line of motion.

REGULAR: This is the ability to keep the footfall the same. It is related to *rhythm* and *tempo* but is *not* the same. (More on the differences later—see p. 63.)

Many people who read this will immediately put their own twist on these three words, but if you do this, you may miss my message. By understanding these words and trying to take the definitions with you into your actual riding, much can be achieved.

As discussed in the previous chapter, a lot of misunderstanding in riding comes from the misinterpretation of words and the associated qualities. These three words and how we use them reverberate in my head when I ride and teach. I urge you to try this approach for yourself.

Forward, straight, and *regular* form the foundation of the majority of our work with horses. Their implementation is closely related to the use of the rider's aids and must be firmly established to achieve the other qualities addressed later in this book. Let's look at each of the three qualities more closely, along with some of the common problems that emerge when trying to execute them.

Forwardness

Without the presence of this fundamental quality in everything we do with horses, *all* of our work is diminished. The desire to move forward forms the basis of a nice riding horse and without it little can be done to correct flaws or sustain performance. Therefore, understanding what *forward* looks like, how it feels and manifests itself, is worth looking at.

The definition of "the horse taking you" is a simple one. Imagine how nice it would feel to go for a hack and not have to continually push the horse along, or to lead him in from the field and not have to drag him at the end of your lead rope but have him walk briskly beside you instead, showing enthusiasm to work and please. This is a good start to any day, regardless of whether we make it into the saddle or not. Having a horse that "goes" in the arena and allows the riding aids to become communication aids, that is a *luxury*.

There is much we can do to encourage this quality in horses, even if it isn't present to begin with. From the definition of *forward* provided on p. 37, it's obvious that this quality is about more than just generating momentum. Forward is a state of mind, one that begins not with the riding aids, but with building the right attitude in the horse from the start of our training. Most horses will conform to their surroundings, so it is our job to set the right tone and explain clearly how we want the relationship to work. It is a two-way relationship, and we should take care to ensure that our horse views us as a consistent, trustworthy partner.

Creating a Forward State of Mind

As you'll recall from the discussion of overfacing in the Introduction (p. 3), it's important that at each stage of a horse's education, he is given the room to "let you in" before you ask for more. Doing this creates a strong connection between what he is learning "now" and what is coming "next." As a rider and trainer, it becomes exciting for me when a horse almost anticipates the next move. This is a satisfying feeling because it indicates that we're on the right path.

We set the tone for learning, for better or worse. If we don't pay careful attention to detail, if we are willing to settle for partial answers, or half-hearted efforts, or if we rely on fear to secure obedience, these are qualities that are likely to be detected and mirrored by our horse. So how should we interact?

Every point of contact with the horse should be crisp, clear, and with the expectation of something happening, that the horse will reciprocate in the same manner. From leading him in from the field to asking him to move over when grooming, setting the right tone is vital. This doesn't mean you have to be brusque or aggressive—it's okay to be his friend and stop for a chat or a cuddle, but prescribe the style of interaction, set an agenda, and be a proactive partner. You will be surprised how this influences the attitude that your horse brings with him into your riding and training.

Every point of contact should also be of value. Each step should be consistent with what came before and what is still to come, and it should also confirm the message you are trying to convey. When the message is inconsistent, the horse is left with an uncertainty of what you want. Every part of your ride time should have a focus, something clear for the horse to grasp. Without clarity it is easy for him to get the wrong message and learn unwanted or unnecessary things.

Take a typical riding session, for example:

- Some people start with a casual hack or walk around the arena (supposedly to allow the horse to loosen up), which might take 10 minutes.
- Engaging the horse's mind and body in the warm-up work (long and low or whatever) might take another 10 minutes.
- Teaching the horse a new task (which may or may not go well) might mean 10 minutes of good work and 10 minutes of bad work.
- Cooling down after work (or thinking about the next horse while talking on your phone) kills another 10 minutes.

Of the 50 minutes of riding time, there might have been 10 minutes of good work and 40 minutes of questionable value. What does the horse remember? What has had the most repetition? Certainly not the 10 minutes of good things.

When horses know that at every point of interaction with us they are expected to turn up and be attentive, they develop the engaged mindset we want. As they see a bridle appear they get ready. As soon as the rider sits in the saddle, the horse is already "at the office."

Every part of our ride time should develop and confirm a subject before moving on to the next topic. It should all be part of a progressive plan that the horse gets used to so he knows things will happen the same way the next time around. While his brain is busy being attentive to a step-by-step ride, we are warming up the body at the same time. The warm-up becomes part of the process.

There are aspects of this progressive work that are more intense than others. Relaxation times interspersed between intense times are needed. Quiet times to recover the focus are all part of being in "class," at "work," and "listening." When we have finished it must be made very clear to the horse with, "We're done, thank you." We give him a loose rein and tell him he's off duty. At each step we are consistent about how we let the horse know what is expected of him.

Addressing a Lack of Forwardness

Although we've just covered the importance of thinking about forwardness as a mindset to be fostered in horses, we certainly feel its absence physically. A lack of forwardness

Examples of Problems Created by Hurrying Training

- If you ask for medium trot before the horse understands connection and impulsion, he's likely to run and lose self-carriage. Judges' comments might include: "More from behind," "Wide behind," or "Losing cadence."

- When security to the rein and an understanding of the leg aid have not been embedded in the training, the horse may go above the bit in the canter transition. The rider's confidence when asking for this in a test will be poor and unsure of the outcome. Scores of "7" or above will be hard to come by.

- When a horse immediately tightens through the body, loses connection, and, as a result, loses his regularity when asked for shoulder-in, he may have been taught the movement too soon. With uncertainty about how to perform the task, he froze!

The solution, of course, is to find a start point from which the horse can reset. In answer to the shoulder-in problem, for example:

- Reduce the amount of bend, return to walk, and explain the mechanics of the movement to the horse.

- When he understands what to do and where to place his body, try it in a quiet and slow trot.

- When he understands this phase, then add to the quality of the trot.

These are common issues encountered in riding and illustrate the need to be patient to avoid creating problems (like them) that then have to be solved later. You need to foresee what can become problematic when possible. This way the horse will join you and retain the can-do attitude required to achieve forwardness, straightness, and regularity, and to bring out all of the other qualities that are our ultimate aim.

and purpose is probably the very first issue that presents itself in our training, but people often fail to recognize the problem in the first place, or they underestimate its significance.

When riders find themselves using more and more leg to make a horse go, it is a sure thing that the horse is doing less and not going happily forward. Without "the horse taking the rider," riding isn't fun and little can be achieved, so forwardness should be considered a must-have.

Some horses are predisposed to laziness and producing just enough—as little as they can get away with. Riders need to look to themselves for allowing this to happen. To rekindle the spark takes attitude on the rider's part. As I have said in my teaching, to start with, the rider must possess an energy that rubs off on the horse.

TRAINING WITH THE CONDITIONED REFLEX

Much has been written about *positive reinforcement* over the last few years. When we add to this a reinforcing stimulus, such as a tap with a schooling whip to draw attention to a certain desired behavior or outcome, or a reward after an action, then that particular response will be strengthened.

When introducing the concept of using a schooling whip, many people will raise an eyebrow. "Why not try something less confrontational, such as natural training or clicker training?" they may ask. Both can be valid forms of training, but for me, the use of a schooling whip has many more merits. Its length allows me to touch parts of the horse that I want to stimulate. I can be at one end of the horse and activate the other end simply by touching. By tapping the horse to produce a response and immediately rewarding him, I am able to draw the horse's attention more quickly to what I want. The whip is not there to chastise or punish, merely to stimulate a response.

This method of training makes use of the *conditioned reflex*, a concept you may remember from the Introduction (p. 6). A conditioned reflex is defined as: *an acquired response in which the subject learns to associate a previously unrelated stimulus with a different stimulus that elicits some kind of reaction.* It was famously demonstrated by Russian psychologist Ivan Pavlov and his dog, which he trained to salivate at the ring of a bell.

A good example of how one might use a schooling whip to produce a conditioned reflex is teaching a horse to lead well. This training activity also happens to be a great start for developing many other responses:

- Start by walking beside the horse's shoulder (remember to do this exercise from both sides).
- With the schooling whip in your outside hand, you want to feel that you know where the back of the horse is so you can touch it without looking.

- Use a brisk voice and a tap with the whip and use an active body movement to encourage the horse to mimic you and move forward. As he does, be very quick to reward him. It won't take long before the horse anticipates your body moving and is ready to go.

The conditioned reflex will become an important part of our toolbox as we dismantle bad or unwanted responses and replace them with good and desirable ones. When teaching humans, we are able to talk and explain why we want something to happen, but with horses, we cannot explain with words, so we must be able to use a different "language"—one that they can understand: *actions*. So *our* understanding of the conditioned reflex is necessary if we are to be helpful to the horse as he learns what we want.

In making the horse's normal response one of "going," "doing," "being there," and "ready to respond," the feeling of *forward* becomes engrained in his mind.

Making a "Forward" Connection to the Hind End

Having produced a forward response from the aids we need to think a little deeper about what we've actually done. To the uneducated horse—and age is irrelevant here, it's his level of training that is important—the conversation we have initiated from the leg aids has produced a simple response on the horse's part: Go!

We need him to understand that the go in "Leg means go " has to come from the *hind legs*—this is an important connection in the horse's mind. It is very simple, but *our* legs must have a connection to *the horse's hind legs*. You must feel a push from the hind legs. *Do not underestimate the importance of this for the future.* Throughout our subsequent training, this connection will be of critical value to progress. At this stage, the horse's education is in its infancy, and the language used is very monosyllabic and in need of refinement, but the important thing is that the link has been made.

Don't be in a hurry to teach anything more subtle than "light leg means go" at this stage. Work at cementing this understanding in the horse's mind. There will be plenty of challenges to this conditioned response later on, so the more secure the response is now, the more we can rely on it later.

This is also the early part of teaching the concept of being *through* (fig. 3.1). It is not nearly a finished feeling, but it is a good start.

This is just the beginning of understanding how *forward* influences every aspect of riding.

Let's now turn to the problems that arise with the foundational quality of forwardness and apply our five-step framework to find possible solutions. To review, our five steps are:

1 What is the problem?

2 How, when, and why did it arise?

3 Why does it need solving?

4 How can we formulate a plan to solve the problem, finding a start point?

5 What do the results of our experiment mean in the context of now and the future?

Note that in the examples that follow, I leave out Step 5, where we analyze results, since that step has to be done in real time.

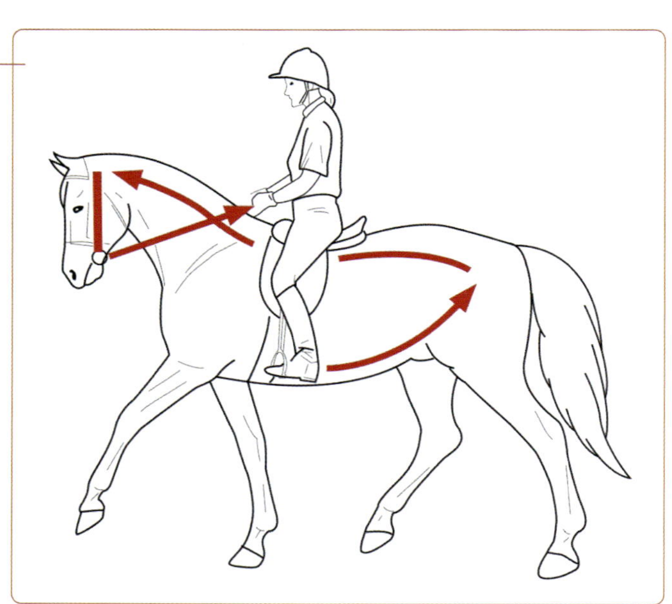

3.1 A horse is *through* when there is no resistance between the leg, hindquarters, back, poll, jaw, bit, and hand. When this happens, the horse is "available" to you.

Forwardness Problems and Solutions

The three qualities featured in this chapter—forward, straight, and regular—form the basis of the majority of our work with our horse. Their implementation is closely related to the use of the rider's aids. We tend to think of forward coming from the rider's leg aids. If, however, we accept that forwardness is a state of mind, then the leg aid becomes merely a communication tool for the rider. In order to access this forwardness, the leg aid must be understood by the horse. The first step is the horse accepting the leg's presence by his side and the next is understanding what the leg is asking.

1 Problem: Rejecting the leg. _

2 Why is the problem there? Many horses reject the presence of a rider's leg at their sides. This rejection of any input you might want to give can be displayed in a number of ways:

- Pushing against the leg.
- Rejecting any input from the aid.
- Kicking at the leg.
- Kicking out behind.
- Bucking.

Sometimes mares that are in season display a variation of these responses Some horses are lazy, some are slow on the uptake of training, some have been trained badly and misunderstand what is required of them..

3 Why does it need solving? By rejecting any input from the leg aid the horse is rejecting any means of communication we might want to give. This is unacceptable, as the leg aid is the primary aid in riding; it is our main source of passing information to the horse.

4 How do you solve the problem? Remove the fear or concern that the horse is showing by refusing to be aggressive with the leg. Keep the presence of the leg next to the horse and be patient as he gets used to it being there.

Work in the stable can help reinforce the message of non-intimidation. Simply ask the horse to move away from your hand when placed by the girth area. Building the horse's understanding that light pressure on the girth area means that we want a quick response from them is a major step in their education.

Beware when you hear a coach say, "Use more leg." The coach doesn't mean it. What is meant is, "Get more from the leg you are using," but that is a cumbersome expression, although technically more correct. Don't get drawn in to using more leg—you'll produce less of a result.

1 Problem: Lack of forwardness to the leg. _ _ _ _ _ _ _ _ _ _ _ _ _

2 Why is the problem there? The aid that initiates the response of forwardness is the leg aid, but too often, horses become unclear about or immune to the use of the leg aid (fig. 3.2). In clinics, I'm presented with a collection of different versions of this complaint:

"My horse is dead to the leg."

"My horse rejects the leg."

"My horse doesn't go forward."

"My horse is sharp to the leg."

"How much leg should I use?"

"I'm very strong with my left leg!"

Forwardness as a mindset and its relationship to the leg aids can very often be a misunderstanding of the training process: the trainer being happy with "quiet" and the "leg being accepted" and the horse content to do "little" or "nothing."

3 Why does it need solving? Without a clear and quick response to the leg aid, little communication can happen. We are then left with whatever the horse decides to give us, which is unlikely to be very much.

The leg should lie comfortably just behind the girth (although this is commonly referred to as "on the girth"). The rider's legs should lie against the horse's sides like wet cloths, wrapping themselves around the horse's sides but without any pressure.

Horses must accept the presence of the leg before any understanding is possible.

In applying the leg aid, there should be no use of strength, no "shout" in the conversation, merely a light ask with the aim of producing a crisp, clean response. What happens when this doesn't work? Or when the horse produces nothing or gives a rather dull sluggish response?

4 How do you solve the problem? The dressage whip is my "go-to" tool in this case (see sidebar, p. 77). The sequence of the aid should go like this:

- Apply a light leg aid on the girth followed immediately by a crisp tap just behind the leg. If the correct response is achieved, then an immediate acknowledgment is important: a pat, the voice, or both.

- If nothing happens then give a sharper tap with the dressage whip, increasing intensity and speed until a response is forthcoming. Always follow up with a reward when the good response occurs.

3.2 No amount of cajoling or pressure can move a horse that is "dead to the leg."

Spurs Are Not the Answer

I seldom use spurs and recommend that most riders ride without them. In my experience, their use tends to make horses less responsive to the leg aid rather than the opposite. It takes good balance and leg control as well as good timing to use them well. They're best left to the experts.

As the horse begins to get the message that a light leg means a quick response and they are praised, we develop a conditioned reflex. This is part of what I call "the leg conversation." It should be exactly that, a conversation, not a shouting match. Strength and force have no place; understanding does.

Having gotten the correct response, our aim should be to look for a quicker correct response. Then we should work on getting a correct response quicker still *and* more often. By increasing the level of response required we automatically improve the mental and physical coordination the horse is asked to produce. This speeds up the creation of new neurological pathways in the horse, and therefore, the understanding of our input.

It is important not to overload the horse's system by asking too much all at once. You will know you are pushing too hard when the response to the leg aids diminishes and the speed of reaction becomes slower. If this happens, go back a step and start again, but don't compromise on the quality of the response; compromise on the number of times you ask for the response to happen. We always want the horse to come with us willingly.

1 PROBLEM: RUNNING AWAY FROM THE LEG (OR BEING TOO LIGHT OR OVER RESPONSIVE TO THE LEG AID). _

2 WHY IS THE PROBLEM THERE? Being light to the leg is often misunderstood as a good thing. It isn't. The horse merely shoots off without really understanding what he is being asked to do (fig. 3.3). Horses' response to the leg aid can and often is very different. Some are quick and almost surprised by its presence. Others take no notice of it being there. The trainer and the horse need to know that the leg aid and its acceptance is paramount to good communication.

3 WHY DOES IT NEED SOLVING? Because of the horse's sensitivity to the leg, the rider becomes reluctant to have the leg anywhere near the horse's side for fear of inadvertently touching him. This produces an incorrect and often unbalanced position for the rider. It also diminishes the rider's ability to communicate with the horse.

4 HOW DO YOU SOLVE THE PROBLEM? To address this problem riders must check their balance and allow their legs to rest by the horse's sides. Any misunderstanding by the horse to move off should be corrected in a quiet, pleasant way, by keeping the presence of the leg aid and using the rein aid to slow the horse down. After all, the horse thinks he is doing what is asked.

3.3 Running away can be caused by oversensitivity to the rider's leg.

"You Get What You're Given"

There are many situations in the training and retraining of horses in which the horse offers something, and we are left to decide whether or not to accept what is being offered. Often the response is not what we asked for or what we wanted, but it seems churlish and ungrateful not to accept it. The response might even be very nice and something that we will want from the horse later on.

In saying "no" in these cases, are we really able to explain to the horse why we are not accepting his answer? Or will the horse think, "Well that's the last time I offer to help!" In going down this road we might have inadvertently closed a door instead of opening one.

As trainers we need to be aware of this dilemma because we need to know how to deal with it. I've said often that I think horses are generous animals and try to help us. They too may be unclear if they are offering an answer, but they give us their best guess. Out of courtesy, we should say, "Thank you, but…" and try to redirect their generosity when it's not exactly what we want.

In all coaching there are times when we must think about this statement. In working with pupils, both horse or human, I often find myself saying some form of, "Yes, but was it what I asked for or what I wanted?"

Sometimes, a horse will say, "Sure, no problem," and march off in a certain direction (different than what I had in mind), towing me behind. I'm delighted that the horse feels positive and keen to go and do, but it wasn't the direction or the speed I asked for.

The horse must be allowed to become accustomed to the presence of the leg and to the rider using it to "talk" with him without moving away. It is only when the horse accepts the presence of the leg that we can teach its meaning. This may be a slow process, beginning at halt before progressing to walk and gradually to trot and canter. Without this acceptance and understanding, we will not be able to have an educated conversation with our horse as our schooling progresses.

Straightness

The next quality we will explore is *straightness* and we will deal with it in the context of the three components of the horse's body: the *hindquarters*, the *forehand*, and the *head and neck* (fig. 3.4).

Often, when asking an uneducated horse to trot around the arena, he will do so willingly once or twice and then be reluctant to continue. To him there seems no point. He hasn't yet come to terms with you directing him as his rider. In the early stages of training, when asking a horse for a working trot, I can sometimes feel the horse holding something back. If I encourage him with the leg aids he hurries, if I don't, the trot is okay but not what I want. I feel him only giving me what *he* wants, at the level of effort where he feels comfortable. This is part of a natural reticence—the horse doesn't want to offer everything.

If we accept what the horse offers, we should know that we are acknowledging that his answer is "correct"...even though it may be only *partially* correct. Therefore, we will have to revise the response later on.

We must continually define and redefine the answers that horses give us, as this is the only way they will know whether or not they have given us what we asked for. (This is also how we raise the level of their response.) If we don't seize the opportunity to redefine where the horse has drawn the line, we will be forever confined by the phrase, "You get what you are given."

Choose the right time to nudge the line and make it *your* line of limitation. The horse needs to accept your definition and come with you, as long as he knows that at all times you are guided by the principle: *If it's a fair and acceptable request, then he should try to help.*

As a reminder of what we are looking for when watching and riding horses, here's a simple definition of straightness: *the hindquarters follow the forehand, which follows the neck and head on any line the rider chooses to ride.*

Most horses go through life with some natural asymmetry. They are seldom born symmetrical and will develop their own way of going, which in nature suits them just fine. It is only when the human gets involved that this lack of symmetry becomes relevant. As a ridden athlete, the horse is asked to be the same on both sides and going in both directions. He is asked to conform to shapes and movements of our choice, which are

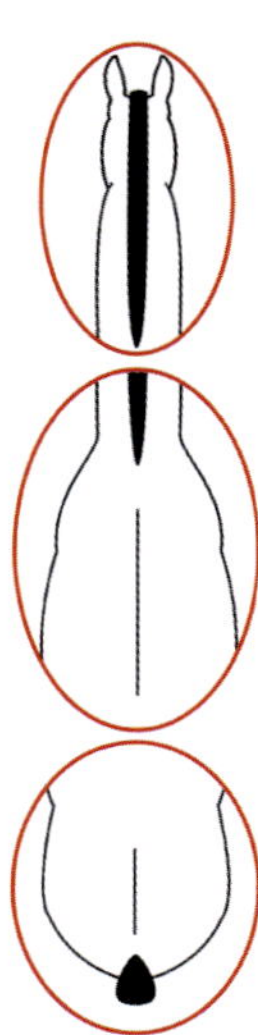

3.4 The horse in three parts: the hindquarters; forehand; and head and neck.

designed to prove our level of competency in training and the horse's level of assimilation of that training.

In order to do this successfully, we need firstly to know what *straightness* is and then what it looks like. We should be able to identify the part of the horse that isn't on the chosen line and is, therefore, *not* straight. Our next job is to explain to the horse what we would like him to do in order to straighten out.

Addressing a Lack of Straightness

All coaches and riders are presented with the same straightness problems:

- "My horse pops his left shoulder."
- "My horse always travels with his hindquarters to the inside."
- "My horse never has enough bend."
- "My horse always has more bend left than I get to the right."
- "When doing lateral work, my horse is never straight."

To solve such problems, we must break them down further. We need to:

- Access each of the three components of the horse (the hindquarters, the forehand, and the head and neck).

3.5 A nice shape when the horse is circling you in the stall or stable should look like this.

- Perform exercises to influence each part.
- Develop the ability to correct and position.
- Translate that to the ability to ride shapes and identify the corrections taking place.

When correcting straightness never underestimate what can be done in the stable or stall. For instance, asking a horse to walk around you as you stand in the middle of his stall, you will likely notice that he finds it easier to go one way than the other (fig. 3.5). This will give you an understanding of how the different directions will feel when riding. The horse that conforms to a correct circle shape on one rein will almost certainly find the other way less easy. His tendency will be to fall in and come closer to you. Being able to identify the part of the horse that falls in or out allows us to make the link to some of our own riding issues.

The same exercise will tell you which way the horse's hindquarters are likely go when not following the desired line of movement.

Begin the correction in the stable by creating a triangle in your positioning with the horse. The rein guides the head and is one side of the triangle. Your extended free arm, or the introduction of a schooling whip to the tail can become another side. The horse is the third side of the triangle, and you are the apex. You can use your body and hand

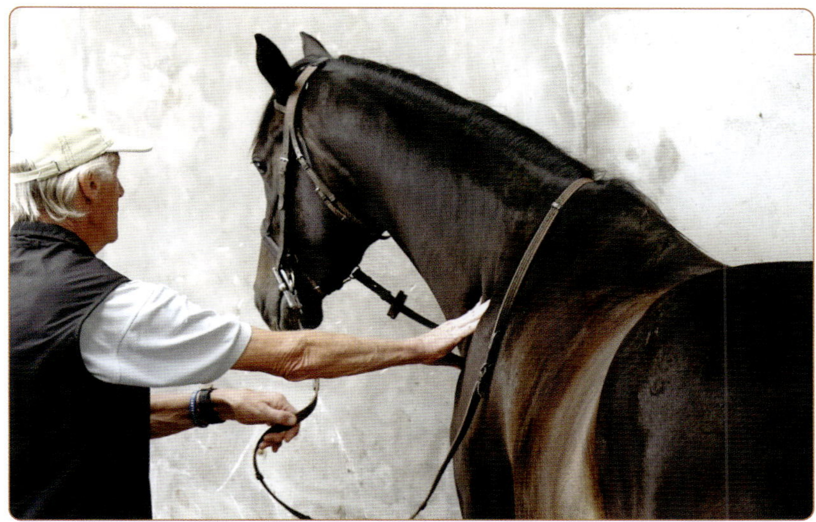

3.6 This is this horse's more difficult direction, which requires I help shape him to the circle using the position of my body and my hand.

to influence the middle of the horse (fig. 3.6). This careful positioning mimics the rider's leg position, and in doing so encourages the horse to bend as he would around the rider's inside leg. The horse's "good" direction will look easy, almost to the extent that he will show a tendency to fall out through the shoulder, while in going the "less good" direction, the horse will drift in toward you and challenge your treaties to stay out. As the middle of the horse falls in, so the hindquarters and the head and neck will stay out. By touching the horse by the girth, with the schooling whip or your hand, you can encourage the middle part to go out and begin to achieve the desired circle shape.

The triangle positioning is a very important part of the early training process (fig. 3.7). Work done in the stall or stable will influence the longeing of the horse at all levels because your position as the apex of the triangle will influence the way the horse goes: moving toward the hindquarters encourages the horse to go forward, while moving toward his head means, "Slow down." Moving toward the middle means, "Move out" (widen the circle).

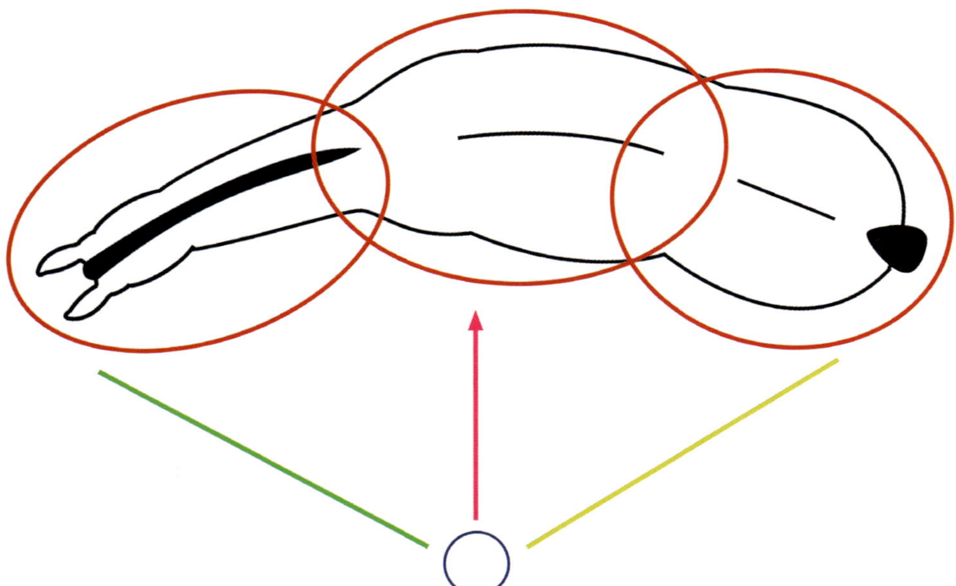

3.7 The Triangle Positioning, with the trainer at the apex, as marked here by the blue circle, is key to effective groundwork.

The key elements of the triangle when longeing are:

1 The longe line. Whether it is attached to the longe cavesson or the bit, this ultimately establishes the contact with the horse.

2 The longe whip. This governs the horse's use of the hind end and encourages the horse to move forward.

3 The trainer. The trainer's positioning and influence can slow the horse, speed up the horse, push the horse out, or allow him to come in. You can produce more or less bend through the horse's body, governing the horse's straightness.

Seeing Straightness

To help you see straightness, or the lack of it, practice looking at different horses as they come toward you and move away: are they moving correctly on the line they are being asked to trace?

Then take this information to your own horse, choosing a line to ride, at walk, and determining if the horse is on that line. His whole spine should follow the same path as the line you want to be on (fig. 3.8). Identify which part of the horse isn't on the chosen line. Developing this "feel" is a big part of the rider's education. To feel and sense straightness will allow you to know when it needs correction. When this becomes instinctive, correcting a fault as it happens becomes the norm.

Earlier in our work with the horse, we introduced the leg aids and their simple function as the request to go. They have other functions as well. They define

3.8 The horse's spine should align with the line you are following. This is a straight horse.

left and right, and in and out, becoming our boundaries. They guide direction and supply the horse with valuable information to enable him to do what we ask.

To help, we have our rein aids, which are, as our legs are, multifunctional. As far as straightness is concerned, the reins assist the legs in supplying the information of what line we want the horse to be on. (The horse has no concept of what a line is. It is a human-defined line to which we ask him to conform.)

Once we have established the line and the boundary aids, we now need to encourage the horse to buy into our interpretation of direction. How he gets from Point A to Point B is irrelevant to him; it is only we who care. We have to ask the horse to comply with the boundaries we give him, to be straight, and this requires us to influence each part of his body separately, so we can correct where and when it is necessary (figs. 3.9 A–C).

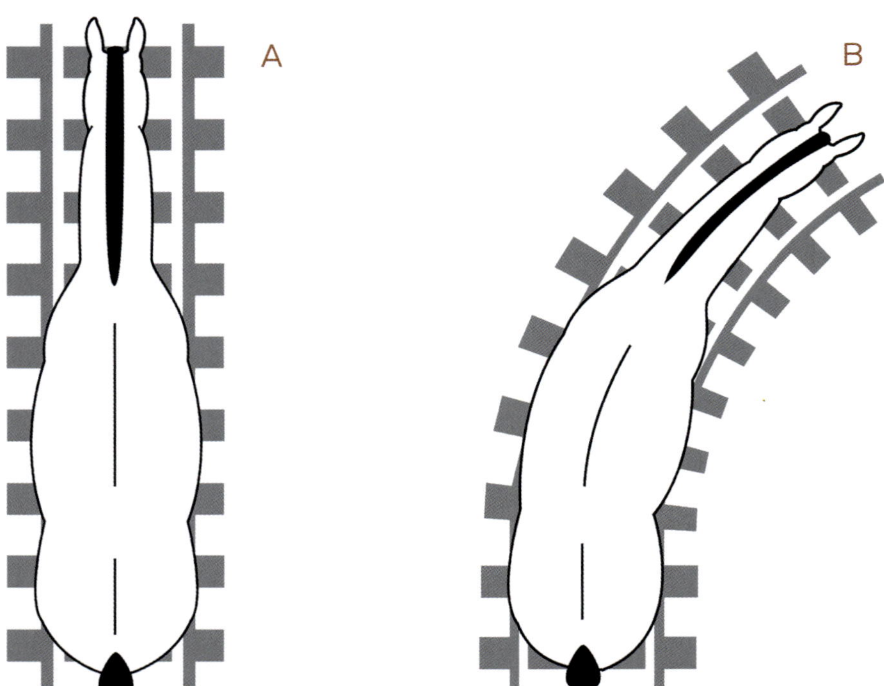

3.9 A–C Our leg aids combined with our rein aids provide the necessary boundaries to keep the horse straight and "on track," whether moving straight ahead (A) or riding a bending line (B).

Be aware: what falls in on one rein is likely to fall out on the other! For example, a shoulder that pops out to the left when going to the right will, on the other rein, be likely to fall in to the left. So in the examples of straightness problems that follow, it is important to think in a very deliberate way about what will happen when the rein is changed. What problems appear? What aid is needed to solve the issue?

Quality versus Control

Any simple movement when broken down will highlight the likely moment of the horse's escape. In knowing this, the rider will develop a feel for being ahead of the horse. Remember, the proactive rider sets the agenda and in doing so preempts the problem.

Anticipating challenges that are likely to arise allows you to guide the horse into

We need to be prepared to correct the horse in the different components of his body, for example, if the left shoulder falls out (C).

correctness. Knowing and trusting the rider's guidance improves the partnership and muscle memory of the horse so that he too can plan ahead with correct and consistent input from the rider.

Doing most of the detailed work on straightness at walk will help both horse and rider to get the message right. Messages need time to be absorbed. Only when they are understood at walk should we see if they are also understood in the faster gaits, which necessitate a quicker input and uptake of the message.

Don't assume understanding. As with all training and re-training, there will be a constant debate in the rider's mind: What's the priority at a particular moment? It is easy to say quality work should always be at the forefront of the rider's mind, but we may have to put that to one side as we grapple with the mechanics. Starting with less quality may allow easier communication, better balance, and better straightness, and hence allow the horse to develop the muscular control to be able to produce better quality *in time*.

Riders must visualize where they want the horse to go in this process. This positive, proactive attitude helps the horse to pick up their intention.

Poles can be a useful way to help the young horse pick up the message about straightness and adherence to the aids (fig. 3.10). By using poles as a guide, the horse has something tangible to aim for and relate to. Each time he succeeds, the process gets a tick in the box of achievement. Horses then grow in trust of the aid and where it actually means for them to go. It also helps the rider learn to apply a correction aid when the horse falls in or out. The horse will then recognize the correction as being a helpful message to get him between the poles. Remember, the horse has no understanding of what a line is or why it is important. He knows about direction, but not about the refinement of a line—that is entirely up to us.

Straightness Problems and Solutions

1 PROBLEM: POPPING THE LEFT SHOULDER. _ _ _ _ _ _ _ _ _ _ _ _ _

2 WHY IS THE PROBLEM THERE? It will be a natural tendency in most horses to fall out through one shoulder or the other. The horse that pops his left shoulder going

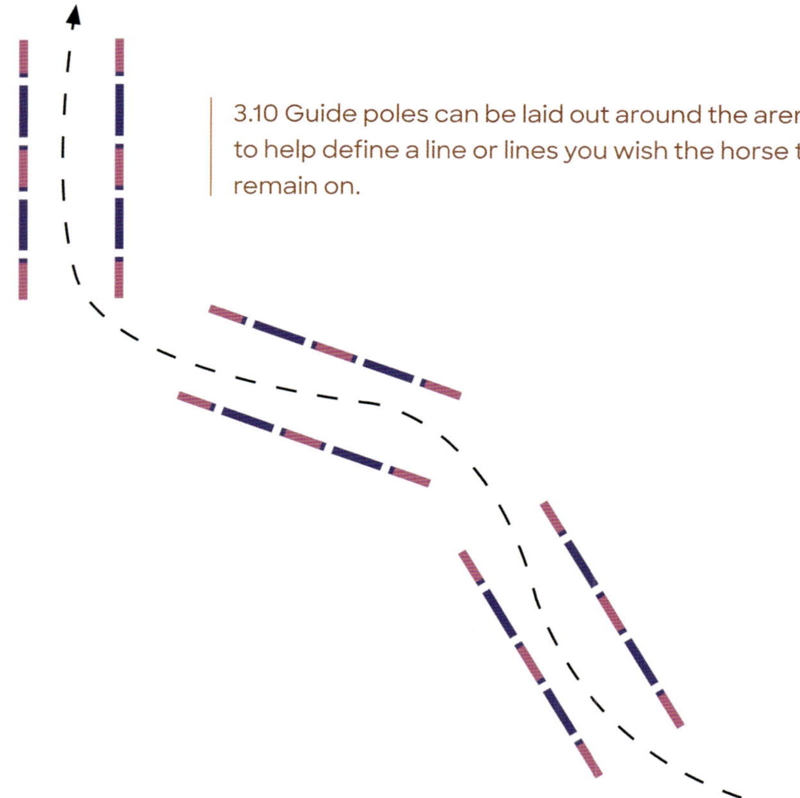

3.10 Guide poles can be laid out around the arena to help define a line or lines you wish the horse to remain on.

to the right will almost certainly fall in onto the left shoulder when going to the left. We should always be conscious that natural tendencies will tend to override what we teach. This lack of straightness will manifest in every movement we try to ride. It shows itself differently in each direction, yet it is a fundamental issue the horse started with.

3   Why does it need solving? Straightness improves efficiency of the horse's way of going, and it's the test of correct education.

4   How do you solve the problem? The left rein stops the horse's neck from bending to the right farther than the chosen line requires. And the left leg is active in supporting the rein and limiting the shoulder movement. The horse may well feel restricted in his movement and unable to comply, but the left rein must be steadfast in saying "no" to right bend and the left leg must be busy asking for the left shoulder to go back where it belongs. When the horse understands that each aid can work independently of the others, he becomes more compliant in being corrected.

Here's another good exercise:

- Ask for left bend with the left rein.
- Use the left leg on the girth or just in front of it, and ask the horse to walk straight ahead. Don't let the horse drift to the left.
- Begin to ask the forehand to go to the right while maintaining the left bend. Develop this "right" direction until you can ride a 20-meter circle with left bend.

Every line we ride requires no more bend than
what's required to place the spine along that line.

What you have encouraged the horse to do is to separate the head and neck from the shoulder and put the forehand in front of the hindquarters. This stops the shoulder from popping out. You can then be creative in moving the horse around the arena in walk and trot, ensuring that the horse understands the message of moving the forehand in front of the shoulders to help produce straightness.

1 PROBLEM: FALLING IN TO THE LEFT. _ _ _ _ _ _ _ _ _ _ _ _ _ _ _ _ _ _

2 WHY IS THE PROBLEM THERE? The same horse that pops his left shoulder (p. 59) will also try and fall in to the left and onto the left shoulder.

3 WHY DOES IT NEED SOLVING? Our reasons for solving this issue remain the same: straightness is key!

4 HOW DO YOU SOLVE THE PROBLEM? As the left rein asks for the left direction, our left leg must become dominant to stop the drift left. The outside rein can help but must not be the main aid as outside bend will result.

By asking for the bend of the curve earlier than required, the rider insists that the left drift is not allowed to happen. Instead, the horse is encouraged to fall a little out of the right shoulder in order to get back to the intended line. If the horse responds to the insistence of the left leg, he should be rewarded by the softening of its pressure.

When the chosen line is reached, the outside leg is applied with enough input to encourage the horse along the line, but not so much that it pushes the horse off the line in the other direction.

This give and take between the leg aids is a conversation the rider has with the horse to provide the necessary information to ride a line that the horse doesn't see, doesn't understand, and is really only doing to please us. If at any stage along the line the horse chooses to ignore the aid and falls left again, the rider must reinstate a strong left leg and ask the horse to go back out again. Always be ready for this to happen.

1 PROBLEM: LOSING STRAIGHTNESS AFTER THE CORNER. _ _ _ _ _ _ _ _ _

2 WHY IS THE PROBLEM THERE? This often happens as a result of the horse still responding to the corner aids or the rider being late in applying the "go forward straight" aids—or both.

3 WHY DOES IT NEED SOLVING? In most dressage tests, one question is followed by another one. In order to be prepared for the next question, the partnership must always be ahead in mind and body.

4 HOW DO YOU SOLVE THE PROBLEM? For a horse tracking to the left, all of the solutions I offered for the previous two problems apply, with some add-ons.

Asking for a light inside bend, we are able to see if the horse's instinct to fall left is being overridden by the use of the left leg. If so, good, as we can feel that the horse is trying to help us.

As we get to the beginning of the curve that describes the corner, the outside aids now come into play to ask the horse around the turn—an important input. As the turn begins to straighten, the rider's right rein and right leg begin to ask the horse to straighten up and conform with the line of the curve and then the straight line following the corner.

There is a moment coming out of the corner that is *very* important to manage: In the horse's mind he will continue the turn and go left, with the result of falling onto the left shoulder and a loss of straightness. The correction is to be ahead of this in *your* mind and to have the left leg aid ready to enforce the line. The outside aids can help finish the turn and focus the horse on the line ahead, but ultimately it should be the inside leg that gets the result.

The same is true going in the opposite direction. To keep the shoulder in front of the hind legs and remain straight requires the rider to focus on the left side of the horse. There will be a tendency for the bend right to appear when it is not wanted and the hind legs to drift right (coming inside the required line) so straightness is lost. As the corner begins, more bend than is required appears, and the horse's shoulder falls to the outside of the line.

The outside rein must be clear to limit the amount of bend to only that required of the line being ridden. As the corner ends and the horse must be straight to follow the line, the bend is often reluctant to straighten and the shoulder is often reluctant to come back in line. Riding this corner with a little outside bend, encouraging the horse with the outside leg and rein, can be a good reminder to the horse to listen to the outside aids.

Be warned: this is easier said than done! This fault (and those described earlier) will cause problems later unless you catch the tendency early. And even then, they can pop up when you least expect it. (The dressage judge will undoubtedly notice!) Catching this fault early will improve not only your balance and straightness in the corner and on the straightaway, but also:

- Preparation for left shoulder-in.
- Preparation for left half-pass.
- Correct use of the arena overall.

Regularity

The final quality we will deal with in this chapter is *regularity*.

Regularity is the ability to keep the gait the same, while as I described earlier, *rhythm* is the footfall of the gait. They are different qualities; both are asked for in a dressage test. The rhythm has to be correct as a prerequisite to all work (we should see no four-beat canters, for instance). Regularity is asking for the correct rhythm to remain constant throughout the work.

I would implore you to read the above few lines over and over again. Please do so for a few minutes and try and see why I am emphasizing this so much. In my teaching I am precise with words because I believe this is only fair to the horse. After all, we ask him to be precise in his work.

The word rhythm is overused in the horse world to cover a multitude of differing qualities, which can—and does—interfere with the understanding of what we watch, how we ride, how we train, and even how we understand the mechanics of the horse. We all sort of know what the word means! That is, until we see it used in different contexts.

Each gait has its own clearly articulated footfall or beat, defined by the species and enshrined in our efforts to preserve its integrity. So we should only talk about the rhythm of the gait being *correct* or *incorrect*: it is either two-, three-, or four-beat—or it isn't. If it is, then there's no need to talk about it again. If it isn't, then it's wrong.

On the other hand, regularity means staying the same, and this word further clarifies the qualities we want from the gait.

A lame horse still trots in a two-beat rhythm, but it is not regular. A four-beat canter is an incorrect rhythm, *but* it can be ridden with regularity.

To use these words in context allows us to be more correct and more precise. We then avoid misunderstanding that results from using one word for a multitude of things.

For example, I might say:

- "You have a lovely trot (it has a correct rhythm), but it doesn't stay the same (regular) for the whole circle."
- "Your medium trot across the diagonal lost its balance, resulting in a loss of regularity."

- "Your shoulder-in was correct in shape; however, a lack of connection meant a loss of regularity."
- "Your horse stays very regular in walk and looks calm; however, the rhythm is incorrect (lateral, pacing)."
- "Your horse has great regularity in canter and is correct in his rhythm, but more impulsion will improve the moment of suspension and give you a better mark."
- "The demi-pirouette lost its rhythm (four-beat walk)."

Tempo is yet another word that is often confused with rhythm and regularity. Tempo means the *speed* of the rhythm. It is often misused. But when we use it in the *correct* way, it can become very helpful and productive. It should in no way confuse the meaning of the other words but rather enhance the vocabulary available to the coach and the rider to improve the overall picture.

For example, I might say to a student:

- "What a lovely, correct (rhythm) trot you have. It is very regular, but to score the extra marks, you need to *up the tempo* (the speed of the rhythm)."
- "Your canter is correct (in its rhythm) and regular but lacks purpose. Up the *tempo* and it will show much more purpose."
- "Your horse is hurrying in trot, the *tempo* is too fast. Slow it down and allow the horse to take bigger and slower steps."

Why can it be difficult maintaining regularity? Well, regularity is closely linked with the word *connection* (see chapter 5, p. 113). I often draw the comparison of a person on a bicycle. When the bicycle is being pedaled there is a connection to the driving force pushing the bicycle. It becomes much easier to ride a straight line or a curve.

There is a similarity with horses, as it is the push from the horse that improves the regularity of the pace or gait.

What follows are all quite common problems encountered with the early stages of schooling as well as in the re-education of horses.

Regularity Problems and Solutions

1 Problem: Hind legs are just "following." _ _ _ _ _ _ _ _ _ _ _ _

2 Why is the problem there? Some horses naturally push from their back end; others don't. When looking at and watching horses, you can easily recognize those that do. There is a much more clearly defined step, and the hind legs will almost always come more under the horse as the horse moves forward.

3 Why does it need solving? The quality of every pace or gait is improved when there is "push" from behind to produce regularity. Performance both in the dressage ring and over jumps is improved when you have it. When it comes to dressage competition, for example, a "6" can be scored with the horse just bringing his hind legs along behind him without much "push." But scores above "6" require the hind legs to engage to ensure regularity and to produce a lift and cadence to the step.

4 How do you solve the problem? To merely allow the horse to "do what he does" is relying on the horse to understand what "better" is when under saddle. To the horse, it doesn't really matter if he has a regular pace, as long as he can keep up with the herd and stay out of trouble.

This issue requires an *intention* from the rider to produce a connection from the leg aids to the horse's hindquarters—and therefore, a response. When the rider has this intention to initiate this, the problem can be solved.

1 Problem: Hesitant transitions. _ _ _ _ _ _ _ _ _ _ _ _ _ _ _ _

2 Why is the problem there? In young horses and horses that require retraining, transitions the way we *want* them done can be an uncertain task for both horse and rider. Meanwhile, it's easy for transitions to happen the way they might in nature.

3 Why does it need solving? Good transitions show proof of a good education, as well as helping the horse become more efficient.

4 HOW DO YOU SOLVE THE PROBLEM? Once the mechanics of a transition has been taught, "quality" can be introduced. The rider's leg initiates the transition. This may seem counterintuitive, as some might think the rein would be the choice. In fact, the reins are applied almost simultaneously with the legs to initiate the horse's responses. The horse must remain secure between the aids.

When the mechanics are secure, the leg aids ask the horse to make the pace or gait in and out of the transition more positive and to demonstrate regularity. This will show a confidence in the process (and allow a "6" or above to be awarded in dressage competition).

1 PROBLEM: A LACK OF A PURPOSE. _ _ _ _ _ _ _ _ _ _ _ _ _ _ _ _ _ _

2 WHY IS THE PROBLEM THERE? This might reflect the character of the horse...or maybe his training or maybe his rider.

3 WHY DOES IT NEED SOLVING? Every part of riding is made so much easier when the concept of *forward* is being displayed. *Forward* gives you a purpose (see p. 38).

4 HOW DO YOU SOLVE THE PROBLEM? Every aspect of regularity is made so much easier when the horse and rider demonstrate a positivity to their work. There isn't a particular exercise or aid that produces this result; it's a state of mind and attitude.

1 PROBLEM: DROPPING BEHIND THE LEG. _ _ _ _ _ _ _ _ _ _ _ _ _ _ _ _ _

2 WHY IS THE PROBLEM THERE? This can be because you have a shy horse, or one who is not clear about what *forward* means (see p. 37). It can also be due to a lack of understanding of the aids or the rider's request, or a lack of responsiveness to the leg aids.

3 WHY DOES IT NEED SOLVING? Both the horse's mind and body must remain "up to the job at hand" and "in front of the aids." Note that does *not* mean *anticipating* the aids.

4 HOW DO YOU SOLVE THE PROBLEM? Much of what has been described in the section on forwardness is relevant to keeping the horse in front of the aids and forward of mind. Without these qualities, it is difficult to find regularity. Transitions within the paces or gaits are a very valuable exercises to keep the horse thinking and trying to be just ahead of the rider. This, in turn, allows the rider to input regularity into a pace or gait that might otherwise drop behind.

A Final Word

In our work, we should always question: "Is the horse *forward*? Is the horse *straight*? Is the horse *regular*?"

It should be remembered that these three words are qualities that can be ridden—they are verbs ("doing words" or actions)—and not just abstract ideals to throw around in order to sound knowledgeable. We should think of them as living, breathing qualities that are crucial to a horse producing good work, being a nice riding horse, and being a pleasure to be with.

Forward, straight, and regular form the basis of the majority of our work with our horses. They live with us as we ride, and they should be at the forefront of our minds every step of the way.

A beginner rider wants to work on better things.
A better rider wants to work on more advanced things.
An advanced rider continues to improve the basics.

CHAPTER 4

Contact

HAVING LOOKED AT *FORWARD, STRAIGHT, AND REGULAR* IN chapter 3 (p. 37), we should bring these qualities with us as we move on to contact. It is impossible to talk about these qualities in an unconnected way. They are, as with all the qualities in the book, related. If we haven't first been through the importance of forward, straight, and regular we are unable to do anything about the contact. Once the foundational qualities have been established and the horse allows some input into their development, only then is it possible to think about the contact and how we want it to evolve.

A good contact evolves as a result of a combination of correct aids and understanding. It isn't "just there"! The rider has many processes to go through before a pleasing picture and feeling can be created. Along this road there are any number of missteps that might spoil the contact.

When dealing with the re-education of the contact in an older horse, there is also the challenge of discarding what was there and then replacing it with what you want. That, in itself, is a difficult task. But when you are dealing with other issues that are undergoing change at the same time, to focus solely on the contact may not be possible. In this case, you may find that the expression, "It's work in progress," pops into your head. Fix a little, secure, move on, fix a bit more, secure, and so on.

What Is a Good Contact?

A good contact is the feel the rider and the horse share between the bit and the hand. The horse should have the bit held lightly in the mouth, be relaxed at the poll, and be happy to *hold* the connection with the rider's hand. It should be a feeling of mutual understanding, trust, and communication—similar to a couple holding hands (figs. 4.1 A–C).

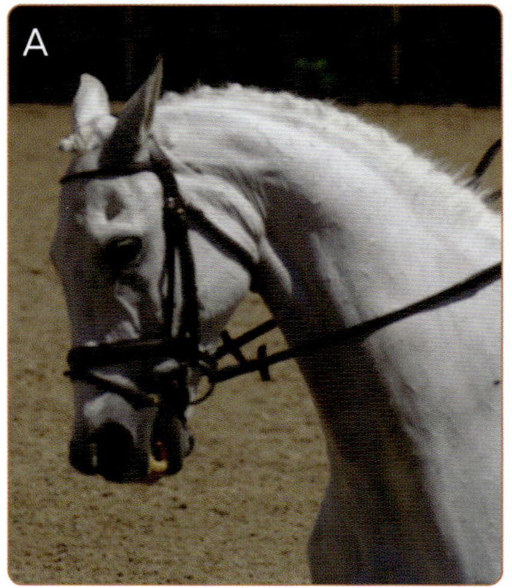

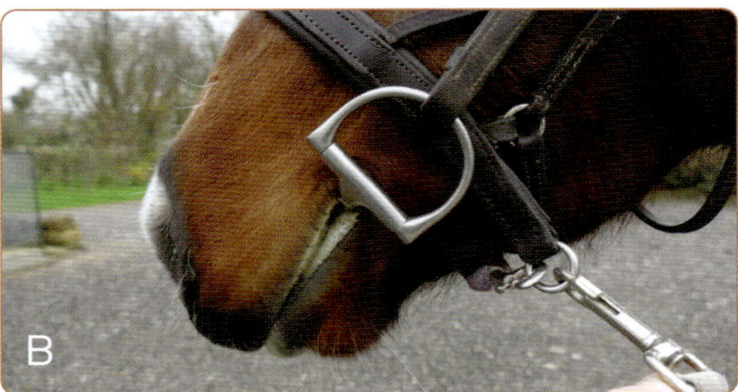

4.1 A–C Resentment of the bit and contact (A), acceptance of the bit in the mouth, although without understanding (B), and the start of understanding of the rein (C).

> *"The head and neck must seek the bit. I hate it if the horse comes behind the vertical and stays there. When the horse is really 'through,' you should be able to open and close the frame, and keep him reaching into the bit. And right now, in the [dressage] judging, in my opinion, this doesn't count for enough. But sooner or later, good riding will be rewarded. You must not lose your patience."*
>
> —INGRID KLIMKE, GERMAN OLYMPIC GOLD MEDALIST

Making and Re-Making a Mouth

In the "making" of a mouth, we are really making a brain. We are asking a horse to willingly accept the presence of a foreign body made of metal in his mouth. Then we are asking the horse to understand, through that piece of metal, all the messages being sent by the rider. At the same time, we want the bit to be quiet and still in the mouth. This is quite an ask. It can take months, and even years, for a horse to learn the desired responses and be comfortable with them.

In the meantime, we are trying to teach him to become a good riding horse. We are often inclined to hurry the making of a mouth so we can get on with other lessons and make training progress. But how can you train without any controls? In the beginning, we have no steering, no brakes, and every opportunity to need both! So you can see why this is a conundrum—to gain control, we may need to move more quickly than we might want with our horse and this may cause problems to arise at an early stage in training, which may prove difficult to correct.

There seems no other way to start a horse than to begin with the head, neck, and mouth, but we must proceed with caution, for once the wrong response is lodged in the brain, it can be difficult to unlearn. For example, if the horse happens to get his tongue over the bit at the early stages of training, it can be a habit that stays with him for life.

Retraining a horse with experience can actually be easier in many instances, as even a poorly educated horse is likely to have some kind of brakes and steering, although perhaps they're not the ones you want. In either case, there are at least partial solutions for many problems with the contact, and these will be the focus of this chapter. Before turning to common problems, however, let's first talk about the correct way to start the education of the horse's mouth.

An Evolution

The phrase "making a mouth" is a much-used-and-abused expression. "Creating an understanding" is better, but it is still incomplete. The process is one of the most important of starting the young horse and becomes a source of much discussion as the horse becomes a little older. *It is an evolution.* It doesn't just happen; there are many steps to go through.

I do not recommend the use of mouthing bits. It seems illogical to ask a horse to play with the bit one moment and the next moment tell him he must be quiet in the mouth. This kind of human inconsistency isn't helpful to horses.

The goal is for the horse to hold the bit comfortably in his mouth and accept its presence, so to begin the education necessary for contact, I prefer a single-jointed, D-ring eggbutt snaffle. A noseband may help keep the mouth quiet. Initially the horse won't understand more than the first step of putting the bitted bridle on. His acceptance of the presence of the bit may take days or weeks, but it is worth waiting for.

The horse may for a time try to expel the bit before he realizes he can't. Holding the bit still in the mouth is the first part of acceptance, and working on this for 10 to 15 minutes a day is plenty. When putting the bit in and taking it out, you should aim for minimal fuss. Try to avoid the bit clanking against the teeth as you take the bridle off.

Normal exercise, such as longeing and hand-walking can continue, but it is important not to have the bit in when doing these exercises. Why? Because new experiences often produce busyness in the mind, which can, in turn, produce a busy response in the mouth, and any association between exercise and a busy mouth should be avoided at all costs.

When an educational exercise is repeated enough to produce a calm response in the horse, then it can be undertaken with the bit in the mouth—but still with *no* contact anywhere near the bit. This gives the horse ample time to accept the presence of the bit without any pressure to understand what it does and builds a quiet acceptance in the brain that the bit "just sits in the mouth." The longer this response is allowed to happen, the more secure that response becomes.

Start in the Stable

I only ever begin to educate the contact with the horse in the stable, and I try to find a quiet moment. A quiet mind has more chance of producing a quiet mouth (figs. 4.2 A–D). You may be brushing the horse, just talking to him or getting to know him. This is a good time to broach the subject.

Get a lead rope, attach it to the bit on one side, and ask the horse to walk around you in his stall. Don't pull, just open your body and offer direction. You are the central figure, just as you are when you teach longeing (think back to the triangle from chapter 3—p. 54). The open, offering rein simulates the longe line, which the horse understands as indicating direction. The result should be that the horse walks around you, looking in the chosen direction with only the weight of the lead rope on the bit. Your body and other hand nudge and encourage the horse forward and outward, linking many key responses, including:

- Forward from behind.
- Outward from the middle of the body.
- Soft, open, looking in the direction of travel from a light contact on the bit.

These are all responses that we want in a nice riding horse, and they should be implanted in the mind quietly, without fuss or confusion. Note that I never try and hurry the production of saliva. It will come in its own time when the horse becomes comfortable with the process.

It is important to remember that the horse is seldom the same in both directions (as you recall from the discussion of straightness—see p. 50). There is not much you can do at this stage to rectify one-sidedness as this might confuse the message about the contact, but it is good to know a horse's natural tendencies early on so they can be addressed later.

In all training the use of the voice is very helpful. It reinforces what the horse feels when we are introducing an aid. The horse will respond to the voice and then associate the command with the aid happening simultaneously and so link the two. Gradually the voice becomes the lesser mode of communication. By this stage in

The re-education of a horse can also begin in the stall as described for a young horse (see p. 52). In both cases, the work must never be seen as "making" the horse do anything. "Asking for submission," "insisting on respect," and "becoming dominant," are all very outdated concepts that should be left by the wayside. Instead, we should be seeking or asking for understanding.

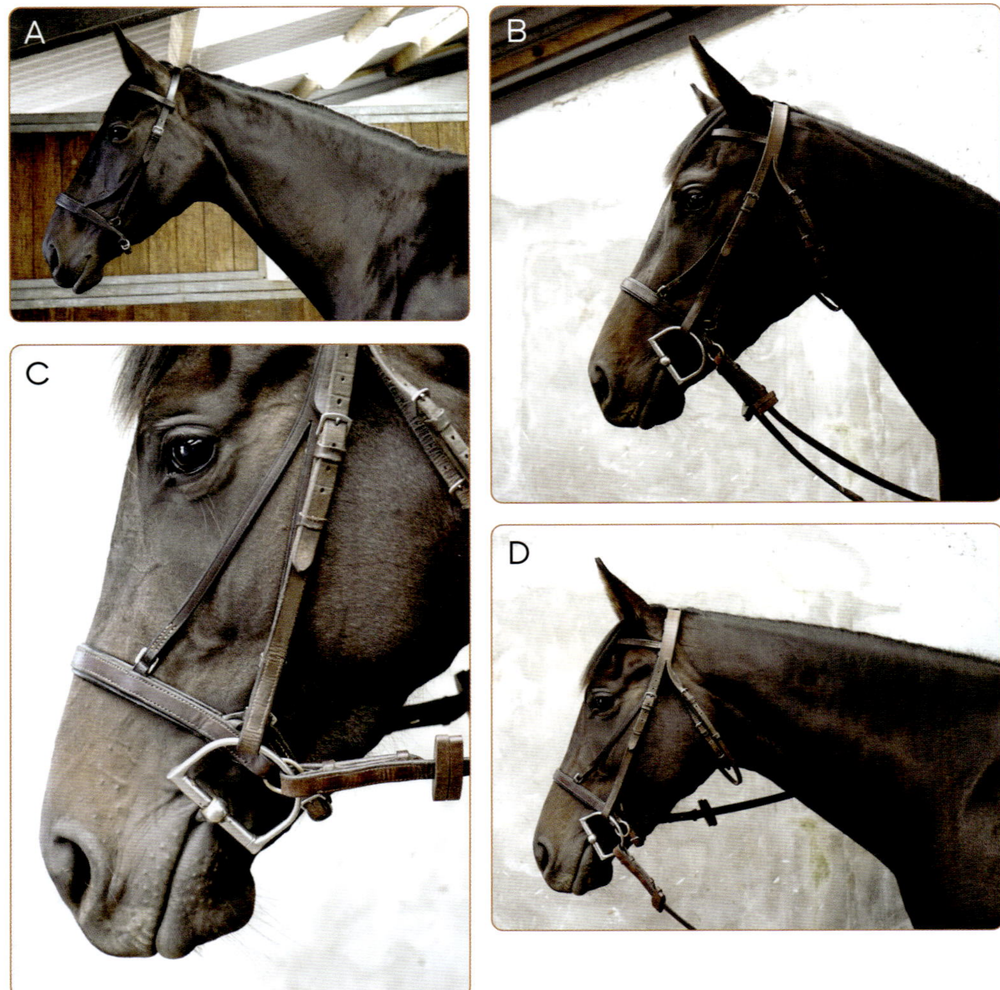

4.2 A–D A quiet mind helps make a quiet mouth. Note here the calm expression with a bridle headstall and no bit (A) and showing acceptance of a bit with the reins attached to the noseband (B). You can gradually introduce the weight of the rein on the bit by first attaching it to the noseband and the bit (C) before eventually, only the bit (D).

our training, the horse should already be accustomed to the use of the voice, understanding commands such as "Whoa" and "Walk on." (Intonation is just as important as the words you use. Soft and soothing will indicate slow; crisp and clean will indicate increased energy.) Adding the word "Whoa" when we apply light rein pressure enables the horse to relate the two messages and stop. Enthusiastic reward should endorse the linking of the two messages.

Other Training Methods and Aids

This is a good opportunity to look at some of the other popular methods of training from the ground that can contribute to the "making of a mouth." These are the go-to processes most riders and trainers use to solve problems with contact, as well as other qualities. But they too have limitations, so we should be careful not to fix one problem and add two more!

As with any task, it is not always "the doing" but the way in which groundwork is done that determines the result. When carried out well, longeing and long-reining (long-lining) are a joy to watch, but they can also be the source of many problems. We need to understand these problems if we are to avoid bringing them with us into our riding.

LONG-REINING

I have never been a fan of long-reining, but I am well aware that there will be others who are in favor of it. Let me explain my position.

Long-reining is a legacy from the era when horses were used as working animals in carriages, pulling farm machinery, and in other capacities. They were an entirely different breed, had a different mentality, and their training was, therefore, fundamentally different from that of modern-day sport horses. Working horses did not need to carry a rider, but for me the biggest difference is the way the rein contact was used and taught.

For the working horse, rein contact went backward, whereas the rein contact for the riding horse is an open guiding one—very different in basic concept and desired outcome.

I have explained my belief that huge care should be taken with making a mouth and avoiding the long-term harm that can occur if the process is done without sufficient thought. An incorrect process has long-term implications, even if that process is well-intentioned.

In our flatwork we are always told by the trainer, "Don't shorten the neck," "Use an open guiding rein," and "Ask, don't tell." But the rein aid, as it is used in long-reining, comes directly from behind, which is likely to shorten the horse's neck (fig. 4.3). It is also likely to "tell" with some insistence because it is not possible to make it open and guiding. It is also very difficult to be light with the hands at the end of 20 feet of reins. To a young, uneducated horse, it is easy to see how misunderstanding, and even physical harm might happen. The handler needs to be super skillful for the horse not to drop behind the action of the bit or become immune to its bidding. It is almost impossible to encourage an open turn with the horse's head and neck looking forward in the intended direction. Turns are more likely to be backward and accompanied by a tight neck or a tilt at the poll, and these issues are difficult to eradicate when riding begins.

Older horses may cope better with this training technique, but in the early days when a young horse doesn't know and is trying to learn, it is hard for them to take many benefits from the process. In the Thoroughbred industry, when horses are started as two-year-olds and are being prepared for racing, they may be too small to ride, so long-reining may be the preferred option. I do understand some of the benefits of long-reining, like encouraging the horse to walk out by himself, cope with new surroundings, and gain experience of the

4.3 While long-reining has its uses and its proponents, I feel it often leads to the horse shortening his neck or coming behind the action of the bit—neither of which we would want to become habits in our horse.

bigger world. These benefits are valuable, but it is better at this stage to attach the reins to a nose cavesson rather than a bit so that the horse does not relate long-reining exercises to subsequent lessons related to contact. Since there are other ways to achieve the same benefits, I avoid long-reining.

WALKING IN HAND

Walking beside a horse is my preference over long-reining. I spend a lot of time walking with my horses, and I do so from both sides so they develop equally and evenly on both reins. This also allows me to develop a good relationship with them (and it's good exercise for me!).

In the beginning with a young horse, walking with tack can be a very peaceful introduction to their new life. It is equally valuable when re-training. There are stages with both educational processes when a horse has to get used to new things. Patience is required every step of the way. For example, every time I introduce a new piece of tack, it is walk time. The horse is encouraged to walk positively and mimic my own strides. This positivity can be further reinforced by the use of my voice, and if need be, with a tap with a long schooling whip.

By introducing the young horse to the "walking hack" from the ground, you are introducing him to another world outside his field, stall, and arena. He learns to trust himself because he trusts you. Your body language and encouragement helps him grow up, and he is less likely to be concerned about the new item of tack you have dressed him with because he is occupied by his novel surroundings.

The Whip Is not a Weapon

I have already talked about the use of the schooling whip and how it must be perceived as an aid and a helpful friend. It can appear to be quite a weapon, but it must not be thought of in this way. It is a piece of equipment that the horse must be comfortable with as another means of communication. It provides access to parts of the horse that are otherwise difficult to get to and allows a trainer or rider to apply an aid at the appropriate time.

At this stage, I try to take the horse on routes that he will likely travel when he is first ridden so when it comes to riding them, he is less likely to be taken by surprise.

When you walk beside the horse, you have many opportunities to continue his education about what the reins mean, what your voice means, and toward the "making" of his mouth. There will be occasions when the horse is receptive and "allows you in," and there will be other times when you shouldn't try. Being beside him will make it is easier to tell the difference.

LONGEING

Longeing is an extension of the work I have suggested be done in the stall (see p. 52). Once again, we have the triangle of positions (see p. 54) so the horse should feel comfortable with the transition. When first going to the indoor or outdoor arena, you should try to confirm what was learned in the stall before beginning new lessons, as the horse is likely to be distracted initially.

Longeing well is a skill at which we should all become proficient. The handling of the equipment, the timing of the input—the voice, body, and whip—and the exercise chosen are all important parts of the education process.

Besides allowing the trainer to "see the whole picture" some distance away from the horse, there are numerous benefits of longeing for the horse, including:

- Improved independence.
- Improved balance.
- Improved communication skills.
- Allowed to find his own way of going.

When things go wrong during longeing, it is likely caused by:

- Poor handling by the trainer.
- Fear or uncertainty of what is being asked.
- Believing that equipment alone can produce a result.
- Having an unclear process.

THE CHAMBON

The Chambon is a very valuable schooling aid *when used correctly*, but it is often misunderstood, so its true value is not always seen. When used to force or cajole a horse into doing something, it becomes an unwanted "gadget." Any training aid is only of true value when it *shows* the way to the horse rather than *tells* him. And it is very important that it is introduced properly.

The aim of a Chambon is to stimulate a response from the horse that encourages a longer and rounder neck carriage. It is useful for horses that have a naturally high carriage, a short neck, or a hollow back, or for a horse that "hides" from taking the bit—several problems that will be explored in this chapter.

The Chambon should be fitted fairly loosely to start, and you should begin by walking beside the horse. Get him walking forward, and then apply a little pressure on the Chambon, which then applies pressure on the horse's lips at the corners. The reaction you are looking for is for the horse to lower away from the pressure. When this happens, immediately praise him, making it very obvious that he has responded in the correct way. Do this a number of times, each time, making the reward very clear.

Do not rush the process and do not overtighten the Chambon or force the response. Remember to always reward the horse and to reinforce the positive response by asking him to go forward. This will sow the seeds of: *forward from behind, over the back, lower in the frame,* and *seek the bit.*

Watch the horse's mouth as you longe him in a Chambon (fig. 4.4). He should show a soft acceptance of the bit, not a tense tolerance. This soft acceptance will become the contact you are looking for when you ride him. Do not force the head and neck down.

*When it comes to working from the ground, the handling of the equipment is **so** important. When trainers are able to deftly handle equipment as if it was part of themselves, they can devote total concentration to the task at hand. All too often, poor handling destroys any benefits that equipment might otherwise provide, and it can also be dangerous.*

When you substitute a pair of reins that give the horse a similar pressure to the Chambon, he is likely to offer you the same desired response by lowering the frame and seeking a softer contact. When you make this transition and you are on the horse, you should take the reins with the same contact and apply a light leg aid. The horse should begin to associate leg and rein contact with softening and lowering the neck.

This process can take a few days for the horse to understand, but the rewards are huge for you have allowed the horse to learn for himself where you want him to be and opened up his topline by removing resistance.

A Simple Rope

Some trainers use a long rope of 14 to 20 feet to encourage the horse to become familiar with the trainer's requests. There should be no force and time should be taken with this method. It is best done in an enclosed area such as a stall, a round pen, or a paddock.

I have watched people desensitizing horses with ropes, and when done well, it is fascinating. I have been privileged to work with Katja Schumann, the daughter of Max Schumann, who was the last director of the famous Cirkus Schumann, one of Europe's most respected circus companies until it closed in 1969. Katja made her first appearance

4.4 The great shape of a horse seeking the contact while being longed in an appropriately adjusted Chambon.

Beware Gadgets

Many "training aids" designed with good intent compound misunderstanding. They can contribute to a false way of going under the guise of "improving the athletic abilities of the horse."

Beware the multitude of longeing paraphernalia on the market, all promoting something that makes it better than another piece of equipment.

- "The must-have method to improve such and such…"

- "As used by…!"

- "Top trainers swear by it!"

Horses will comply without understanding to a lot of these gadgets, most of the time by finding a comfortable way to avoid the pulleys and ropes trussing them up (fig. 4.5). The outdated words "submissive" and "dominant" come to mind. Once removed they tend to revert to their normal way of going. It takes very skillful longeing to explain to the horse any benefits that might be possible when gadgets are in use. Note that the Chambon, which I describe as potentially beneficial in this chapter, should not "position," "restrict," or "hinder" the horse but merely guide the horse in the correct way of going.

4.5 Gadgets in general, and certainly in longeing, should be avoided. I find they confuse more than they clarify, and they generally require tremendous skill and experience.

in the ring of the family circus at age 10 as a ballerina on horseback. She subsequently worked in her family's outstanding equestrian acts, notably in high school dressage (the highest from of classical riding) presentations, alongside her father (fig. 4.6).

I was able to watch Katja train horses and work with her, and she used ropes in a most delightfully educated way. The horses appeared to enjoy the process and were so engaged with her (figs. 4.7 A–C).

I have also watched some Western trainers using ropes. Good horsemen make it look easy and do so in a humane way. One example is the legendary American horseman Gene Lewis. I wish I had been around to work with him. I have heard so much about him from two of his former pupils, Darcy and Robin Sundeen, from Lynnleigh Farm in Sandy, Utah.

4.6 Katja Schumann performed in her family's Cirkus Schumann until it closed, and then found engagements with some of Europe's other leading circuses where she established a strong reputation as one of the best high school riders of her generation. She participated in the first International Circus Festival of Monte Carlo in 1974, where she won *La Dame du Cirque* award, given to the best female performer. In 1976, she won a Gold Medal at the Circus World Championships in London.

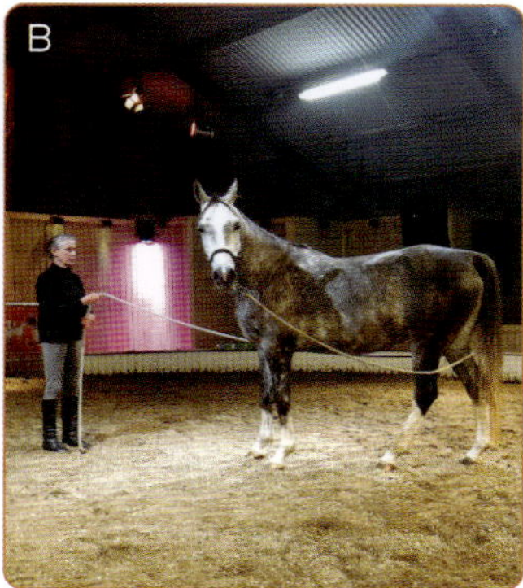

4.7 A–C Katja Schumann using a long rope in a gentle way to familiarize the horse with contact around his feet and legs (A), hind end (B) and girth area (C).

Lewis grew up in Idaho and worked on a cattle ranch until he enlisted in the United States Air Force in 1944. After WWII, he entered the horse show world, first in Western divisions, but then in the jumper divisions where he could make more money. He applied his Western training knowledge and experience to the preparation of top jumpers, and soon made himself a riding career on the West Coast as well a popular clinic schedule throughout the Western United States (fig. 4.8 A & B).

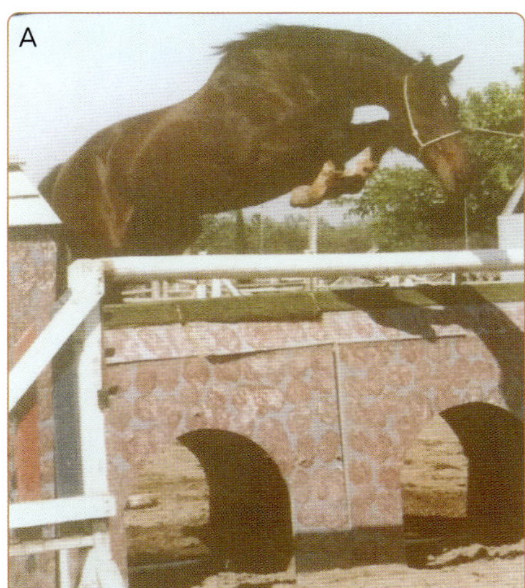

4.8 A & B Gene Lewis was known for turning green horses into successful jumpers in no time. He used to say that when a rider didn't "mess around" with a horse too much, "things worked pretty well."

Using ropes during the early handling process, as Katja Schumann and Gene Lewis proved, could encourage horses to "open the door" and "welcome you in." The techniques they used encouraged the horse to become part of and not afraid of the training process. He became trusting of the journey and the ultimate outcome…*being partners.*

While using ropes needs care in learning the skills, which takes time to learn, by watching experts, you can learn a lot.

RIDING WITH A NECK STRAP

Once we are able to ride a horse, we should develop the skill of riding with a neck strap from the very first stages. Contrary to popular belief, a neck strap is not only an old person's or a beginner's aid. Used skillfully, it has many benefits, including:

- Allowing freedom of the horse's head and neck.
- Improving horse and rider balance.
- Teaching the horse to rebalance.
- Giving peace from busy hands to the horse's mouth as he learns about contact.
- Allowing the horse to find his "fifth leg" when jumping (he quickly reacts when getting too close or far away from a fence, or when slipping or tripping, and adjusts as needed).
- Allowing the rider to stay out of the way as the horse learns his own skills.

A neck strap is not a technical piece of kit. An old stirrup leather will suffice (fig. 4.9). Note that if a neck strap is used in competition, FEI (Fédération Equestre Internationale) rules dictate that it must have an independent attachment to the saddle to stop it from falling forward and possibly becoming caught in the horse's legs.

Riding with a neck strap is something that should become a habit and should be done equally well with both hands. Start by taking a light rein contact, one that does not restrict or annoy the horse but encourages him to go and seek more. The horse may feel slightly abandoned and unsure of himself with a light contact, so allow time for him to get used to walking and gently trotting along tracks, lanes, or around the arena. The rider may feel inclined to shorten the reins if the horse goes faster, but avoid doing this whenever possible.

Instead, pull the neck strap, which will also produce a very light (additional) feel on the reins. The horse will slow down to the neck pressure. This is the beginning of the all-important *rebalance*—one of if not *the* most important lessons taught to horse and rider. This is my preferred substitution for what many might refer to as the "half-halt," and what I find many don't fully understand. All rebalances happen when the horse's weight is moved from the front to the back—a mechanical redistribution.

As the horse gets used to this feeling, he will develop an understanding that a light rein and the leg closing means *rebalance*, without the rider having:

4.9 A correctly fitted neck strap can be of aid when making the horse's mouth. This one is an unused stirrup leather.

- Shortened the horse's neck.

- Manhandled the horse's mouth.

- Upset the horse's balance.

- Upset his own balance.

When retraining horses, especially racehorses, we have to reeducate the notion of grabbing the bit and running, something racehorses are taught to do. By using the neck strap to train the rebalance, we can break the links the horse may have mistakenly made that:

- Rein contact means, "Go faster."

- Rein contact means, "Curl up and hide."

- Rein contact means, "Shorten the neck."

The neck strap will thus be a useful tool in finding solutions to several of the problems covered in this chapter (and beyond).

Addressing Problems with the Contact

If we are lucky enough to start with an untouched horse and have a blank sheet of paper to begin with, we can follow the logical course of installing the qualities of forward, straight, and regular before moving on to establishing the contact. Knowing how mouths are made in the early stages of training can be helpful when attempting to improve what you have. Knowing what you want to achieve gives a feeling of how to encourage the horse along the right path.

Any method of communication that works through a bit in the mouth is open to much abuse in the wrong hands, and so a thorough understanding is vital if we are to avoid discomfort and pain for the horse. Getting it wrong can leave the horse with uncomfortable memories and an incorrect habit that may remain with him for life.

Let me offer a reminder here of the conundrum at the center of our quest to establish a good contact: In order to remain safe working with an untrained horse, we need to retain control. But the horse doesn't understand the controls yet. We must, therefore, find ways of gaining control without taking hold of the reins too much and creating lasting problems through misunderstanding. (That's why I like to use a neck strap—p. 84.)

At the same time, we are trying to let go of the reins and encourage the horse to find his own balance while he gets used to a bit in his mouth, and we are also applying our leg aids to the sides of the horse. As the desired responses have not been firmly established at this point, misunderstanding of both aids can occur. For instance, instead of the horse going quietly and listening to the legs' "conversation" (which he doesn't yet fully understand), he may become too responsive and go too fast, encouraging us to use too much rein, which he *also* doesn't quite understand.

I repeat this here only to emphasize how complicated this process is. Whichever way you look at it, it must be a compromise. As I've tried to make clear, it's not always possible in the beginning to do it correctly, however much we may want to. Problems, like the ones that follow, are bound to arise.

Contact Problems and Solutions

1 PROBLEM: A BUSY MOUTH. _

2 WHY IS THE PROBLEM THERE? Many horses can be heard "chattering," grinding their teeth, or just being "busy" in their mouths when they have a bridle on and bit in. Some horses are just naturally busy. Busy mouths tend to come from busy minds. There are many reasons for this. It may be induced by the rider or trainer, but often it is simply a reflection of the horse's character. Some horses are of a nervous disposition and find the bit a comfort to play with; some horses play with the bit as a response to the rider's hands being busy; some grind their teeth when they are tense, anxious, or irritated; others simply *like* to play with the bit; sometimes early training with a mouthing bit can encourage long-term mouthing.

Asking the horse to understand the rein before he has accepted the presence of the bit is sometimes to blame. Asking too much change of a horse too soon can likewise cause the problem, as can general anxiety about the surroundings, or simply a misunderstanding of what's being asked.

3 WHY DOES IT NEED SOLVING? The ideal mouth, as explained earlier (see p. 70), should be calm and quiet, reflecting the qualities of the mind, and showing that the schooling of the horse has been calmly and progressively taught.

4 HOW DO YOU SOLVE THE PROBLEM? Whatever the reason for a busy mouth, it can be a challenging problem to solve. A sound principle of corrective training is to remove the source of the problem and re-educate the response, but with horses this is not always possible. Once they develop a bad habit, it is difficult to explain to them that they are doing something undesirable, even if you remove the source. Simply stopping them, when it is possible, doesn't correct the habit or the horse's desire to continue doing it.

Here are some things to try:

- Re-educating the rider to have quieter hands is always a good place to start.
- Close the horse's mouth (within humane and legal limits, such as with the use of a flash) in order to limit the movement.
- Test different bits in an effort to find a comfort zone for the horse.

Each of these solutions has merit but employed alone may not be the total solution. In some cases, you will need to try all of the above, along with a return to the exercises on the ground that I described in the section on making a mouth (p. 71). A re-education of what a good contact and connection really is can often be your best bet for improving the situation and producing a solution you can live with. As the horse grows in confidence with a contact that is quiet, secure, predictable, and with feeling (like a nice handshake between humans), he becomes more able to reciprocate those feelings. The connection coming from the rider's leg aids also supports our request for the horse to take the contact and grow in his confidence of what's good and wanted.

1 PROBLEM: A DRY MOUTH. _

2 WHY IS THE PROBLEM THERE? This is when the mouth remains dry with no production of saliva. The production of saliva is an indication of an acceptance of the bit. It should be a creamy color and not produced in large quantities of white froth (which is generally an indication of fear, worry, or anxiety). It indicates a relaxation of the lower jaw, which activates the mandibular saliva gland under the lower jaw. If the mouth becomes clamped around the foreign object, no saliva is produced, and the mouth remains dry.

3 WHY DOES IT NEED SOLVING? The clamped, dry mouth renders contact with the bit unproductive or even counterproductive.

How often have we heard riders say: "My horse has a hard mouth," "My horse doesn't turn right/ left," "My horse was a racehorse, and he still runs away with me," "My horse is very sensitive in the mouth"? All of these are issues that begin with a poor understanding of what the bit is to the horse in his education. This, in turn, often leads to stronger bits being used to compensate for the horse's lack of understanding. But this is not the horse's fault!

4 HOW DO YOU SOLVE THE PROBLEM? Trying to prompt the production of saliva may also prompt unwanted movement in the mouth. I have yet to find a horse that left quietly to become accustomed to the bit will not in his own time begin to produce this important sign of acceptance. Beware of hurrying things with the making of a mouth. Allow the horse to get used to work from the ground and in the stable to improve the acceptance and understanding of the bit. Avoid trying to "work" the bit and push the horse to understand. Saliva will begin to appear on its own as this acceptance happens naturally.

1 PROBLEM: A HARD MOUTH. _

2 WHY IS THE PROBLEM THERE? It might sound as if a "hard mouth" is a physical problem, but it isn't. This term refers to cases where the horse desensitizes himself to the action of the bit. This unresponsiveness can be for many reasons, including:

- The horse doesn't understand.
- The horse doesn't want to understand.
- He is avoiding the actions of bad hands.
- He has experienced previous discomfort with the bit.

3 WHY DOES IT NEED SOLVING? Little will be accomplished with our communication if the correct understanding of the bit doesn't happen.

4 HOW DO YOU SOLVE THE PROBLEM? Unresponsiveness is in the mind, not the mouth. Our priority must be to open the mind to become more responsive and understanding of what we are asking. Be very aware of falling into the trap of believing that it has anything to do with the type of bit you are using. It can be easy to be persuaded to go down that cul-de-sac.

The key is to reactivate the horse's brain so that he *wants* to understand. If we can open the door, the education process can begin anew. As he begins to understand what you want him to do, make sure he receives a reward. This will encourage him to open the door wider. Quiet work in the stall is a good place to start with the remedy. Begin as you would with a young horse (see description on p. 52).

Use a guiding rein to offer right and left. As this gentle request becomes willingly accepted, begin to apply slight pressure with two reins. Wait for the horse to offer a response of the lower jaw relaxing and then reward him. Repeat the exercise until the horse understands that light rein pressure on both reins means relax the lower jaw and at the poll. Then do the same when mounted. Be patient when asking. As the horse's understanding improves, go on to apply a light leg aid and rein pressure at the same time, and the horse will begin to connect the two aids. When the horse feels a light rein and leg, he should soften his lower jaw and poll—the very beginning of being "on the bit," which I will discuss at greater length (beginning on p. 95) and of riding a *rebalance* or a half-halt (see p. 150).

1 PROBLEM: TONGUE OVER THE BIT. _ _ _ _ _ _ _ _ _ _ _ _ _ _ _ _ _ _ _

2 WHY IS THE PROBLEM THERE? This is a more common problem than people think—sometimes they don't even realize their horse has his tongue over the bit. There are many reasons why this happens in the beginning: poor fitting of the bit when it's being introduced to the horse; the bit being too low in the mouth; a bit that is the wrong size and shape for the horse; or sharp teeth, which cause the horse discomfort.

3 WHY DOES IT NEED SOLVING? It is important to recognize when this happens and what it feels like. The sensation and feel the rider gets through the reins back to the hands will change and the contact will become less consistent, sensitive, and responsive. The horse may be fussy and give the feeling that he is uncomfortable (which he undoubtedly is). He will often open his mouth in an effort to get his tongue back over the bit.

There may be times when the tongue comes out the side of the mouth as the horse tries to find a comfortable position for it. From the ground, it is a fairly easy problem to see. However, some horses hide it well as they become practiced at doing it.

Apart from the difficulty you're likely to have making the horse comfortable and finding a good contact, there is the chance that he will be frightened by the experience and bolt in an attempt to avoid the pain or discomfort.

Do not underestimate this problem or avoid doing something about it—we must help in its correction.

4 HOW DO YOU SOLVE THE PROBLEM? Getting the tongue over the bit is not an easy habit to correct. First, make sure tack fits correctly and consider whether you, as a rider, could be the source of the problem: Busy hands produce a busy mouth (see sidebar, p. 92).

It is possible to physically stop the tongue from going over the bit, with a "tongue grid" (fig. 4.10). There are various styles and fittings available, but the horse will still always be trying to find a way to avoid its function.

Tightening the noseband may seem like a solution, but it is not. It can discourage bringing the tongue over the bit, but it won't stop the issue.

There are many reasons why horses put their tongues over the bit, and the seed can be sown as early as the first time the horse has a bit in his mouth. This is a really bad habit for a horse to develop. He would have to be an exceptional performer for me to even consider buying a horse that habitually got his tongue over the bit because once a horse starts doing it the habit is likely to remain with him forever. It is very distracting for the horse as well as the rider.

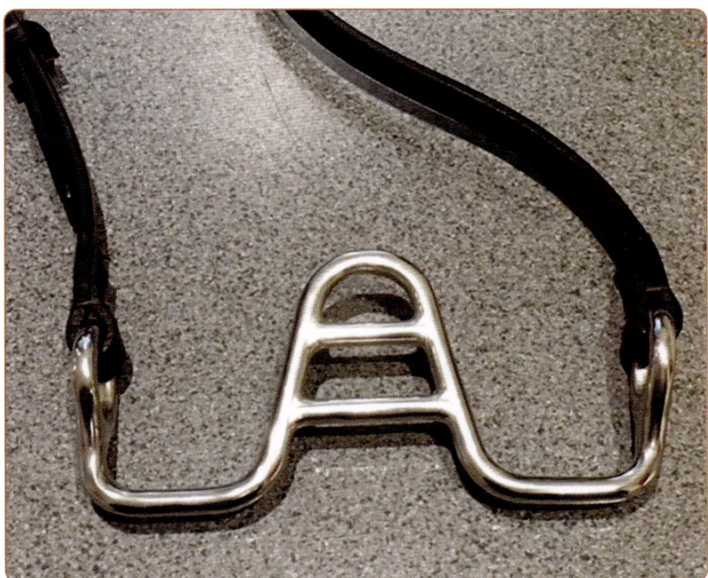

4.10 A "tongue grid" can physically prevent the horse's tongue from coming over the bit.

Busy Hands

Riders need to know that they have the bad habit of busy hands before they will be able to do anything about it. Some riders never know, until it is pointed out to them. When their attention is drawn to the issue it can be a whole new education for them.

Some trainers encourage riders to be busy with their hands in order to "keep the bit active and alive" in the horse's mouth. However, to ask the horse to be still and quiet with the bit while the other end of the reins is busy in the rider's hands is illogical and very confusing for the horse. If we want the contact to be quiet, then the hands must also be quiet.

Changing the way riders hold the reins can very often help. Having the reins come through the forefinger and thumb, rather than the usual way between the fourth finger and pinky, can be a good solution.

1 PROBLEM: NO CONTACT. _

2 WHY IS THE PROBLEM THERE? When the horse drops any feel through the bit and rein, we have no contact with his mouth. As I've mentioned already, dropping the contact is often thought of as a good sign of the horse accepting the bit. Riders can and do ask for this to happen but are mistaken in doing so. Some horses willingly comply.

3 WHY DOES IT NEED SOLVING? To have nothing in front of you, no *feel* at the other end of your rein, is a difficult sensation to ride—it's hard to know where the horse actually is, and what he's thinking or going to do. There can also be a tendency for the horse to shorten the neck and drop behind the bit when he should seek the contact.

4 HOW DO YOU SOLVE THE PROBLEM? It is important to make every effort to encourage the horse to take *some* contact. It doesn't matter if this is a resistant contact, a rude contact, a light contact—anything will do at this stage in the training. The old adage rings true: "You can educate something, but you can't educate nothing!"

A soft-mouthed bit such as a Nathe will often encourage a horse to hold the bit— always worth a try, even if it is only a step along the path to something else later on.

This is true for the early stages of training a young horse just as it is for the re-education of the older horse.

It can also be helpful to ride with a neck strap (see p. 84). Holding a neck strap and the reins at the same time can steady the rider's hands. This in turn will steady the contact and encourage the horse into a friendly connection between the bit and rein. The neck strap also has the effect of slowing a horse down, complementing the message the rein aid is giving without the reins having to do much, if anything. This can also encourage a shy horse to take a contact with the rider's hand.

Holding the neck strap allows the horse to find his own balance by leaning on the bit. Never reprimand the horse for holding the bit too much. This is a good sign and often a prelude to taking a contact that can be educated.

Common Misunderstandings About the Contact

When the word "light" precedes the word "contact" there is often the misperception that this means that the contact is almost not there. Light can be quite firm in the hand, but the horse must feel happy to take up the contact.

When the horse is asked to "accept" the bit, there is likewise a misperception that if he then drops any contact, he has done what was asked of him. Acceptance should not feel like avoidance, but rather like a reaffirmation.

1 PROBLEM: TOO MUCH CONTACT. _ _ _ _ _ _ _ _ _ _ _ _ _ _ _ _ _ _ _

2 WHY IS THE PROBLEM THERE? There can be many manifestations of this problem, from leaning on the bit, to running away, to being unresponsive or just ignorant. Fear, ignorance, or ill-fitting tack are the likeliest culprits.

3 WHY DOES IT NEED SOLVING? For the same reason that having no contact with the horse's mouth is a problem: without a good contact, our communication with the horse is impaired.

4 HOW DO YOU SOLVE THE PROBLEM? There are slightly different solutions for different manifestations of the problem.

If the horse is *leaning* on the bit, then we must teach him the rebalance (see p. 150). As with the challenge of a hard mouth (p. 89), the remedy is to return to groundwork until the horse understands that a light rein contact combined with the leg aid should result in a softening of the poll and the jaw. This is the very beginning of the horse's understanding of "being on the bit." The connection in the horse's mind between the rider's leg and softening to the bit is critical. It cannot be overemphasized.

As this book progresses, you will see how the relationship between leg and hand develops. It is *so* important not to overload the understanding of either aid too early as the horse will be unready (mentally and physically) to oblige. As with any conversation, we should begin with a vocabulary that is understood and only then move on to use more complicated words (that might have more nuanced meaning).

If the horse is *running away,* then you must teach him to *stop,* any way possible!

If the horse is *unresponsive* or shows that he *doesn't understand what is being asked,* then we must reopen the horse's mind to being attentive to the aid. Once again, groundwork is the solution. Then we need to address the rebalance and the ability to ride with a regularity to the gait (see chapter 3, p. 63). Many small rebalances eventually make up a big difference. Be careful to avoid asking the horse to "give" too much as the outcome might be to drop the contact and drop behind the leg.

Throughout a horse's training there will be continual adjustment of the amount of contact desired. Riders may have differing preferences (based on personal style, balance issues, or the way they have been taught) as to the feel they want through the hand. But everyone should have *some* contact. It is part of the demonstration of good education.

Addressing Problems with Neck Shape, Outline, and Being on the Bit

One of the questions I'm asked most often is how to get a horse "on the bit." We should all appreciate that being truly on the bit is a feeling that pervades the whole being of the horse and is not just about the bit or where the horse's head and neck are, although the two things are very much related to one another (fig. 4.11).

Putting a horse on the bit is a measure of achievement for a lot of riders and a source of interest for many others. I will deal with it in pieces. There are many parts to the subject and each part should be understood in order to make up the whole picture.

4.11 David Taylor demonstrates a lovely frame, in a light seat, allowing the horse to work on to the bit.

The first part is to look at the conformation of your horse. What does the neck shape look like? How is it attached to the rest of the body? What happens to this shape if I do X, Y, or Z? We should bring certain qualities with us from learning to watch horses, qualities that help us recognize a pleasing picture as well as a happiness and willingness to work and an attentiveness to the aids. (In fact, it may be helpful to revisit the section on neck shape in chapter 1 before proceeding—see p. 20.) Most importantly, having understood the problem how do you correct it?

Neck Shape, Outline, and Being on the Bit Problems and Solutions

1 PROBLEM: ABOVE THE BIT. _ _ _ _ _ _ _ _ _ _ _ _ _ _ _ _ _ _ _

2 WHY IS THE PROBLEM THERE? When the horse is higher in the neck than normal and carrying his head with the nose out, well in front of the vertical, this is what's known as being "above the bit." There are many reasons for this, from conformational defects to a misunderstanding of or resistance to the aids. If it is a conformational defect, we must look at how best to help the horse carry himself in a more correct way given the body he has to work with.

Horses that are "hollow-necked" or "ewe necked," for instance, often have difficulty understanding what good carriage is. Sometimes the prescribed solutions can be worse than the original problem, so don't be in a hurry to try and correct it.

3 WHY DOES IT NEED SOLVING? Assuming that the problem is not one of conformation and can be corrected through training, we should aim to do so as part of educating a good contact. Being correctly on the bit is also necessary to achieve *throughness*—a correct representation of being between leg and hand.

Going above the bit during transitions is a common problem. Horses will often go above the bit when being asked to do a number of tasks at the same time. The problem is often particularly apparent in canter transitions, which are hard to do correctly, because the horse is distracted and accepting the correct shape becomes secondary to the request for a change of gait.

Most people's focus in this transition is the crispness of the depart; having the horse respond instantly to the aid is deemed a success. But if we allow this sequence to become the accepted norm, it can be quite hard to re-wire the horse's neurological pathways, and without this re-wiring, we will always get a transition with the horse going above the bit. This is a very common problem and one that we will revisit later in chapter 5 on connection (see p. 113).

4 HOW DO YOU SOLVE IT? If a horse is above the bit as a result of a misunderstanding or resistance to the aid, then ask yourself a few questions:

- Has the horse been taught the subject?
- Has he been asked the question in the correct way at the right time?

If, when the rider's leg aid is applied, the horse responds by going above the bit, then we must re-educate the response. The response of "leg to rein" must always produce a softer, rounder, and more secure outline. When the leg aid initiates a request, the reins must make it clear that it is not acceptable for the horse to go above the bit. They do this by holding against this tendency. Meanwhile, the leg aid continues to ask the question until the horse finds that a lower, softer, less resistant contact on their end produces the same from the rider. This will now enable the rider to allow the horse to answer the question the legs were asking (for example, a transition). It also sets the tone of future requests—that is, leg to rein means acceptance of both before answering the rider's question.

1 PROBLEM: BEHIND THE VERTICAL. _ _

2 WHY IS THE PROBLEM THERE? Not to be confused with being *behind the bit* (see p. 103), being behind the vertical is when the imaginary line that runs down the front of the horse's nose is deemed to be behind the vertical plane (fig. 4.12).

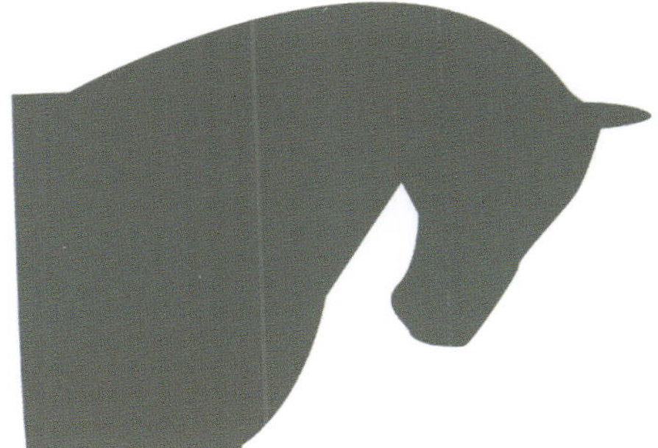

4.12 A silhouette showing a horse behind the vertical.

This way of going may have been asked for by the rider or trainer, so the horse may think behind the vertical is where he is expected to be. Of course, this is not a correct way of going.

3 WHY DOES IT NEED SOLVING? The horse's nose should be on or just in front of the vertical. The overriding proviso is that the horse must remain on the contact. Without the contact, it will not be possible to retrieve a correct outline.

There is one notable exception: sometimes when schooling or re-training, behind the vertical can be a more secure position to put a horse into while other issues are being dealt with. Horses will sometimes find it easier to work "through the back" when slightly behind the vertical (I will explain how later in chapter 5—p. 120), for example, so there *can* be merit in asking horses to be in this position.

4 HOW DO YOU SOLVE THE PROBLEM? The key is very much in the horse taking a contact, as already mentioned. Without a contact, this issue becomes very difficult to solve. Once a contact, however light, is achieved, the rider can ask for the nose to come back in front of the vertical. Rider balance and an offering hand are the key to the horse understanding you want him to "take the contact out." Exercises such as leg-yielding and transitions can be helpful as they require balance from the horse, and the horse seeks the rein to achieve this.

1 PROBLEM: CARRYING THE HEAD TOO LOW. _ _ _ _ _ _ _ _ _ _ _ _ _ _ _ _

2 WHY IS THE PROBLEM THERE? When a horse carries his head too low, it can be the result of a conformational issue, or it can be trainer- or rider-induced. It can also be accompanied by being behind the vertical (see p. 97).

3 WHY DOES IT NEED SOLVING? Whatever its cause, there are few, if any, benefits. Being too low with the head and neck should not be confused with working "through the back" or "over the top line." They don't necessarily go together.

You may have heard about the idea of working "long and low." It's important to understand that there is a right way and a wrong way to do this (fig. 4.13).

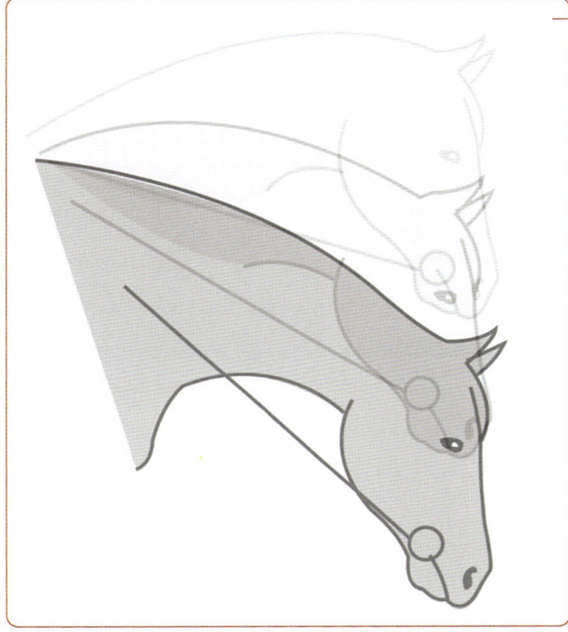

4.13 A really nice sequence of shapes, where you can see a horse working correctly as he comes "long and low" with a contact to the bit and the correct shape to a lower frame.

4 HOW DO YOU SOLVE THE PROBLEM? To resolve this issue requires a plan, which involves rebalancing the whole horse. We need to be able to encourage the hind legs to come in under the horse to carry a little more weight. The rein aids limit the amount the horse lowers the head and neck and reduces weight going onto the forehand. This transfer of weight from front to back changes the balance.

To maintain this, the horse needs to get used to the change in biomechanics. Trotting poles are helpful. Cantering smaller schooling figures can activate the hind legs. Decreasing the size of figures can help the balance.

As the access to the horse's "engine" improves, so the lightness of his forehand and position of the head and neck also get better.

1 PROBLEM: TILTING THE HEAD. _

2 WHY IS THE PROBLEM THERE? Ideally, we should be able to trace a line down the center of the horse's forehead and nose, which should be perpendicular to the ground.

Sometimes, however, the head tilts to one side or the other (fig. 4.14). Horses seldom have a natural head tilt, so this fault it is more than likely the result of improper training.

It is important to recognize a head tilt as early as possible as any prolonged time riding with such an issue makes it a habit that can be difficult to correct.

Acceptance and understanding of the aid is at the root of the issue. Head-tilting usually first appears when a horse is being started off as a two- or three-year-old. The first few times a bit is put in a horse's mouth, the observant trainer should notice if the trait appears and slow down or go back in the training to correct it. It will be obvious that early. Young horses tilt their heads in the early stages of teaching them what the bit is as a way of showing a rejection of or resistance to the foreign body. This resistance can be apparent in the mouth or at the poll.

If we inherit a horse with this tendency, it is something we should address immediately.

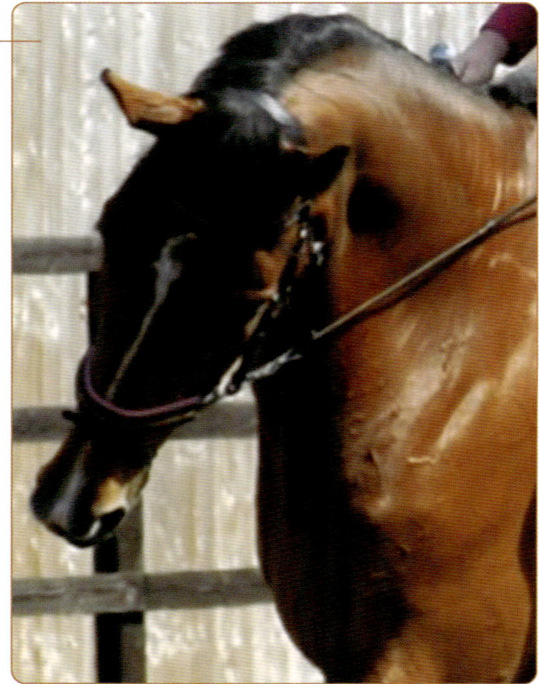

4.14 This horse is resistant to the left rein and hanging on the right rein. It is also possible that he may not be listening to the left leg. The result is the rider having problems keeping him out to the right and having to use too much right rein. The horse's nose is reluctant to follow the left rein, so the head starts to tilt.

3 Why does it need solving? Our aim is to have a horse that is symmetrical and evenly developed on both reins. The horse is more likely to work in an efficient manner if he is. If you watch horses trotting down the centerline in the arena, you will see this issue more times than you might expect. It may make no difference to a horse's jumping, racing, or general riding performance, but it will in a dressage test, and it is a sign of a general schooling problem. Head-tilting will affect overall straightness and the athletic performance of the horse, because it is a sign of resistance.

In most cases, a head tilt is correctable with the right work. It can take time as, once again, we can't talk to the horse and explain the issue!

4 How do you solve the problem? Firstly, make sure that the head tilt is not a result of some physical pain or discomfort. A routine visit from your veterinarian will confirm one way or the other.

Solving this problem under saddle can be difficult, as there are normally other issues that distract us. So it is best to begin the solution in the stable as explained earlier in this chapter (p. 72). The process described in the section on addressing a lack of straightness in chapter 3 may also be helpful (p. 50).

We want to encourage the horse to follow a guiding rein. We are asking his mind to be interested in what we are doing. This will remove any resistance, and he will want to look and go in the requested direction. *Ask* him; don't tell him. When progress has been made from the ground, then try from the saddle. The open and guiding rein should be applied in the same way. Begin at a halt and then progress to walk. At the same time, use your body position to control the horse's shoulder from falling in or out. In the case of the horse in photo 4.14, for instance, using the right leg to control the shoulder, and the left rein, will guide the head and ask the neck to follow. By linking these two requests—opening the rein and controlling the shoulder—we encourage the horse to release the outside muscles of his neck and to soften to the bit on the left. When he gives the correct answer, make sure he has a clear reward to let him know that he has done what you wanted.

The bend to either side also comes from the relaxation of the two bones of the spine at the poll—the atlas and the axis (see p. 21). These bones allow the spine to have a degree of rotational movement, and when the horse understands what is being asked, he will release tension at the poll (longitudinal acceptance), and the head can flex either way (lateral acceptance—figs. 4.15 A & B). Each and every time he offers the correct answer, reward him. Offering a guiding rein will encourage the horse to look in the desired direction. When your horse understands, he will be more inclined to truly follow the line being asked of him in a correct way and physically, he will develop more evenly on both sides.

Be aware that bad habits will reappear when the horse feels pressure or tension. So avoid them when explaining things to the horse. A horse that works correctly is also more likely to cope well with the pressures and tension of competition.

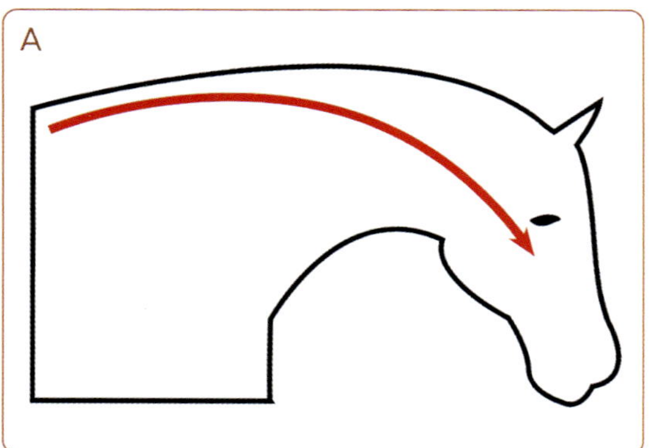

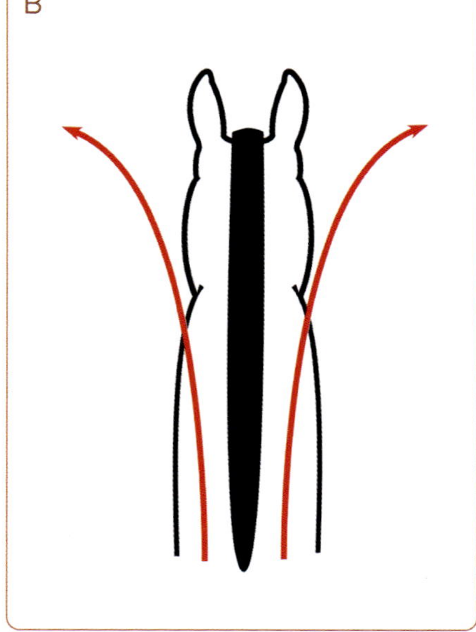

4.15 A & B Longitudinal acceptance (A) is more likely to produce lateral acceptance (B).

Beware Too Much "Inside Leg to Outside Rein"!

"Inside leg to outside rein" is a phrase often used and nearly always misunderstood. When passed along to the horse, this misunderstanding can teach him to tilt his head or have too much inside bend.

The rider's inside leg (inside the bend) stops the horse from falling in. It defines the inside of the line you are riding on. The rider's outside leg conversely defines the outside of that line. The rein aids guide the front of the horse on the chosen line.

"Inside leg to outside rein" is often misunderstood as an active aim to push the horse into the outside rein. This should not be so. If the horse isn't falling in, don't push him out! Each of the four aids (two reins and two legs) have a responsibility to position the horse on the line of motion. The inside rein should have a guiding or "offering" role, and the outside rein defines the amount of direction and bend required to stay straight on the line being ridden. Both reins should have a fairly even contact.

If this is ridden badly and too much pressure is applied to the outside rein, the head tilts.

Often you will hear instructors say, "Keep your horse on the outside rein"! This is not what they mean but it is what they say. We would all be wise to use the outside rein judiciously.

1 PROBLEM: OVER-BENDING OR BEHIND THE BIT. _ _ _ _ _ _ _ _ _ _ _ _ _ _

2 WHY IS THE PROBLEM THERE? Over-bending is normally the result of a horse being asked to be too compliant or submissive (fig. 4.16).

4.16 The over-bent horse is often being asked to be too submissive.

> ## Don't Confuse Over-Bending with Suppleness
>
> Suppleness is a mental acceptance of the aids and *not* something physical. Bending the horse inside out does not produce a supple horse, but encouraging the horse to understand what the aids are asking for does.
> *Please read this again.*

3 WHY DOES IT NEED SOLVING? When asking the horse to accept and go on the bit, we are in danger of asking for too much submission. It may seem like a better issue to have than being above the bit, for example, but in many ways this might not be so. Once a horse drops the contact, it can be very hard to convince him to pick it up again. Being over-bent with a contact should be an easier problem to resolve than being over-bent with no contact.

We must beware of asking for too much submission; it's an outdated concept. And it produces a horse being over-bent. In dressage, it will be marked down. In show jumping, the horse will lose vision ahead. In cross-country and racing, the horse will lose both vision and length of stride.

4 HOW DO YOU SOLVE THE PROBLEM? The solution lies in the connection from the back of the horse to the front. (Connection is discussed at greater length in the next chapter—p. 113.) To achieve true connection, we must ask the horse to remain *on* the contact and to *seek* to take the contact *out*. This encourages him to re-evaluate our request to be on the bit and allows us to show him where we want him to be.

1 PROBLEM: A SHORT NECK. _

2 WHY IS THE PROBLEM THERE? This is when the horse's neck appears too short in relation to the rest of his body. Conformation can be to blame. Some horses just naturally have a short neck! If they are born this way, then it is ever more important *not* to draw attention to it by the way they are ridden and trained.

The expressions "over the back," "seeking the contact," and "allowing the neck" are especially relevant for the training of a horse that is naturally short-necked. The danger comes when the concept of collection, rebalance, and true contact begins. When a rider focuses on the front end rather than the back end of the horse, then it is easy to shorten the neck even more. If our training is to *enhance* the neck shape, attention must be paid to the contact and the horse's understanding of it.

Conformation isn't the only culprit, however: visibly short necks are often a sign of a shortcut or a misunderstanding in the horse's education. While we are often encouraged by trainers *not* to shorten the horse's neck, but it is not always clear *why* or *how* to recognize that we are doing it.

As you look at a horse being ridden, from the side, with the rider in the middle, there should be roughly the same amount of the horse in front of the rider as there is behind. A horse being ridden in a less-advanced shape will have a longer, lower outline compared to the more educated horse who will be in a more collected outline. The problem arises when we see a collected front end—a short neck—without the equivalent shortening behind. This shape tells me that the shortening of the neck has happened as a result of incorrect schooling.

3 WHY DOES THE PROBLEM NEED SOLVING? Short necks limit stride length. They can also make it harder for the horse to work through and over the back. Our aim is to *enhance* the natural paces and gaits, not restrict them.

4 HOW DO YOU SOLVE THE PROBLEM? As with the problem of over-bending (p. 103), the solution to a short neck lies in the two words *contact* and *connection.* Asking and encouraging the horse to stay on the bit and to take the contact *out* (in front of the vertical) at every opportunity is important. As we will talk about in the next chapter (p. 120), having a connection will support this request to take the contact out.

Offering the horse the freedom to regain the use of his neck for balance and length of stride will also help. I recommend the use of a neck strap here to help you let go of your hold on the reins and encourage the horse to seek a longer neck shape (see p. 84).

The Perils of "Collection"

A short neck sometimes arises as a misinterpretation of the word "collection"—a much misused and poorly understood word, as I have mentioned. Collection can only happen when the horse and rider understand the rebalance (p. 150) and the availability of energy from the hind legs. If there is too much focused on the front end and not enough on the hind, the rider may shorten the neck without achieving true collection. Without this understanding, other problems may also appear, including:

- A short step.
- A hollow back.
- A struggle with the rebalance.
- A reluctance to stretch the neck.
- Running, when asked for lengthening.

Trotting poles can be helpful too. Begin with poles about 4 feet (1.2 meters) apart and ask for regularity of the trot. Encourage a contact. Then make the distance longer—4 feet 6 inches (1.37 meters) apart. Encourage the horse to stretch his neck as he needs to stretch the stride to make the distance. Make sure to reward him for taking the contact with him. Try and get to 5 feet (1.52 meters) as the horse learns to open out his frame. Your leg aids will be an important part of this process as they encourage a push from behind to happen during the exercise.

As I've mentioned, a constant evaluation of what the horse's neck looks and feels like is important. Once the neck has been over-shortened, the horse will readily over-shorten it again. We must be on our guard that we don't ask for this to happen. In fact, we should do the opposite, and at every opportunity.

1 PROBLEM: "BROKEN-NECKED." _

2 WHY IS THE PROBLEM THERE? Sounds awful, doesn't it? The term "broken-necked" describes the shape of a horse's neck that has had flawed training or that has a conformational defect. It will appear as a "break" to the smooth shape of the topline of the neck, about 9 to 12 inches behind the ears (fig.

4.17). If its origins are conformational, it will take very clever training to avoid it appearing when ridden. Dressage judges will recognize it as such and will deduct marks.

4.17 "Broken-necked" is a "break" to the smooth shape of the topline of the horse's neck.

When not due to a conformational issue, a "broken neck" appears as a result of the misunderstanding of "acceptance of the bit," "forward to the contact," "over the back," and "being through". All these are well-used expressions in the dressage world and in training horses in general and refer to important steps in the horse's education. So, if horses begin to show this characteristic in their early training, we need to be aware and ride them differently.

3 WHY DOES IT NEED SOLVING? The "broken neck" is a sign of incorrect education and so should not be present. Often horses that have been "broken in" using mouthing bits and too-tight side reins will display a "broken neck." This display of poor schooling has no place in riding.

4 HOW DO YOU SOLVE THE PROBLEM? This issue is a difficult one. Revisit over-bent (p. 21) and encourage the horse to take contact. Look to work with a Chambon to try to lengthen the neck (p. 78) with his nose in front of the vertical.

1 PROBLEM: SNATCHING THE CONTACT. _ _ _ _ _ _ _ _ _ _ _ _ _ _

2 WHY IS THE PROBLEM THERE? Watch for this problem of snatching at the reins and searching for more freedom during a "stretchy" trot or free walk. Fixed or forcefully positioned outlines will often produce a horse that snatches, an action that is prompted whenever a glimmer of freedom is offered. To drop the contact or to snatch at the contact demonstrates a misunderstanding of what being correctly "through" looks and feels like. By "fixed" I mean a position held or placed by hands that are too rigid. Side-reins used in too fixed a manner can also produce this result.

3 WHY DOES IT NEED SOLVING? By trying to find more freedom away from the contact, the horse is demonstrating a schooling fault, and the two movements I've mentioned (stretchy trot circle and free walk) are doing what they are intended to do: show where the horse's education has been correct and incorrect. To pass the test of whether the horse is comfortable with the contact, he should take the contact forward and remain on the bit as he is allowed more rein—not snatch for more.

4 HOW DO YOU SOLVE THE PROBLEM? Begin by retracing your steps, starting with work from the ground on straightness to encourage the horse to be comfortable with the contact rather than feeling fixed or held by it. Work in an outline should be followed by a relaxation phase, where the rider and horse show that taking a contact forward and down is done so as a reward for good work at the end of a ride. The horse takes the rein contact politely and just as far as the rider allows. This will become a natural form of relaxation.

We must frequently test this feeling of willingness and desire to stretch. Periods of work in the frame must be mixed with periods of work longer and lower—but always on the contact.

1 PROBLEM: A RELUCTANCE TO STRETCH. _ _ _ _ _ _ _ _ _ _ _ _ _ _

2 WHY IS THE PROBLEM THERE? When a horse is offered the stretch and doesn't take the contact forward and down, but instead drops the contact, stays in a frame, or

The Highjacking of Stretching

Stretching and its use and understanding has been highjacked by those who would have the equine athlete warm up as a human athlete does. In recent years, more attention has been focused on the value of an athletic warm-up in human athletes, and its relevance to performance. It was a natural follow-on that a comparison would be made in equine training. After all, horses are performing athletes too.

However, a horse's natural way of going does not require a warm-up. When a horse is grazing in the wild and is startled, he will take flight. There is no warm-up in advance and the horse will seldom come to any harm.

Moreover, the process of riding and confirming the acceptance of the aids at the beginning of our daily ride will warm the horse up sufficiently without stretching. Teaching horses to stretch as a prerequisite to work seems counterintuitive to most horses. As soon as they have stretched, the rider asks them to come back up into a frame again! But they will stretch automatically when asked *after* good work. So all the "stretching" and "athletic warm-up" at the beginning of the ride time may be unnecessary and indeed, even become an irritation to the horse.

Asking the horse to take the contact forward, out, and down should be a reward for working well and a form of relaxation following work, not a prerequisite. If you look at Figure 4.13 on p. 99, you'll see there is a halfway point that fulfills all aspects of the warm-up: This horse is on the aids and warming up in a pleasing frame.

Applying the same reasoning, there is also little logic to riding in a casual or sloppy way at the beginning of a ride and expecting the horse to pay attention moments later (fig. 4.18). Why not begin asking him to pay attention as soon as you have mounted? This is a clear message of intent to the horse: "Tack on, pay attention."

4.18 Sloppy riding does not communicate the right message to the horse. If you expect him to pay attention, you should pay attention.

goes above the bit, these are signs of a horse that is not connected, working through, "between the aids," or on the bit.

3 WHY DOES IT NEED SOLVING? Both the stretchy trot circle and free walk are required in dressage tests. They provide proof of the correct training and way of going.

4 HOW DO YOU SOLVE THE PROBLEM? It is important to keep in mind the words *contact* and *connection* as we continue to strive to work our horses through from the leg to the hand so the muscles of the back work harder. Trot poles help us do this. Raised trot poles in a spoke-shaped arrangement and long- and short-distance trot poles are all helpful to work the horse through the back. As we connect the horse's back to the contact, the horse will look for a moment to relax his frame. He will seek to take the contact down and out. This should be encouraged, however little to begin with. More can be achieved as the horse gains understanding of the concept.

The Importance of Timing

I hope that it is perfectly clear after reading this chapter how the contact relates to the shape of a horse's neck. The two things are linked in a way that says much about a horse's education. And yet we also require more pieces of the jigsaw puzzle to complete the picture. The solutions discussed here are subject to compromise and so the "picture" may not be perfect but should be considered a work in progress. The compromises will be determined by an individual horse's conformation, level of education, and reactions to training. There is seldom one answer that fits all scenarios.

Knowing when the time is right for learning is an important skill to acquire in our training. There will be times when your horse's mind is not attentive to the job and to persevere would be unproductive. Forging on when the mind is not in the right place may teach the horse something you don't want him to learn—something that might require retraining later on. Windy days are not good with youngsters, for example. They hear, see, and imagine things and so will be much less attentive to a trainer. The same applies to a new horse in a strange environment, a change of routine, workmen doing something noisy in the vicinity—anything that is different to the norm will tend to distract horses from learning.

> ## Did You Know?
>
> The horse has a far smaller ratio of brain-to-body size than the human. The human brain is able to think in the past, present, and future, and controls memory, communication, and association. The horse's brain, however, is mainly busy with muscle coordination, balance, and body functions.
>
> As a result, a horse is not able to reason through a skill (which, by the way, is the definition of intelligence). Horses learn by repetition. They learn to associate things with pain or pleasure, and to associate cues and signals with behavior—for good and bad. The choice rests with us.

Young horses have to get used to the hustle and bustle of everyday life, but they also need to focus on what you want them to learn without too much distraction. Once they have started to develop a base understanding of certain skills, and some social manners and boundaries, then it is appropriate to introduce more. At this stage the test becomes listening to you at the same time as watching what is happening around them.

Training has to provide a consistency and clarity that the horse can live with and understand. The same goes for instruction of the rider. When consistency and logic is not applied, we cannot blame the horse for taking a best guess at what we want or opting for the easiest way to stay out of trouble. The horse may be simply avoiding what he doesn't understand, which he achieves by hiding behind the contact or becoming insensitive or immune to the contact, or one of the other things we've discussed in this chapter.

Contact is an important quality to educate correctly, but it is often hurried over. Take time to study the horse's responses and development at this critical time in his education, and I assure you that the rewards will be worthwhile.

Stoke the fire from within, the glow will be seen for longer.

Connection

I N THE NEXT TWO CHAPTERS, WE WILL BEGIN TO SEE THE LINK between many of the qualities we've covered in the previous chapters.

Of the many components in play, connection is one of the most critical to the overall picture of a horse working well. Understanding how to connect the components of the horse (hindquarters, forehand, head and neck) is vital to being able to sustain and improve the picture. And the ability to connect the various parts of the horse and appreciate how they work together is essential to the development of horsemanship too.

Many would call this quality "working through." Being "through" for the horse is like writing for us: we need to understand letters, the formation of words, how to make a sentence, and what we want to say before we can put all the pieces together.

In the training we've covered thus far, we have made the link in the horse's mind from our leg to the hindquarters and from our hand to the contact with the horse's mouth. But now we must ensure that we can join the back end to the front end! This is what I call the *connection.*

Transitions within the gait, transitions from one gait to another, direct transitions, and lateral work are all good tools for improving connection. We'll look at problems that arise within each category. First, to help us understand the mechanics of connection, we should look at the conformation of the back half of the horse. The structure of the

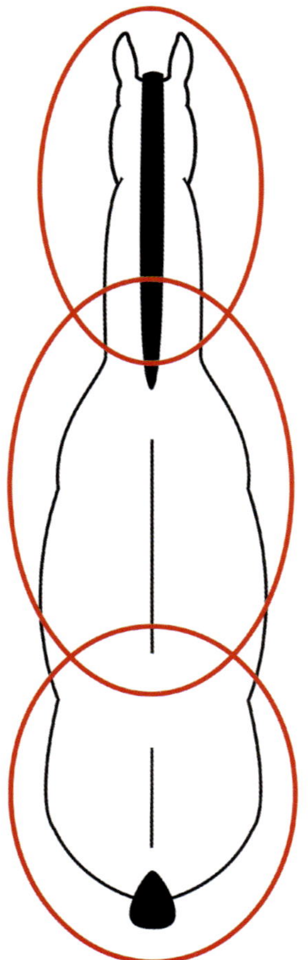

horse is an important part of the equation; the rest is in the mind, the education, and how the horse uses his body.

Up to this stage in the book, we've dealt with the horse's three sections (front, middle, and hind) separately. As we begin to connect each part to the others in an effort to join up the whole working animal, we need to retain an awareness of how to contact each part individually for the purpose of correction, as well as how the three parts can actually connect with each other (fig. 5.1).

The Back

There is little one can do about the conformation of a horse's back. There is, however, a lot you can do with how you live and work with it. Some of the most common conformational problems we find in the back include:

- No clear withers
- Too prominent a withers
- A narrow back
- A wide back
- A sway back
- A flat back

Each has its own issues related to riding, and importantly, saddle fit:

No withers makes it difficult to secure a saddle. There is always the tendency for the saddle to slide around, which is irritating and unsafe.

Too prominent withers also makes it difficult to fit a saddle. There should be enough space between the withers and the saddle tree at the pommel, when the rider is sitting, to ensure that no pressure point is created. Space should be sufficient to allow movement of both horse and rider.

A narrow back needs a narrow tree in the saddle fitting. Attention to fitting a narrow-backed horse is important to avoid pinching of the back and pressure points.

A wide back is difficult in saddle fitting. Finding a wide tree that causes no pressure points but nonetheless sits comfortably and secure is a challenge.

A sway back involves a very hollow shape behind the withers, which makes saddle fitting extra difficult and extremely important.

A flat back is where the withers' end and the correct saddle position isn't clear, so it's difficult for the saddle and rider to become "at one with the horse."

Where the neck, withers, and saddle position converge is an important part of the horse. The shape of this area affects how the horse is able to use his neck to influence balance, which ultimately affects performance. It also affects how the horse's shoulders function, which is critical for all athletic movement of the horse.

Where and how the saddle nestles onto and into the back determines the rider's level of comfort on the horse but, just as crucially, the horse's level of comfort with the rider. The right shape allows for a good fit for both, and that's a good start for a strong connection and clear communication.

Saddle Fit and the Balance Sweet Spot

"Start with rider balance by placing the rider in the deepest part of the horse's back. (Not in-front or behind the sweet spot.) Then the rider can be placed in a pelvis-neutral position, and from there a saddle can be fitted to the rider.

"From the flattest to most swayed of backs, all horses have that sweet spot of balance where they are able to carry the rider's weight and perform to the best of their ability. As a saddle fitter you need to have a wide variety of tools in the box to accomplish this. Access to a variety of saddle tree specs is key.

"A saddle should not be thought about by the rider or horse when they are riding. It is purely a communication tool with which the rider transfers information to the horse. Constant adjustment by the rider means the rider is out of balance. Horses hollowing away from a saddle means they are not comfortable."

Joanna Dillon is Head of US Distribution and Retail and a saddle fitter for Equipe Saddles (equipeusa.com).

The Loins

I'm sure you are aware of the expression, "A chain is only as strong as its weakest link!"

There is merit in having this thought in our minds when we look at the loin area of the horse, just behind where the saddle sits. After all, this part joins the "engine" to the rest of the horse. If it is weak or the conformation is poor, the overall efficiency of the horse will be diminished.

What we are talking about specifically is the broad band of muscle behind the saddle, the *longissimus dorsi* and the *gluteal* muscles, which, in simple terms, join the back end to the middle of the horse, and are a major source of power.

The Hindquarters

A human sprinter produces power from muscle bulk that propels him horizontally. A high jumper can produce power from less muscle bulk to propel himself vertically.

Most ridden horses need a combination of horizontal and vertical ambition to perform

With Mares in Mind

One thing to note is that mares tend to be longer in the back and loin area than geldings to provide more space for carrying foals. The reason to mention this is that this extra length *may* have implications in other areas of the mare's life. For instance, mares sometimes:

- Find it more difficult to over-track in the walk (the hind feet step clearly *in front of* the prints left by the front feet), which is a requirement in dressage tests.
- Find it more difficult to bring their hind legs underneath them when asked for a more collected movement.
- Have a hard time being "through" as a result of their long backs.
- Take longer to find their balance.

I do mean *sometimes*, and this in no way precludes mares from performing on an equal footing to their male counterparts. But it is a physical attribute to watch along the way.

Horses Aren't the Best Jumpers Around

A cat is only about 8 inches (20 centimeters) at its "withers," yet it easily jumps 4 feet (around 1.20 meters), at least six times its height. Horses are bigger, around 5 feet (1.50 meters) in height, and stronger, so using the same formula, they should be able to jump almost 30 feet (9 meters) high! But this is impossible. Horses, unlike cats, have very limited use of their backs to produce the whiplash necessary to propel cats to such relative heights.

The lesson here is that in order to produce power, there needs to be muscle *plus* the correct bone or joint angle. The hind legs also need to function in the correct way.

such varied skills as piaffe or passage, or to clear a jump of 1.60 meters. It's the muscles and joints that allow them to perform these skills.

If we stand upright and without bending our knees try to spring in the air, we might make it a few inches off the ground. If we try the same thing but this time bend our ankles, knees, and hips, the result should be better. The ability to flex our joints and use the spring action created by doing so allows us and many other mammals the ability to jump.

Evolution has left the horse standing on the equivalent of the human's middle finger, with our wrist being equivalent to the horse's knee and our heel being equivalent to the horse's hock! As I have said many times, *natural* outdoes *trained*, so if the hindquarters and the legs naturally perform well, it will make all our schooling easier (figs. 5.2 A & B). Watching young horses play is a great indicator of how they will turn out later on in their life. I spend hours observing my young ones in their natural state—it's educational and fun!

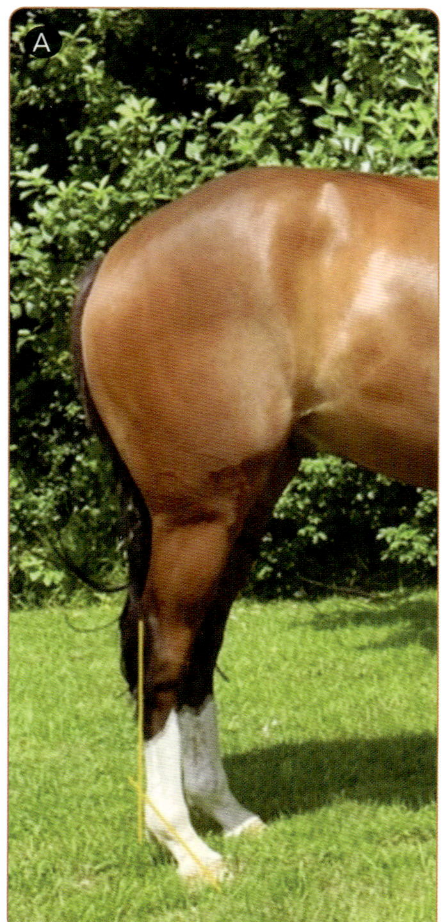

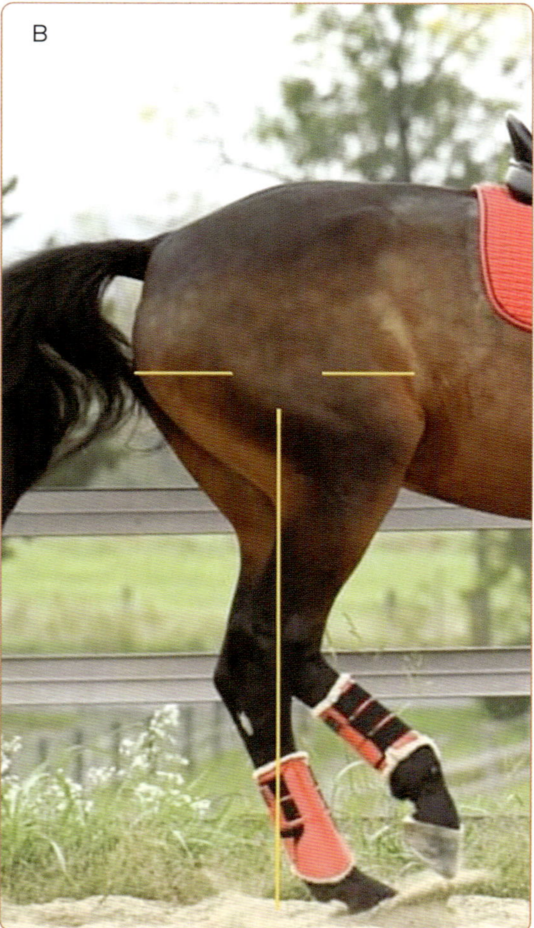

5.2 A & B In A, we see a good hind leg in a horse standing still. Note how it is comfortably underneath the hindquarters. A straight line can run perpendicular to the ground from the point of the hock, and there are clearly defined angles at the point of the buttock, the stifle, and the hock. The pastern/fetlock relationship is good; so too is the pastern-to-hoof relationship (50 to 55 degrees). This conformation is deemed to be ideal and should cause minimum stress to the limbs and produce maximum function under the right conditions. In B we see that kind of function in the angle of the back leg at work.

Exceptions to the Rule

I am very aware that although we may look poorly on the less-than-ideal conformation and its correlation to diminished performance, there are endless examples of horses that have performed at the very highest level with conformational defects. There are always exceptions to the rule.

One example was a show jumper called Retina Z. She was a star in the 1990s, winning multiple European and Olympic medals with the German rider Ludger Beerbaum. She had hind legs that I'm convinced were bought at a yard sale!

Another example is a horse called Tiny, who is not old and a proven performer. He, too, is a good reminder that conformation isn't everything. It is only part of the jigsaw puzzle. The heart and mind, which we can't see, are more important.

5.3 A & B The show jumper, Retina Z (A), and Tiny (B)

How the Rider Influences Connection

We sit on the horse's back—the area that is most crucial to connection. Our weight and balance will, therefore, have an influence on how the back performs. If we use them correctly, the back is able to function in a way that allows for the connection of the hindquarters to the front of the horse.

Sit in an incorrect way and the connection has difficulty and sometimes doesn't happen at all. Sometimes the horse just carries us along in a merely functional way. Our goal is for the "conversation" from our legs to encourage the horse's hind legs to create the power and push to take us forward and upward, sometimes both. The back must allow for the passage of this power, which should travel through the horse all the way to the contact and ultimately to the rider's hand. The connection we are looking for through the back is, therefore, one of the back, up underneath us, carrying us, but loose enough to allow the passage of energy to happen. As riders, we need to be able to sit in balance and allow the horse's back to move with us and underneath us, to enable the transfer of this push from back to front.

Our conversation through the legs will regulate the push and so influence the connection. Without this leg influence and connection from back to front, the horse is like two separate parts traveling along a similar line, each doing their own thing. Comments you are likely to see from the dressage judge indicating a lack of connection include: "More engagement needed!" "More push from behind required!" and "Not enough connection."

Let's talk about one of the problems we can see with this element of the connection.

Back Problems and Solutions

1 PROBLEM: A HOLLOW BACK. _

2 WHY IS THE PROBLEM THERE? From behind the withers to the loin area, a "hollow back" describes a lack of the back being up under the saddle and rider.

Although this may be the result of a conformation issue, it may also be that a horse isn't working "through" or using the back properly. The back is the functioning part of the horse that not only carries the rider but is a vital link between the power source (the hindquarters) and the front of the horse. This can also be an issue during transitions (see p. 122).

3 WHY DOES IT NEED SOLVING? To be described as being "through," the horse's back must be an active part of weight-carrying and locomotion. The complete cycle of energy is: rider leg, to horse's hindquarters, back, poll, jaw, bit, to rider's hand. If, for some reason, any of the links in this chain stops working, the horse will stop being "through."

Having either a short neck (p. 104) or a hollow back can create a "block" to the back working "through," diminishing the overall quality of work.

4 HOW DO YOU SOLVE THE PROBLEM? The solution is to rekindle each of the parts of the horse that make up "throughness," especially the connection. This will allow us to lengthen the neck and remove the blockage to the back. Trot poles are the first "go-to" exercise. They allow for a lightening of the load the rider can become and also an activation of the back as it becomes motivated. This can clear the blockage and reopen the "dialogue" between horse and rider. Trot poles also encourage the horse to look down to see where he is placing his feet. As he does this, the back becomes more suspended. The poles also encourage the step to be more animated and expressive; this, too, activates the push from behind and through the back.

Start off with the poles distanced to suit the horse: a short stride at 4 feet (1.20 meters), a bigger stride at 4 feet 6 inches (1.40 meters) and so on. Once the horse becomes accustomed to the distances, open the distances out by 6 inches (15 centimeters). This will encourage the frame of the horse to stretch, his stride to become bigger, and the back to develop more swing. Each time the horse offers to stretch his frame, reward with the use of your voice and a pat on the neck.

Poles placed on a circle as spokes of a wheel are a natural progression from work on a straight line. They develop lateral acceptance and flexibility as well as longitudinal flexibility.

Raised trot poles can also be used. They are, however, less effective in this scenario than poles on the ground.

I keep trot poles in an area of my arena to be used whenever I feel the need. If I find the horse becoming a little "fixed" in the back, then I can "refresh" its proper use by using the poles.

Training a Strong Connection

My definition of impulsion is "available energy." Once energy from the horse is available to us we can use it for whatever we want. Add speed, and now we have the tools to improve connection.

Transitions

Transitions can be helpful in many ways. Much is written and said about transitions in books, videos, lectures, and in lessons, but like most exercises it is not the *doing* that is important, but *how* they are done. There are two main types of transitions: progressive and direct.

Progressive transitions are as they sound (going from halt to walk to trot, for example) while *direct transitions* skip one gait and go directly to another (for example halt-to-trot or walk-to-canter). These definitions apply to both upward and downward transitions.

We also have transitions *within* the gait. From a working trot or canter to a bigger trot or canter and back, for example. Or from a working trot or canter toward a shorter trot or canter and back to working. "Bigger" and "shorter" eventually becomes "medium" and "collected." There are many more variations. Transitions allow us to test the horse's response to and understanding of the rider's aids, and at the same time, develop physical and mental flexibility, adjustability, and ultimately, a better connection. They are an integral part of our toolbox when we work with horses.

As we incorporate transitions into our work, doing them correctly must come first. Practicing things incorrectly is never of value. The horse doesn't know one from the other, so we must be the guide.

Let's turn to some examples of problems that occur with transitions.

Transition Problems and Solutions

1 PROBLEM: GOING ABOVE THE BIT IN UPWARD TRANSITIONS. _ _ _ _ _ _ _ _

2 WHY IS THE PROBLEM THERE? Say you use a transition from walk to trot to improve the horse's reaction time, but while you achieve a quick, immediate response to the leg, the horse goes above the bit. You are pleased with the reaction time, but less so with the evasion. What should you prioritize? The answer is to do the transition well, but slowly.

The horse has prioritized speed of reaction over correctness, but he doesn't know the difference. The "conversation" of leg and rein has been ignored or not learned well enough. The rider may also be at fault with the timing and incorrect use of the aids.

3 WHY DOES IT NEED SOLVING? A good transition has a number of components. Each has to be done well for the overall transition to be deemed good and of value for the reason it was chosen.

4 HOW DO YOU SOLVE THE PROBLEM? Do not accept "quick" at the expense of "good." Do the transition again—well—but ask the horse to be better in his response to the aid.

Any "conversation" from the leg aids should produce a response that travels throughout the horse's body to give us a feeling through the reins to the hands. When getting a good response from the leg aids and feeling that a quick clean transition is about to happen, the rider will often feel resistance happening through the reins. To correct this, the rider should apply a pressure against the horse's resistance to indicate that it is an unwelcome response. Reapply the conversation with the legs to remind the horse of the relationship between both aids and only accept a transition that is accepting through the hands as well as the legs.

This attention to detail is part of a horse's initial training and should also be part of re-training. It will give both parties confidence that correct is desirable and achievable, making it more likely to happen when in competition as a result. This relationship between leg and hand will appear more often from now on. This progressive transition from walk to trot should be practiced to confirm the relationship and a correct response.

Switching On and Off

As we've discussed, the horse's conformation can affect his ability to come "through" (see p. 120). It is true that a hollow shape, for example, can limit his ability to use his back, but this shouldn't be used as an excuse!

Riding school horses very often "switch off" the feeling of connection in their backs as a protection against beginners or unbalanced riders banging up and down in the saddle. These types of horses can initially be reluctant to offer the use of their backs for fear of being hurt, yet when encouraged by a good rider, they will begin to allow the feeling to be reignited and produce better work. These horses are fully able to compartmentalize information and skills.

That's half the fun—looking for and finding the key to the right compartment.

1 PROBLEM: HOLLOWING THE BACK AND GOING ABOVE THE BIT ON A DOWNWARD TRANSITION. _ _ _ _ _ _ _ _ _ _ _ _ _ _ _ _ _ _ _

2 WHY IS THE PROBLEM THERE? This is a sign of the horse-and-rider partnership losing the connection form back to front.

3 WHY DOES IT NEED SOLVING? It is an indication of a lack of understanding or a lack of physical control on the part of the horse that the back "clicks" out of gear on the transition.

4 HOW DO YOU SOLVE THE PROBLEM? To correct this, begin working with transitions within the gait. Start with walk first, similar to teaching the rebalance (see p. 150). When the horse responds to the rein aids when they ask for a slower gait, and at the same time, responds properly to the leg aids asking for the hindquarters to maintain the forward momentum and there is no change to the frame, then try this in trot.

When the horse complies with this request in walk and trot, we know we have connected the hind end to the front end through the horse's back. Now it is a good time to ask for a transition from trot to walk. Maintain the leg aid asking for the horse to push from behind at the same time as you ask with the rein aid for the horse to slow down (both legs to both hands). The voice can help support the process with a calming tone and a good downward transition will result. Again, practice the process a number of times until the horse understands what is required of him and for the rider to improve feel and coordination.

To enable connection to remain, a rider's balance and position must be supple enough to sit in the saddle and still allow the horse's back to work.

- Rising or posting trot will make it easier, rather than attempting to sit.
- A light seat in the canter is also good for getting the horse's back to remain up under the rider and connected.
- Trot poles help improve connection in many ways (as already mentioned in the section on addressing a hollow back—p. 120).

Lateral Work

Some would say lateral work is a panacea, but I say, beware. Often taught as a way to improve understanding of the aids, suppleness, balance, and a horse being "through," for me it is more often performed by the horse as a way of avoiding being "through" and balanced. To go sideways and retain the connection requires physical and mental coordination. It also requires a willingness on the part of the horse to keep trying.

Some horses find it difficult and give up by losing the connection. When this happens, it becomes harder to maintain the forward, straight, and regular qualities of the gait required of a good movement. Others shorten their step, losing their swing through the back and the feeling of supporting the rider. It's like a blockage to the energy traveling from the rider's leg to the hindquarters and through the back. So lateral work should be introduced with caution to ensure the horse retains his "can-do" attitude and can reap the benefits it can produce.

Lateral work shouldn't be undertaken until *some* connection has been established. To attempt it earlier runs the risk of switching the connection in the horse off. However, lateral work may help us to *improve* the connection. This is the sort of dilemma we face on a daily basis with horses.

What Is Suppleness?

I believe there is a huge misunderstanding of the word *suppleness* among judges, trainers, and riders alike that compounds the problems associated with lateral work.

When comparing human exercise and equine exercise, the word suppleness is often invoked. Humans understand why exercise is undertaken and how stretching and improving joint articulation improves the body's overall suppleness—horses less so. When horses undertake exercise of their own accord, they demonstrate extreme suppleness. But to do so when asked by the human, the horse must firstly accept and understand the rider's aids, and secondly, be sufficiently engaged to willingly comply with the rider's wishes (he must be forward of mind, in other words). Without this attitude, the movement by the horse can only be functional at best and tolerant at worst.

Suppleness is, therefore, primarily a word that denotes the horse's acceptance and understanding of the rider's aids and his compliance with requests to do what he does naturally, on demand. *It is a mental rather than a physical quality.*

It's fun playing with lateral work, and it can be so rewarding when we feel that the horse is trying to understand what we are asking. As we teach lateral work, we should be aware that to understand and do it well is sometimes hard for the horse, and to do it badly is much easier. As the horse doesn't know what's good or bad, he will most likely take the line of least effort, which means doing it badly.

Some of the most common problems seen in lateral work are:

- Losing forwardness.
- Losing regularity.
- Losing balance.
- Losing connection.
- Becoming unresponsive to the aids.

Being aware of these issues makes us more apt to ensure that they don't happen. Sometimes it's not easy. But it is only when the horse allows himself to become and remain connected when being asked to go sideways that lateral work has its true benefit.

The feeling of connection while teaching the horse any lateral work is vital. An ability to influence the hind legs and keep the push taking us forward is key to the work being of quality and the beginning of engagement. We want the horse to develop a physical and mental understanding of doing it correctly and not avoiding the effort. Once he learns to avoid this connection, it's very difficult to encourage him to pick it up again.

As the horse becomes more familiar with lateral work and the rider and horse understand the independence of the aids better, it allows us to test and explore further aspects of the education to improve connection. Lateral work can be both an *aim in itself* and a *test*. It is truly exciting to find your horse going sideways knowing it is something you have taught

The Trainer's Dilemma

We need to continually remind ourselves as we travel down the education road, "Is what we are being offered helpful to where we want to go?" If it takes us "sort of" in the right direction, should we say "Okay, I'll take it," knowing that it will require a change later on? Or do we say, "No, it's not right." As I've mentioned in previous chapters, this is the constant dilemma trainers and riders deals with.

My granddaughter, aged five, offered the word "pushion," instead of "cushion." Not a bad try, but not correct. Constant efforts to pronounce the "c" sound succeeded in producing the word "c-pushion!" Still not right, but in the right direction. More entreaties to drop the "p" and leave the "c" eventually produced the correct answer. That took over a year.

One might have said she could have learned the right way the first time, which would have saved a lot of effort. But her mind didn't work that way. By drawing too much attention to the mistake, the mind can create a block to any correction happening at all. But, by avoiding drawing attention to the mistake, we are endorsing the error, which then becomes more engrained in the mind, making it harder to correct.

There will be occasions that we can resolve the trainer's dilemma by a correction and practice of the correct answer, ending in the creation of a good habit. There will be other times when the horse's mind won't allow itself to be corrected. Don't make an issue of it, move on to something else, and come back to it later and try again.

him. Asking the horse to compartmentalize his brain to produce leg-yielding, shoulder-in, demi-pirouette, and more is good work. To accomplish it correctly is even better work. To also be able to use lateral work as a *test* or *tool* when working on the correctness of each movement is the mark of *horsemanship*.

It should be understood that the acceptance and understanding of the aid goes in tandem with an exercise. As the aid is accepted better, the exercise is improved. They are mutually beneficial.

Lateral work is a vital tool in our training of young horses, as well as retraining and further education. It can improve the balance and muscular development of the horse as well as the Three Cs: contact (p. 69), connection (p. 113), and consistency (p. 147). Before beginning, however, remember that we must not lose the constant qualities of *forward, straight*, and *regular* (p. 47).

These are the typical exercises used in schooling, some of which are also tested in competition:

- Turn-on-the-forehand
- Turn-about-the-forehand
- Demi-pirouette
- Leg-yield
- Shoulder-in
- Half-pass
- Travers (haunches-in)
- Renvers (haunches-out)

Let's look at each of them with the eye of a trainer who knows "what happens next." The goal is to empower the rider to anticipate what might happen and do something about it—before it becomes a bad habit.

To make this easy to follow I'm going to use the same example throughout this section: A horse that finds it easier to turn right and is, therefore, more likely to fall out through the left shoulder. Your horse may have different faults or tendencies, but the principles will be the same.

Turn-on-the-Forehand

To some, this exercise has merit. It requires much understanding by the horse of what each aid is asking him to do. It also requires the rider to develop the feel necessary to ensure good qualities remain constant throughout.

In a lifetime with horses, I have yet to see it done well. I have also seldom done it well myself. For me, it creates so many problems that I feel the exercise should be removed from the training process altogether. So I'm not going to give it the time of day!

Turn-about-the-Forehand

This is a very different form of exercise. You will see why as it is explained.

Performed from a good walk, the horse is balanced and slowed using the outside rein while the inside rein asks for a small amount of bend (for the purposes of our example horse, to the right). The inside (right) leg comes slightly behind the girth and asks the horse's hindquarters to move over to the left, while the outside (left) leg receives this movement and maintains the forward motion.

The horse describes part of a circle around the forehand with the movement of the hindquarters. Forwardness remains, the walk rhythm remains, the regularity of the walk remains. The horse should remain through the back and on the bit. There is a lot happening and a lot to get right. To do all of this from halt—as is required in a turn-on-the forehand—is almost impossible.

It is also important to say that striving to do the turn-about-the-forehand correctly from the start will solve (or preempt) some of the issues we will tackle next.

Turn-about-the-Forehand Problems and Solutions

1 PROBLEM: FALLING OUT. _

2 WHY IS THE PROBLEM THERE? As we ask the horse to slow down with the outside (left) rein, he is likely to resist and fall out through the left shoulder. The right rein, as it asks for the small amount of right bend, is likely to be presented with much more bend than is needed or wanted, and the horse will fall through the left shoulder a little more. The rider's right leg, as it asks the hindquarters to move over, is likely to be met with a dull, non-compliant feeling, which gives the left leg nothing to receive. And the horse will fall out the left shoulder a little more.

3 WHY DOES IT NEED SOLVING? The result is a difficulty moving the hindquarters around while there is too much bend in the neck and the horse is undoubtedly trying to escape through the left shoulder. These are all very common faults.

4 HOW DO YOU SOLVE THE PROBLEM? Control the amount of bend, being firm with the left rein. This will stop the left shoulder from escaping. Now the horse may feel hemmed in and reluctant to listen to the right leg asking for the turn. The rider must be firm and clear that the hindquarters must move over before a release of the outside rein will be allowed to happen. This is part of the rewiring of the horse's brain that takes place when training.

There are several benefits to this exercise:

- It develops a better understanding that the outside rein helps control the amount of bend and helps rebalance the horse.
- The horse will begin to understand that the inside leg should be listened to and not ignored. (A schooling whip can also be very helpful in this regard.)
- The horse will work out that the inside rein asking for a little bend should indicate the rider's desire for him to look and think right, even if the hindquarters are going left.
- The rider's coordination of the aids and the horse's understanding of the independent use of the aids will both improve.

Demi-Pirouette

I really like this exercise, which has many benefits and is very satisfying to teach and ride. It is best left until the horse has some understanding that the rider's leg aids influence the horse's hind legs. To teach it too early in his education can sever the connection of the rider's leg aids to the horse's hind legs—a bad result.

The demi-pirouette is performed from a good walk. To the right, the right rein asks for right bend, while the left rein allows the bend and slows the horse down. The walk keeps marching but covers less ground.

The right leg should remain on the girth to keep control of the right shoulder, while the left leg, positioned slightly behind the girth, asks the body of the horse to move the forehand to the right following the lead of the right rein. In doing so we are describing a partial circle around the hindquarters.

Benefits of the exercise:

- The rebalance required allows the horse's hind legs to come more underneath his body.
- It also lightens the forehand.
- The horse begins to understand the early stages of collection.
- It improves understanding of the aids for both rider and horse.
- Eventually, the same feeling will be useful for corners and turns in both dressage and jumping.

Demi-Pirouette Problems and Solutions

1 PROBLEM: FALLING OUT ON ONE SIDE AND OVERBENDING ON THE OTHER. _ _

2 WHY IS THE PROBLEM THERE? In the demi-pirouette, similar issues are likely to arise to those I described for the turn-about-the-forehand (p. 129). As you ask for right bend, you will likely get more than you want. The horse will try to bulge out through the left shoulder and think "left" instead of following the intention of the lead rein to the right. The rider's right leg will all too easily control the shoulder as the horse falls away to the left. The rider's left leg will find it difficult to help the left rein keep the shape and stop the shoulder from falling out (see fig. 3.9 C p. 51). You will also find the horse reluctant to move over to the right. He may even swing his hindquarters to the right through misunderstanding.

3 WHY DOES IT NEED SOLVING? I hope it is clear by now that we can't allow a problem to persist or we risk the problem persisting forever, or simply stalling out in our and our horse's education.

4 HOW DO YOU SOLVE THE PROBLEM? As the right rein offers bend, so the left rein must limit the amount. In doing so it will assist in controlling the horse's left shoulder.

The rider's right leg, in this case, should be quite passive, as using it too much will be unhelpful. The rider's left leg shouldn't be too far away from the girth so as not to cause the hindquarters to go right, but also, it has more chance of helping the rein control the roving left shoulder in this position. The left leg should ask the *forehand* over to the right, supported by the right rein as it encourages the horse over.

It is also worth thinking about what might happen when the direction is changed and these movements are performed on the opposite rein. The horse will demonstrate the same issues in a different way:

- Left bend will be harder to achieve.
- Controlling the left shoulder will be harder.
- The hindquarters are likely to escape to the right.
- As the movement evolves, the horse is likely to ignore the rider's aids and revert to falling through the left shoulder.

Knowing this ahead of time ensures a methodical approach to practicing the movement on the opposite rein.

Leg-Yield

The leg-yield is a forward-and-sideways movement, as much forward as it is sideways, with the horse perfectly straight, and an imperceptible bend *away* from the direction of movement at the poll (fig. 5.4). This is a great exercise and has many uses.

In a leg-yield to the right, the left rein creates a *slight* bend to the left. The right rein allows the bend and controls the forwardness. The rider's left leg goes slightly behind the girth to ask the horse to go sideways. The rider's right leg is on the girth to "receive" the horse and limit the amount of movement sideways, while at the same time ensuring a forward and connected pace or gait.

Benefits of the exercise:

- Improvement of the coordination of the rider's aids.
- Improvement of the horse's understanding of the rider's aids.
- Improved balance and connection.

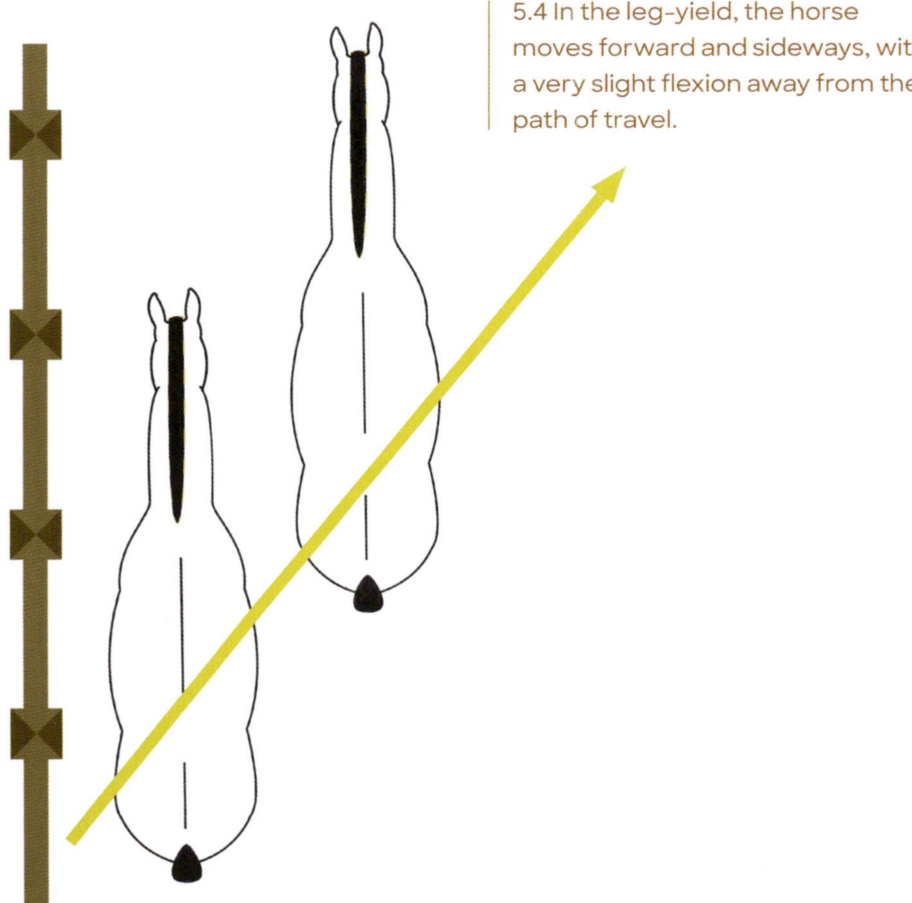

5.4 In the leg-yield, the horse moves forward and sideways, with a very slight flexion away from the path of travel.

Leg-Yield Problems and Solutions

1 PROBLEM: STOPS GOING FORWARD IN LEG-YIELD. _ _ _ _ _ _ _ _ _ _ _ _

2 WHY IS THE PROBLEM THERE? As we've discussed, it's because the horse has dropped the connection.

3 WHY DOES IT NEED SOLVING? It's a prerequisite of being correct that the horse goes forward in all movements.

4 HOW DO YOU SOLVE THE PROBLEM? Think of traveling from one parallel line to another. As already directed, in a leg-yield to the right, the rider's left leg is slightly behind the girth, asking for the sideways movement. The right leg (on the girth) is the aid that ensures the forward (as much forward as it is sideways), so use it actively and send the horse straight for a few steps to reconnect the push from the hind legs. Then go sideways again. Get a few more steps sideways and then go straight again to ensure you reconfirm the connection.

As this exercise becomes more refined and the conversation between the horse and the aids is better understood, you'll be able to accomplish both sideways and forward in the moment. It is as if your sideways aid "gives" the horse to the forward aid, which says, "thank you" and ensures connection at every step. The aid becomes unobtrusive.

It's a physical exercise that depends on a mental understanding. Balance improves through the physical control, and thus the quality of the gait can be maintained. Now the "7" or "8" mark that you achieve while going straight in the dressage arena will stay a "7" or "8" when going sideways as well.

When your horse tries to convince you that it is enough just to go sideways without also going forward, you may need to alter your priorities. Reduce the amount of sideways in favor of going forward, and be quick to remind the horse of the importance of this connection. Often you will feel a lovely, lively trot when going in a straight line suddenly disappear when the horse is asked to go sideways. It's difficult to maintain forward and regular when the connection has been dropped. Your score of "7" or "8" going straight suddenly gets reduced to a "5" or "6."

Riders must be very alert to feel when the connection gets dropped and reconnect with the help of the forward aids as quickly as possible. Either abort the movement to ensure connection remains, as that is the priority, or if the horse allows, continue the movement with regained connection.

The horse must never be allowed to develop the mindset that, "I'll drop the connection at the hint of lateral work."

1 PROBLEM: THE HORSE'S HINDQUARTERS LEAD. _ _ _ _ _ _ _ _ _ _ _ _

2 WHY IS THE PROBLEM THERE? In this instance, the act of asking for the slight left bend will automatically block the natural drift of the left shoulder. The horse then becomes too responsive to the left leg. The issue will now be ensuring that the hindquarters don't lead and that the horse brings the shoulder in line with the hindquarters (fig. 5.5).

3 WHY DOES IT NEED SOLVING? Remaining parallel to the direction of movement is always difficult, but it's necessary to properly execute the leg-yield.

4 HOW DO YOU SOLVE THE PROBLEM? The rider's aids must be coordinated to communicate what is desired. Each aid has a role—to ask and correct. The horse must pay attention to the correction the rider seeks to maintain the right position. Bending left will most likely be harder to encourage than bending right. Work in hand can help this (see p. 000). The hindquarters will be inclined to drift to the right, so the use of the rider's left leg has to be subtle and the positioning not too far back from

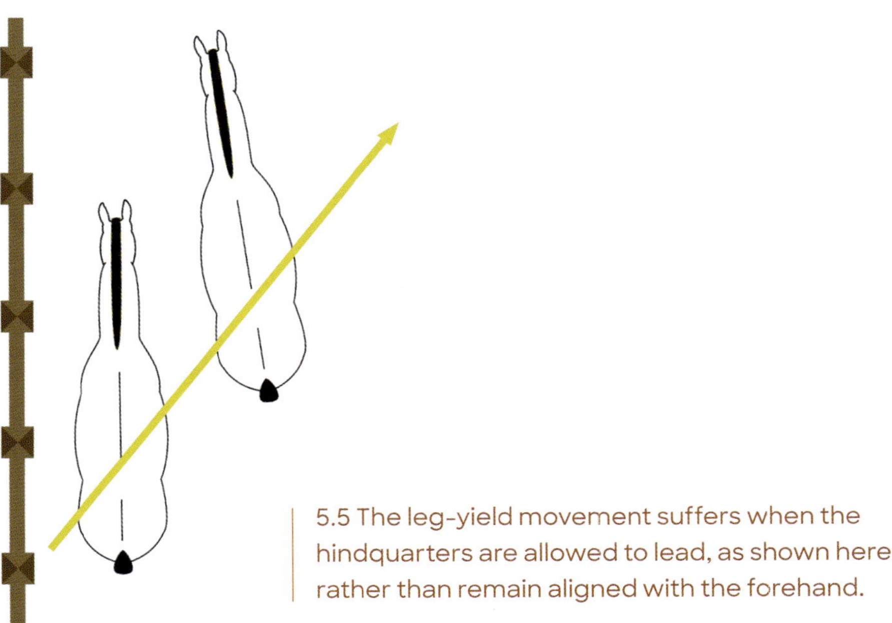

5.5 The leg-yield movement suffers when the hindquarters are allowed to lead, as shown here, rather than remain aligned with the forehand.

the girth. The forehand will be the reluctant part to move over, so the rider's left leg may actually need to come forward closer to the girth area as the right hand gently leads the forehand to the right. Too much use of the right hand and the bend to the left—part of the leg-yield to the right—may disappear.

Throughout the movement to the right the horse mustn't try to move the hindquarters more than the forehand. The forehand is the part of "this" horse that will tend to get left behind, so we must be constantly aware of that likelihood.

Shoulder-In

It is a good idea to start the shoulder-in exercise in walk. This gives the rider more time to explain and the horse more time to understand what is being asked.

Right rein initiates the uniform bend throughout the horse's body by asking the shoulder to come off the track. The left rein allows for the bend and controls the amount of it, at the same time allowing the forehand to move off the track. The right leg is fairly passive as the hindquarters will follow as desired. The left leg is busy supporting the left rein, controlling the amount of bend and ensuring the hindquarters don't swing left (fig. 5.6).

Benefits of the exercise:

- Improvement of the coordination of the rider's aids.
- Improvement of the horse's understanding of the rider's aids.
- Improved balance and connection.

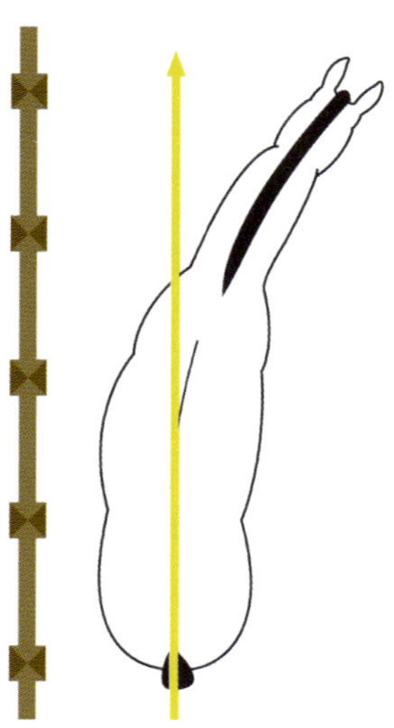

5.6 In the shoulder-in to the right, the horse bends slightly to the right and his shoulders move to the inside as he moves straight down the track.

Shoulder-In Problems and Solutions

1 PROBLEM: OVERBENDING, STIFF-NECKED, OR FAILING TO MOVE OFF THE TRACK.

2 WHY IS THE PROBLEM THERE? The horse may not understand what is being asked or have difficulty moving his shoulders off the line of movement. Too much bend or not enough bend in the neck may therefore appear (figs. 5.7 A & B).

3 WHY DOES IT NEED SOLVING? Shoulder-in is one of those movements that will be repeated throughout the horse's lifetime, so it's best to get it right at the start. It is of little value if it is done incorrectly.

4 HOW DO YOU SOLVE THE PROBLEM? Read through the solution for a turn-about-the-forehand (p. 129) as there are similarities between the two movements. Control the drift of the left shoulder and the bend with a limiting left rein and clear support from the left leg. Ensure the uniformity of bend remains consistent—an amount of bend similar to what would be required for an 8-meter volte (small circle).

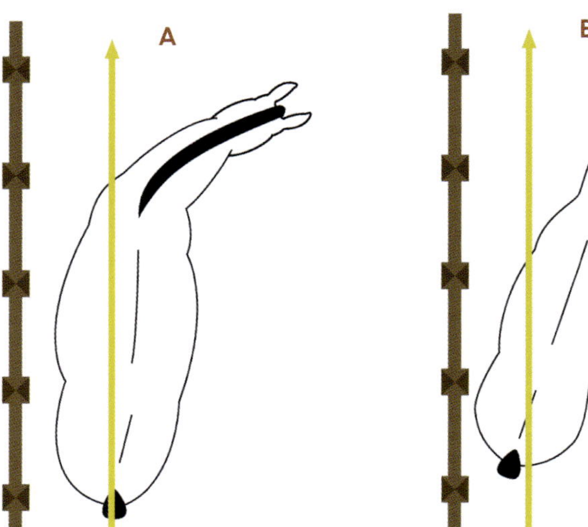

5.7 A & B When a horse lacks understanding or is stiff, he may overbend his neck (A) or have no bend (B) when asked for the shoulder-in.

The rider's right leg in right shoulder-in must be careful to encourage, not demand forwardness along the line of direction. The right leg must also be careful to not push the hindquarters to the left. On this rein, bend will likely be offered too easily and the shoulder will be reluctant to come "in" off the track. (In left shoulder-in, you'll tend to find there's not enough bend through the horse's body and the shoulder will happily "come in." There should always be a uniform bend through the body.

Half-Pass

Begin this exercise in walk. To ride a half-pass right on a horse that tends to offer more bend to the right means the positioning of right bend with the right rein will be easier this way than the other, partly because the horse's right shoulder will allow itself to be held by the rider's right leg. The degree of positioning right will need to be controlled by the left rein to stop the horse's left shoulder from falling out to its favored place (the left). The rider's left leg, which is the sideways-moving aid, will be slightly behind the girth to move the horse to the right.

Benefits of the exercise:

- Improvement of the coordination of the rider's aids.
- Improvement of the horse's understanding of those aids.
- Improvement of the horse's balance and athleticism.

Half-Pass Problems and Solutions

1 PROBLEM: TOO MUCH BEND OR THE HINDQUARTERS LEADING. _ _ _ _ _ _

2 WHY IS THE PROBLEM THERE? The hindquarters will be keen to go to the right because that is what is easiest for them, and they may sneak ahead of the forehand.

3 WHY DOES IT NEED SOLVING? This issue creates a half-pass with too much bend and the hindquarters ahead of the forehand (fig. 5.8). The horse's left shoulder will be reluctant to stay ahead of the hindquarters. As this happens, an incorrect shape in the horse's body will appear, which will restrict the horse's movement.

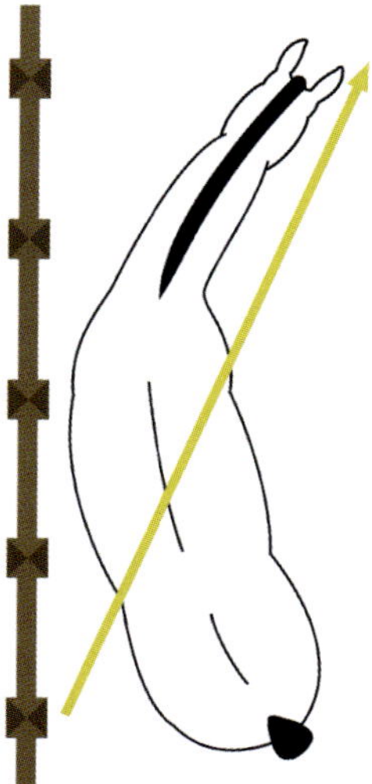

5.8 The half-pass with the hindquarters leading.

4 HOW DO YOU SOLVE THE PROBLEM? The left rein has the responsibility for managing the correct amount of bend. It is also responsible for containing the horse's left shoulder (remember, the left shoulder will want to be too much to the left). You will need to be careful about where your left leg is positioned to avoid the hindquarters going to the right too easily (the hindquarters leading is a common fault).

The rider's right leg will be tempted to drift back to stop the hindquarters from leading, but the rider must be careful not to allow this to happen. The right rein may need to be proactive in offering a direction for the forehand to go. Having "closed" the left side, there must be somewhere on offer for the horse to go (the horse often feels restricted when bend is being contained).

Travers (Haunches-In)

Going to the right, the right rein initiates the bend right. The rider's right leg controls the position of the horse's shoulders and stays around the girth area. The left rein allows for the bend and controls the amount of forward movement. The rider's left leg encourages the hindquarters to move to the right onto the inner track. The rider's right leg controls the shoulder position and acts as a sort of "post" that the horse wraps around (fig. 5.9).

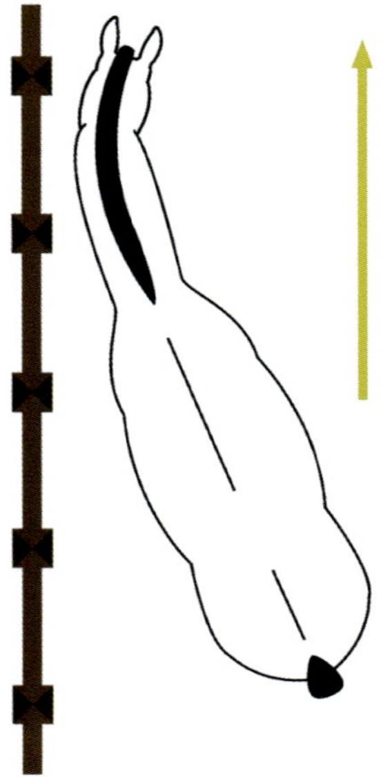

5.9 In travers (haunches-in) to the right, the horse bends toward the right (inside) as his hindquarters come of the track.

Benefits of this exercise:

- Improved balance.
- Improved coordination of the rider's aids.
- Improved understanding of the aids by the horse.
- Improved straightness and athleticism.

Travers (Haunches-In) Problems and Solutions

1 PROBLEM: TOO MUCH BEND AND A LOSS OF FORWARDNESS OR REGULARITY. _ _

2 WHY IS THE PROBLEM THERE? The horse in our example above will tend to move his hindquarters willingly in this direction so he will be inclined to create too much bend and angle.

3 WHY DOES IT NEED SOLVING? The result will be a difficulty in retaining forwardness, regularity, and a connected pace or gait.

4 HOW DO YOU SOLVE THE PROBLEM? Again, the left rein will need to actively limit the amount of bend as the horse will be inclined to show right bend too easily. The rider's left leg must be careful in its positioning and use as the hindquarters will move right too readily in reaction to an active leg aid. The right leg will need to control the amount the hindquarters come off the track at the same time they retain the forwardness.

Angle vs. Bend

These concepts are often confused by trainers and dressage judges! It is important to understand the difference (figs. 5.10 A & B).

- **Bend describes the amount and type of bend the horse has through his body.**
- **Angle describes the angle of movement the bend is placed on.**

Too much or too little of each can be a problem. If the bend or angle is too great, it is also difficult for the horse to remain forward and retain his regularity. Care should be taken in understanding each concept as they can greatly influence the quality of the gait and the connection. In particular, too great an angle is a major fault.

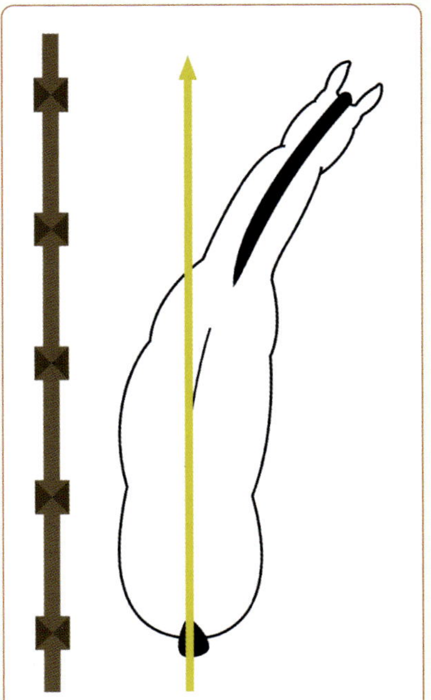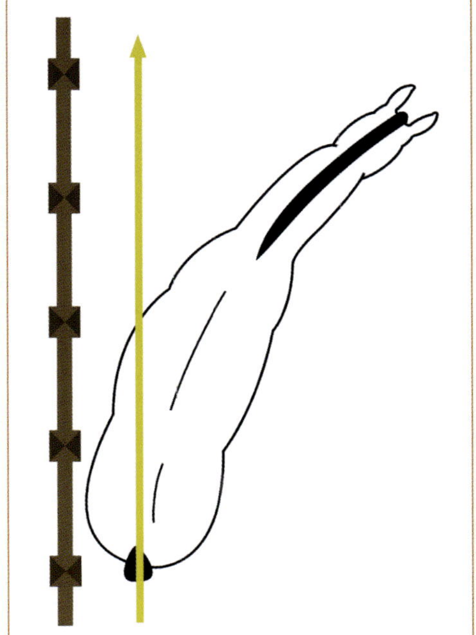

5.10 A & B show a horse with the same bend but different angles in relation to the direction of movement.

Renvers (Haunches-Out)

The issues in the renvers (haunches-out) will be very similar to the half-pass described on p. 138 as the horse is asked to adopt the same basic shape. The direction of movement is different, however. In renvers, the horse will continue to travel in a straight line in relation to the arena, rather than moving sideways as he does in half-pass. The shape is similar to half-pass and the aids are also similar to half-pass, so the problems and solutions are as well.

Two Non-Lateral Movements

I'm including the halt and the rein-back in this chapter because of their importance to the subject of connection. Both cause significant issues in their training and much concern to riders and trainers when there is a lack of connection.

The Halt

A good halt is hard to perform and should not be taught too early in a horse's education. It can be difficult for the horse to understand what is being asked, and as a result, he may become anxious. This is the last thing we want when a halt begins and ends many dressage tests.

It is a test of connection of the horse's hind legs to come in squarely underneath him. Until this connection begins to be understood by the horse, he will produce uncertain responses.

Halt Problems and Solutions

1 PROBLEM: RESISTANCE TO THE REIN AID, LOSS OF OUTLINE, HOLLOW THROUGH THE BACK, NOT SQUARE, LACK OF A REBALANCE PRECEDING THE HALT, FALLING ON THE FOREHAND.

2 WHY IS THE PROBLEM THERE? Problems with the halt tend to be the result of a misunderstanding of the rider's aids.

3 WHY DOES IT NEED SOLVING? A good square halt is proof of good education, so it is beholden on us to initiate and pursue it.

4 How do you solve the problem? It's difficult to perform a good halt until the horse understands a rebalance within the gait. The rebalance will display elements of connection being understood. Once this has been grasped, the halt becomes so much easier.

With the constant qualities ever-present (forward, straight, and regular) and the "Three Cs" (contact, connection, and consistency) we should begin the training or retraining, asking the walk to be big and then small and then big again. In doing this, the horse should start to alter the length of his step and bring his hind legs under his body. This will redistribute some weight from the forehand onto the hind legs, producing a readjustment of the balance (a rebalance).

When we slow the gait, the horse is tempted to think "halt," he begins lightening the forehand while the hind legs keep walking in underneath him, ready to absorb the forward momentum. Now the horse is ready to attempt a full halt. Don't be too fussy with the first few attempts. Feel for the horse thinking his way through the rebalance and remaining attentive to the hand. If he doesn't come in square at first, it is not the end of the world.

He must, however, be comfortable remaining immobile, on the bit, and secure between leg and rein. Without this security, it can be difficult to correct any lack of squareness behind.

The use of a schooling whip to gently tap the offending leg that doesn't quite come in square will highlight to the horse what is needed. As he moves the leg and replaces it square, there is a need for you to give him a clear reward. Once the horse allows the correction and begins to seek squareness himself, you have improved the connection.

The transition from halt to walk will test this connection. The transition from halt to trot further tests the horse's responsiveness.

Keep practicing.

The Rein-Back

The rein-back is a valuable test of a horse's acceptance of the rider and the aids. It demonstrates an acceptance of the aids and a willingness to do what the rider asks.

There is a risk for it to be introduced too early in the horse's training or retraining, with the result that problems can be introduced unnecessarily.

Rein-Back Problems and Solutions

1 PROBLEM: TOO STRONG A REIN, WITH THE CONTACT SOMETIMES BECOMING A PULL; SHORTENING OF THE NECK; TENSION OF THE LOWER JAW AND NECK MUSCLES; NOT HALTING SQUARE; HOLLOWING OF THE BACK; DRAGGING THE FEET; INCORRECT RHYTHM OF THE FOOTFALL; LOSING FORWARDNESS OF MIND; LOSING STRAIGHTNESS; RUNNING BACKWARD.

2 WHY IS THE PROBLEM THERE? The rein-back is often used to improve submission and compliance in the horse, neither of which are appropriate words or qualities. Very few horses are ever taught to rein-back at the right time or in the correct manner.

These faults are caused by similar problems:

- Too strong a rein, shortening of the horse's neck, and losing straightness often happen when the horse is unresponsive or misunderstands.
- Tension of the lower jaw and neck muscles is due to resistance to aid of leg to hand.
- Not halting square and hollowing of the back demonstrates a lack of connection.
- Dragging the feet or incorrect rhythm of the footfall means the horse is lacking the impulsion needed to lift his feet cleanly.
- Losing forwardness of mind means the horse has not retained a readiness to immediately spring forward.
- Running back indicates he is afraid of the aids, misunderstands the task, or is poorly trained.

3 WHY DOES IT NEED SOLVING? Many horses "go backward," which may be the rider's aim and may, as a result, please the rider. But to introduce this movement in the correct way, in a way that is understood by the horse, requires many skills. It takes time for the rider and the horse to develop them. But done well, the rein-back is a very satisfying exercise as it demonstrates good education that is well understood.

4 HOW DO YOU SOLVE THE PROBLEM? There is a right way to ride the rein-back. Before going backward, the horse really needs to understand what being "in front of the leg" means, as well as being "between leg and hand," and being "through." He needs to understand what a "resistant hand" means and how to respond to a leg aid that "talks" rather than "tells."

A rein-back is as much forward as any other movement. Rein-back should be preceded by a square halt, which, as we now know, is a tricky thing to ride in itself (see p. 143). That is why I am inclined to leave the rein-back alone until a horse is well along in his education, when all the riding qualities are in place and firmly understood. Once riders are able to use their legs to bring the horse into halt, they can ride him up to be square behind, "through" the back, and on the bit, and then the rein-back will be easy. I am not in favor of using the rein-back in the early stages of training or retraining to gain control.

The trick is to ask the horse to go from the rider's leg at the same time as the rein aids are resisting any move in a forward direction, encouraging the horse to seek another outcome. The only direction that is available is backward. To assist the horse in understanding this subtlety of aid, the rider should lighten the seat and move both legs very slightly behind the girth. When taught often enough, the mere application of the aid will produce the desired response.

When the horse knows the direction of travel, he will not be confused by the apparent contradiction of the use of the rider's legs. The rider's legs need to stay active, asking the horse's legs to stay active as they step back with clearly defined steps. Losing activity results in the horse dragging his legs.

When the rein-back is done correctly, the horse's legs move in diagonal pairs, in an almost two-time rhythm. The rein aids should not be used to pull the horse back. Instead, they should resist the inclination of the horse to walk forward, but at the same time stay on a good contact that doesn't shorten the neck. There is a subtlety to this that takes a little getting used to. The messages can appear contradictory.

Positioning horses with a barrier in front of them can often reinforce the message that you want them to go backward. It is important not to hurry the horse as he assimilates the message and finds the appropriate answer. Once the correct answer has been produced a number of times, the process becomes more clear and the delay in reaction will lessen.

To ensure that the mind retains the intention of forwardness, when doing a rein-back, alter the number of steps asked for. Also ensure that a clean transition to walk or trot is asked to finish the movement.

The Common Link

Connection is critical for all the exercises we've covered in this chapter to be of good quality. Without it, a score of "6" in a dressage test might be achievable, but with connection, a score above "6" becomes possible.

The movements we've discussed are school exercises that can be both a test of the level of education of work being produced and a means to improve the quality of connection. Used in an understanding way, they will also confirm the qualities of forwardness, straightness, regularity, and contact, as well as consistency, the subject of the next chapter.

Train like you want to win; compete like you've never lost.

CHAPTER 6

Consistency

Consistency: "Adhering to the Same"

ONSISTENCY IS AN IMPORTANT AIM IN COMPETITION RIDING across movements, gaits, and disciplines. It might mean making a 20-meter circle look the same all the way around, or ensuring the horse's outline looks the same during a transition, or maintaining the regularity of the gait on both reins. It is part of what we are tested and judged on. But to achieve it requires understanding from the horse and active riding from the rider.

Remember the concept of a start point from the introduction (p. 9)? A start point is a point of security and stability—a knowing place. It is somewhere the horse and rider can recover a correct moment if things go wrong, tension arises, or a misunderstanding occurs. It is a good tool for training because it requires consistency. For example, a trot that remains regular for a whole 20-meter circle and scores a "6" in a dressage test for being satisfactory is a good start point from which to move on to the next level of work. The gait and the movement of the circle can both be ridden with consistency. A trot that scores a "6" for part of the circle and a "5" or a "7" for other parts demonstrates inconsistency and still needs work.

The same applies when jumping. A consistent canter has a greater chance of ensuring a predictable arrival at the jump than a canter that is inconsistent. It is the rider's role in the partnership to ride the consistency, as the horse does not understand the concept. To do this there must be a step-by-step input from the rider. At times it will be a very light and almost invisible confirmation, indicating to the horse that he is doing well. At other times, there may be a more insistent input to correct or keep the work the horse is producing up to the mark.

Inconsistency is a sign that something is not working as it should and must be noticed and addressed. Remember, success does not come from what you do occasionally, but from what you do consistently.

In this chapter, we'll look at some of the exercises we can do to help achieve consistency as well as the common problems that can arise when doing them.

Transitions within the Gait and from One Gait to Another

Performing transitions within a gait is an often-used exercise with many benefits (fig. 6.1 and 6.2). Playing with the pace by increasing and decreasing the length of the stride while maintaining the constant qualities of forward, straight, and regular, and the Three Cs—contact, connection, and now consistency as well—not only allows us to test the horse's responses to the aids but also improves the balance. The change in balance is the beginning of the road to collection, but more importantly, is a response of preparation for something else.

Consider again figure 5.2 B on p. 118. Note how the horse's hind legs are endeavoring to remain in front of the perpendicular line, coming as far as they can under the horse's main body of weight. This is the beginning of collection, an improvement of balance, and a more uphill frame.

The use of this exercise allows us to keep the horse constantly in front of the leg and ready for whatever comes next. I'd also like to emphasize that decreasing and increasing the stride are equally valid options.

Increase Decrease Exercise

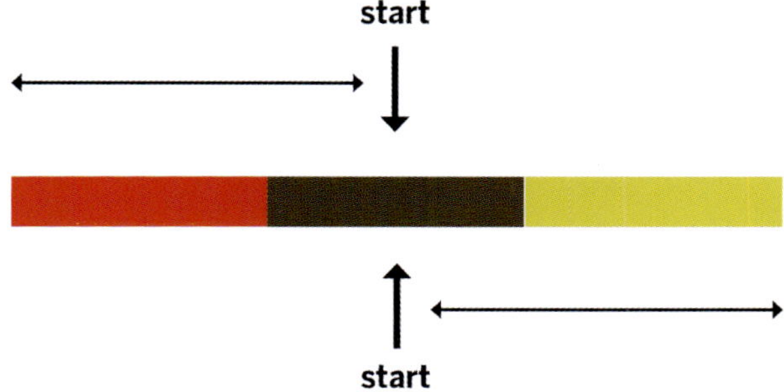

6.1 This illustrates what happens if we only increase and decrease the stride from a single point: Effectively we only practice two variations of the gait. If we also use the middle (working) as our starting pace and then decrease, return to the middle, and then increase, we will have practiced three different variations of the same gait.}

Length of Stride

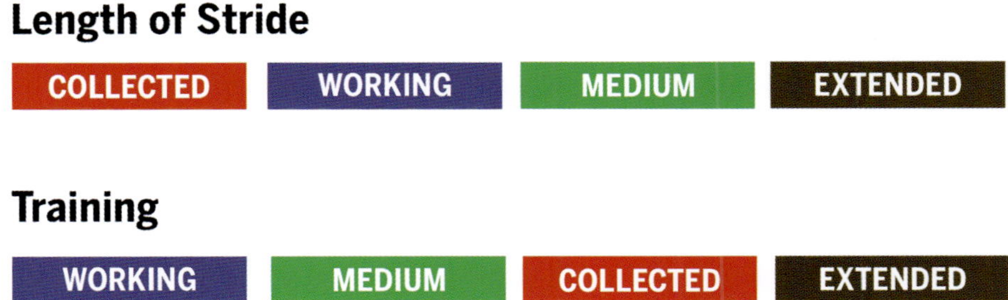

Training

6.2 This diagram illustrates how using increase and decrease in training produces different stride lengths. We start with a working gait and decrease—we are working toward a more collected pace. Then we increase, and we work toward a medium gait (see the markers under Length of Stride). But true "collection" only comes out of much training in working and medium gaits. And true extension only comes out of a true collection (see the progression markers under Training). That's why these last two gaits become the last to be mastered by the horse. Collected stride length is the shortest stride and extended is the longest stride length, both very hard for the horse to do, physically and mentally.

Transitions Problems and Solutions

1 PROBLEM: NOT SHOWING ENOUGH CHANGE IN LENGTH OF STRIDE WITHIN A GAIT.

2 WHY IS THE PROBLEM THERE? Riders are often reluctant to be too demonstrative, opting for a smooth transition rather than an expressive one.

3 WHY DOES IT NEED SOLVING? Clear, quality changes in the length of stride show control and availability of power and demonstrate an educated and "available" horse.

4 HOW DO YOU SOLVE THE PROBLEM? School movements and shapes are the bread and butter of our work with horses. They test and measure where we are. Accuracy and quality must become the add-on to functionality.

The Rebalance

As I said earlier in the book, "half-halt" has to be one of the most overused and misunderstood expressions in riding. It has a different meaning and execution for everyone. I use the word rebalance to describe the process instead. I explained the concept earlier (p. 85), but revisit it here because I find that repetition of important ideas never hurts—and the rebalance is one of the most important tools in our toolbox as riders. We will need to employ it, over and over again.

The rebalance precedes just about everything we ask the horse to do. It gives him a "heads up" that something new is coming. It is a "nod and a wink" to get ready, and it is something every horse must come to understand. Without this understanding, riding can be like speaking in a foreign language: It doesn't matter if you say what you want louder or more often, the horse still won't be ready and able to give you the right answer. So clarification of the language is the first step.

I have talked a lot about the link between the rider's leg aids and the horse's hind legs. The rider's legs are the primary aid that initiates everything, from the plain language we have to use to converse with the young horse to the invisible language exchanged with the educated horse, and from the simple request to "go" to the more complicated nuances of the canter pirouette. Both of the rider's legs are involved.

Ride a 20-meter circle. After every three or four strides in working trot, shorten the stride for two strides. Return to the working trot for three or four strides, and then ride forward to a longer stride for two.

Every time you shorten or lengthen, the constant qualities (forward, straight, and regular) should remain, as they must do when you transition to working trot again. Your leg aids ask for the push from the horse's hind legs to be more noticeable, while the rein aids ask the horse to shorten or lengthen the stride without losing the contact or shortening the neck. Both legs and both hands are used in your "half-halts" or rebalances. The horse should be starting to understand the Three Cs—contact, connection, and the beginnings of consistency.

The legs are assisted by the rein aids in their unique language. From the uneducated pull, which is sometimes necessary, to the advanced whisper that cements "togetherness." Both reins are involved. Without the horse understanding both ends of the conversation— the rider's legs and reins—nothing much can happen. Only when there is understanding is a rebalance possible.

The word rebalance can mean to:

- Reassess
- Rethink
- Return
- Readjust
- Recalibrate
- Reinvite

Something has to happen for the rider to start thinking there is a need for a rebalance. It might be that a transition is coming, the horse has fallen out of balance, or a movement needs fine-tuning. Something prompts a reassessment.

A conversation between the rider's leg and rein, when both horse and rider understand the language, will produce a rebalance at the appropriate time. With the young or uneducated partnership, it may be a slower, more simple conversation, while with the educated partnership it can happen in a heartbeat with a mere thought.

1 Problem: Going above the bit, speeding up, being sluggish, losing straightness, the horse "collapses" or goes against the hand, hollowing of the back, or lacking purpose in the first stride of walk.

2 Why is the problem there? There are many reasons for these issues to show up. The main one is probably a lack of preparation and clear communication on the rider's part.

3 Why does it need solving? Because a good transition is a demonstration of good training, it is important to demonstrate our ability to do them consistently well.

4 How do you solve the problem? The old adage applies: "It's not the doing of it, but how well it is done!"

A horse is very capable of doing crisp, clean, and correct transitions on his own. With the rider on board, he is still physically able to perform good transitions, but problems arise due to poor communication, misunderstanding, and a lack of preparation.

Your *start point* must be to do transitions correctly. Then you should strive to do them correctly in a crisp manner. Walk-trot-walk is the go-to. Each gait should retain its integrity. You may find that one or two steps on either side of the transition are initially upset when ensuring correctness. As the horse's understanding of the request improves, the quality will return.

As I mentioned in chapter 5, I recommend that you avoid riding walk-to-halt transitions as it is too easy to get them wrong with a bad result that will last. In asking for a transition, we want the horse to remain secure to the aid and in an outline that is appropriate for his level of education.

When considering problems and solutions, let's break down the movement into two parts: walk-to-trot and trot-to-walk.

Common flaws from walk to trot include going against the rein or above the bit, speeding up, or being sluggish to the leg. Riding transitions within the pace is always a good way to begin correcting transitions from one pace to another. Doing this requires the necessary response to the rider's leg and rein while at the same time maintaining a forward feeling. It also allows the horse time to assimilate the information and organize his response.

- In walk, ask for two or three increase and decrease transitions (as described on p. 148) before you ask for a walk-trot transition. This will allow you to check for the correct responses, ensure the horse continues to accept the bit, maintains the outline you want, and listens to the leg aids.
- The response to the leg aids must produce a push into trot, a spring forward, showing an enthusiasm to "take the rider along." You might need the assistance of the schooling whip once or twice to remind the horse what is required.
- The rein contact must allow the horse to go into the trot while retaining an accepting feel. You must not allow the horse to go above the bit. It is the rider's job to feel for the sensation of the horse being over the neck and on to the contact.
- Should you feel resistance, especially to the rein, abort the transition and start again.

Common flaws from trot to walk include the horse "collapsing," going against the hand, hollowing the back, or lacking purpose in the first stride of walk. We can solve this when:

- The rider's leg aids ask for the horse's hind legs to be active and listening so the horse can manage his weight and momentum.
- The rein aids ask for a slowing down of the momentum.
- The rider's voice can assist by using a calm, slow tone, often a "Whoa" type noise.

(The combination of these aids will indicate to the horse that he needs to get ready to move down a gear.)

- You should carefully time your aid to ask for a bright, cheerful walk—too soon and the horse will trot again; too late and the walk will already be flat and sluggish. Careful timing will ensure the horse understands that "good" requires a rebalance of the trot, and a clean transition immediately into a purposeful walk.

Transitions are the go-to exercise to ensure that the horse and rider are in sync with each other. Done correctly they are rewarding; done badly they are proof that there is work to do.

Changing Direction Across the Arena

Changing direction sounds so easy to do, but it is often when a partnership loses its consistency. There is often a lot happening in the rider's and the horse's mind and body.

Changing Direction Problems and Solutions

1 PROBLEM: LOSING ONE OR MORE OF THE CONSTANT QUALITIES OF FORWARD, STRAIGHT, AND REGULAR; LOSING BALANCE. _ _ _ _ _ _ _ _ _ _ _ _ _ _

2 WHY IS THE PROBLEM THERE? We are asking the horse to do many things at once.

3 WHY DOES IT NEED SOLVING? As crossing the diagonal of the arena to change direction is a test of consistency, we should strive to do it well. Good diagonals (the shape) add flow to a dressage test, a round of jumps, and even a cross-country ride.

4 HOW DO YOU SOLVE THE PROBLEM? The diagonal (the shape) is made up of three components: the line you ride, the bend change, and the new direction (figs. 6.3 and 6.4). You may need to break down the components to achieve consistency in execution.

- Start in walk, as there is more time to prepare. Give ample warning that a change in direction is coming. Change the direction the horse is looking. Change the aids to the new direction. Ensure that the horse doesn't anticipate the change, but that he does respond when asked to go in the new direction.

- In trot there is even more going on in the horse's mind when you ask him to change direction, so it's helpful to separate the three components (the line, the bend change, and the new direction) and allow the horse to perform each element correctly separately before asking him to put them together at once.

- Don't rush: if you're in a hurry, each component can produce a fault that is difficult to correct because the next part comes quickly. When re-educating an older horse or training a young one, the assimilation of information may take a second or two.

- Change the trot diagonal well before changing the bend.

- Change the aids before changing the bend.

- Change the direction only when the bend has been changed successfully.

You now have the chance to perform each component correctly before the new direction arrives. Repetition of a process produces a well-worn neurological pathway that creates a habit. So practice directional changes often—slowly at first to get them right, then reduce the time allowed for each part, gradually speeding up the horse's responses.

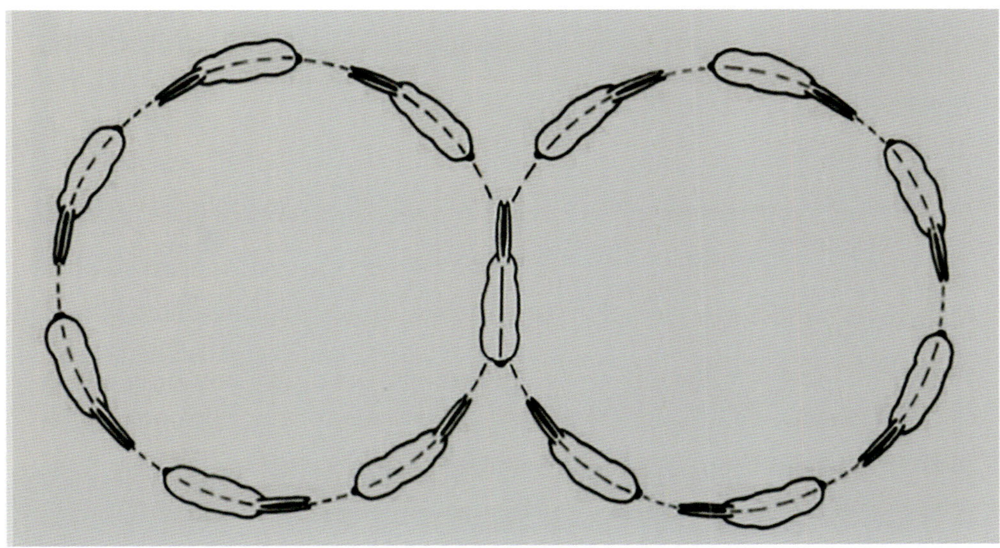

6.3 A predictable and methodical change of direction—like that of a well-ridden figure eight—will become a good one.

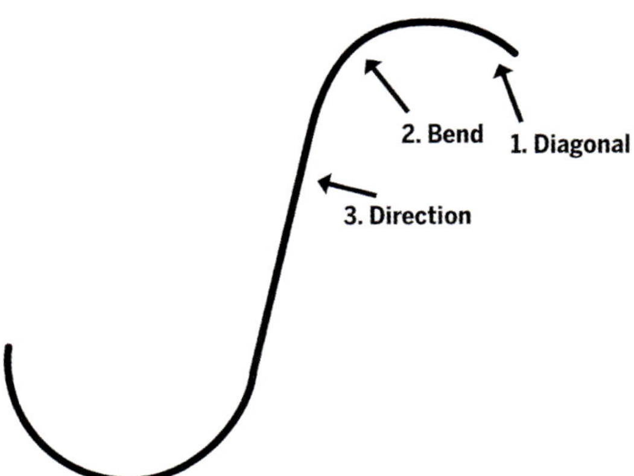

6.4 Strive to change direction well by first changing the trot diagonal (1) before changing the bend (2) and finally changing the direction (3).

Combining a Direction and a Gait Change Problems and Solutions

1 PROBLEM: EVEN MORE IS HAPPENING WHEN WE CHANGE DIRECTION AND HAVE TWO TRANSITIONS THROWN IN AS WELL—FOR EXAMPLE, A CHANGE OF DIRECTION IN CANTER, THROUGH THE TROT (OR THROUGH WALK FOR THE MORE ADVANCED). COMMON FAULTS INCLUDE A POOR DOWNWARD TRANSITION, POOR BALANCE INTO THE TROT OR WALK, LOSS OF STRAIGHTNESS, HESITATION, A POOR UPWARD TRANSITION, DIRECT TRANSITIONS TURNED INTO PROGRESSIVE TRANSITIONS (SEE P. 122).

2 WHY IS THE PROBLEM THERE? The more that's involved in a movement, the more there is to go wrong.

3 WHY DOES IT NEED SOLVING? Transitions like these are a test of the more advanced horse. They demonstrate the level of training achieved.

4 HOW DO YOU SOLVE THE PROBLEM? As I have already explained, when dealing with something complex, it is important to separate each component and perform it well individually before trying to piece everything together.

Start by riding canter to trot:

- The weight and momentum of going from canter to trot can be difficult for a horse to manage. The rider must prepare the horse with a rebalance to discourage the horse from falling onto the forehand.

- Some horses will brace with an extended front leg to absorb the momentum. As it comes to the ground, each front leg slows the horse down and allows him to rebalance himself. This is an indication of the horse's difficulty with the rebalance. The better the horse becomes at rebalancing, the less likely it is that this misuse of the front leg will occur. With an improvement in pre-transition balance, the horse's hind legs will slow the momentum and allow the front legs to take a normal stride.

Move on to the trot and direction change:

- As the downward transition happens, the timing of the rider's aids should encourage a spring and positivity to the step, which is critical to the quality of the gait. Apply the aids too early and the horse keeps cantering, too late and the horse has collapsed into the transition.

Now address the trot-to-canter transition:

- Once in trot, the change of bend and direction need to be managed before we can ask for the new transition to canter. Horses will become "wise" about the transition to canter and often anticipate its coming. Be prepared for this. Anticipation can be a useful educational process; however, it can also appear when you don't want it. Vary the number of trot strides taken to ensure the transition is "on demand." Each stage must be clearly understood and be "good" in practice, before you ask for multiple things in close succession. (Being in too much of a hurry allows flaws to creep into your work without the opportunity to correct them.)

Give each component time to be logged in the horse's brain, as this will not only allow him to do it well once, it will allow him to retrieve the information next time you ask and do it consistently.

Now try for the canter-to-walk transition! Direct transitions (where we leave out a gait) tend to feel harder for the horse and rider when they are downward rather than upward. There is more momentum for the partnership to control.

- Giving the horse plenty of warning that the transition is about to happen will improve the result.
- Make sure you establish the walk before thinking of the transition back to canter. It is a mistake to hurry this. It's important that the walk steps are of good quality, especially if you want high marks on a dressage test.

In all of these transitions, you should practice repetitively the process of preparing the horse using a rebalance, followed by a well-understood aid that allows the horse to prepare a correct result. The consistency of input allows the horse's neurological process to produce a consistent response.

Practice perfect, perfect practice.

Developing Consistency in Lateral Work Problems and Solutions

1 PROBLEM: A LACK OF CONSISTENCY IN LATERAL WORK. _ _ _ _ _ _ _ _ _

2 WHY IS THE PROBLEM THERE? Lateral work gives a horse the perfect opportunity to drop behind the aids. Horses can anticipate this moment, and when they seize it, inconsistency is the result. To avoid losing consistency in lateral work, it is important to be aware that the horse might be looking for an "out" and to be ready for the moment when it arrives. Let's look at one example, the working trot to leg-yield, which very often produces problems, such as:

- Loss of connection.
- Loss of correct shape.
- Loss of forwardness.
- Loss of straightness.

3 Why does it need solving? Avoiding the fault is always easier than correcting it. Remember, that is why the movement exists: to test the training.

4 How do you solve the problem?

- Ride a 20-meter circle in working trot. When you feel you have a consistent trot, decrease the size of the circle to 15 meters (by spiraling in) and make sure this size is established.
- Next, play with your inside leg slightly behind the girth. The trot must not change but the horse should start thinking that he should be responding in some way. Return the focus to riding the horse straight on the circle.
- Try the same aid again and the horse will begin to offer to move away from the leg. Now help him with a slight pressure on the outside rein and he will move out in leg-yield. Your outside leg should "receive" the horse and ask him to stay forward. This should not feel like the horse is "falling out."
- Two or three steps of leg-yield are enough, then go forward and straight again.

This forewarning allows the horse time to find the correct answer when the rider next asks for leg-yield at the trot. It also allows the rider time to correct an incorrect offering from the horse.

As we know, consistency is easier to achieve when we are not thinking about going sideways. Staying connected in lateral work tends to be harder for the horse, so there is every chance he will take the easy option and drop behind the leg and ignore the rider's leg aids if he is allowed. This will show itself as an inconsistent trot—sometimes

---

A Note of Caution

I talked a lot about lateral work in chapter 5 (p. 125), but I want to emphasize this point: All too often we hear what lateral work can do to improve the horse's way of going, but in reality, it does little or nothing if it is not connected and consistent. It can be quite fun to feel one's horse going sideways and that may be an achievement in itself, but for the work to be that of a true education, it must include these qualities.

---

irregular, sometimes of differing stride length, and often lacking weight-bearing and push. The solution is always to keep the horse up to the mark and honest to the leg. Do not ask for too much lateral movement before confirming the forward. Two or three steps may be enough in the beginning before the forward aids are required to ensure that the forward feeling is still there. Keeping the body on the line of the circle is important—*do not* let the horse drift out through the outside shoulder.

Adding Impulsion

Impulsion (available energy) and connection are qualities that go together. They are, however, subjective and how they are expressed depends on the individual horse.

When there is a feeling of connection combined with the ability to maintain consistency, the feeling of impulsion can be produced in any of the exercises I have described so far. Some horses demonstrate this quality more than others. Once available, the energy has many uses:

- To produce a cadence to the stride.
- To improve a more collected pace.
- To ask for a lengthening of the stride.
- Or even just to improve the basic quality of the gait.

Impulsion Problems and Solutions

1 PROBLEM: A LACK OF IMPULSION. _ _ _ _ _ _ _ _ _ _ _ _ _ _ _ _ _ _ _

2 WHY IS THE PROBLEM THERE? This is an exciting point in a horse's education, but it can be fraught with problems. There is the perceived need for "more impulsion" or "more collection," which are remarks that are bound to appear on a dressage test. The unfortunate result is often a horse changing their "good" way of going for something less good. The "8" now becomes a "6."

3 WHY DOES THE PROBLEM NEED SOLVING? As the rider tries to create more to satisfy both statements, faults tend to appear in the horse's impulsion and outline— the very things you are trying so hard to get right.

4 HOW DO YOU SOLVE THE PROBLEM? A horse's conformation and natural way of going should be taken into account when you try to improve both impulsion and collection. The horse should continue to seek the contact as his hind legs are activated to produce more impulsion. Riders should not feel they are "holding" the horse from going faster as more energy is produced, nor should the horse have his neck shortened to look collected.

More impulsion comes from the horse wanting to respond to the rider's leg request to produce more, and the rider redefining what "more" means. What was acceptable now isn't, and the horse is being asked to produce a little above the previous accepted level. This allows the horse an understanding that with more response to the rider's leg aids, he can transfer more weight onto his hind legs. The result is less weight on the front end and the appearance and feeling of a lighter forehand that is more uphill, with the hindquarters more engaged.

Repetition Leads to Consistency

You may have noticed that many of the exercises in this chapter appeared in previous chapters as well. They appear again here because consistency in doing them is the ultimate goal, as is the case with all things. We must be able to do more than perform something once correctly if we hope to achieve the descriptor "consistently excellent."

"Excellent isn't perfect but both take practice."

CHAPTER 7

Jumping

THERE CAN BE MANY ISSUES WITH JUMPING THAT CAUSE RIDERS and horses concern. As with work on the flat, the first step is to analyze the problem. So often with a perceived problem, we may confuse the symptom with the cause. "My horse knocks poles," says the student who arrives for a lesson. We need to delve a little deeper into the why before we can help. As I've emphasized throughout this book, to solve problems in a lasting way, it is important to get to the root issues and address them.

Also, keep in mind that a lot of jump problems are in the rider's mind! Many of them are placed there by what riders are taught. In quenching the thirst for knowledge, teachers often give more information than necessary, irrelevant information, or inappropriate information to riders who may be incapable of applying this information. In doing so, we create a difficulty for the partnership of horse and rider.

Mixed Messages

The well-intentioned rider tries to apply some theory without the practical ability to do so. The well-intentioned horse does his best to guess what he should do. The outcome is unsatisfactory. Riders lose confidence in themselves because they believe they are doing as instructed, but it isn't working. The horse loses faith in himself and trust in the rider because he's getting mixed messages.

Some common examples of the mixed messages and misunderstandings are as follows:

- "Control the canter."

- "See your spot."

- "Look for your distance."

- "Half-halt!"

- "Ride a corner."

- "Set up."

These phrases are all commonplace in jump training yet seldom are they acknowledged as being part of the cause of bad jumping.

7.1 My student Camilla, who had to learn not to try (so hard).

When I began teaching my student Camilla, all of the above sample instructions were ringing in her ears (fig. 7.1). And at each competition, she would have at least four poles down. She is an amateur rider who works hard to do as asked. The more she tried the more the horse gave up trying. What was the trouble?

Sound Principles

A good jump comes from a good canter on the correct line, with both partners knowing their responsibilities. I doubt if this would be disputed by anyone.

Once Camilla began to understand this principle and the horse developed a conscience—the desire to jump clean—clear rounds appeared.

Before we get into the process of dismantling the tasks of jumping, highlighting the problems, and finding solution, let's clarify the responsibilities within the partnership.

Five Phases

There are five phases in jumping:

- The approach.
- The takeoff.
- In the air.
- The landing.
- The getaway.

We should understand each of the five phases and the responsibilities within each phase. Together, horse and rider make up the complete package and each partner becomes empowered to make decisions at the correct time.

A good partnership works when there is mutual support and no interference from the more passive partner at each phase. For example, when the horse is jumping well and doing his job in the air over the fence, the rider must sit quietly in balance and not interfere. This clarity about roles and responsibilities allows for a trust to develop and if one partner needs help they become more comfortable receiving that help from the other.

In my career as a rider, trainer, and coach, the partnership works best when the responsibilities are divided up as follows:

The rider is responsible for the approach and the getaway, otherwise known as the line and pace. This involves managing the type of canter and the straightness of the approach and the getaway. The horse doesn't know where he is going without the rider, so he becomes the supporting partner in these aspects of the jump.

The horse is responsible for the jump itself, including the takeoff, in the air, and the landing. The horse knows what effort is required to jump, so the rider becomes the supporting partner in these phases.

There should be a seamless join as one partner hands over to the other from main role to supporting role. We should keep these roles and responsibilities in mind as we work our way through the following common jump problems and look for possible causes and solutions:

- A lack of forwardness.
- Rushing.
- Running away after a jump.
- A lack of straightness.
- Poor jumping technique.
- Hitting rails (what I call "carelessness").
- Stopping.

Before dismantling these problems, however, I'd like to revisit an important concept from earlier in the book: *overfacing*.

Overfacing

As you will recall from the introduction (p. 3), overfacing is a term that is used to describe asking a horse or a rider to do something that is beyond their capability. Although it is a word that is normally associated with presenting a jump that is too big, I think it is important to link the concept with all aspects of training, including flatwork (fig. 7.2).

Doing flatwork well is not just functionally doing it correctly; it's much more. It comes with the confidence of knowing that each step in the education process is understood. How it works, where it fits in, why it's done in that order, how one step leads to the next one.

This confidence allows the horse and rider to feel brave in their performance—the type of confidence Valegro would show as he entered the arena with his rider Olympian Charlotte Dujardin or when performing the extended trot.

When overfacing occurs on the flat, horses and riders demonstrate an uncertainty, a lack of confidence in execution, a physical inability to perform...a lack of self-belief.

At each stage of the journey of education, a horse should "let you in" before you ask for more. In doing so he will know that what he is learning now relates to what is coming next. This goes for jumping as well as flatwork.

7.2 We commonly think of overfacing being associated with too-big jumps, but it is symbolic for all kinds of challenges.

Instilling the "Can-Do Attitude" When Jumping

The first jump of a young or newly acquired horse is a moment when my imagination either runs riot with excitement at what I have, or my training brain kicks in with how to make it all better.

For any horse that shows a degree of ability, the industry asks for too much of this ability to be tested and put on display with loose-jumping competitions, sale videos, and longeing over jumps. Some high-performance sales horses are jumping enormous obstacles to impress prospective customers.

I believe that by asking for too much too soon we abuse a young horse's natural generosity and at the same time diminish his "can-do attitude."

Most young horses give their all when jumping at the early stages. This is a fragile attitude that we need to nurture and look after. It can be easily destroyed. There is much going on in a horse's brain at this time: *How do I get to the jump? What will I meet when I get there? What does it look like? What question is it asking? How do I get to the other side, leaving it up?*

And the jumps keep coming.

Very few horses take all this calmly. To add size to the jump question very often puts one too many challenges to the already busy mind of the young or untrained horse. The result is a stop, a run-out, a knock down, a speed up, a slowdown, or even a "won't try"!

The rider is also placed in a difficult dilemma. Having presented the horse to the jump the rider has to jump it. It's bad practice to turn away. The rider hopes it goes well, because dealing with all of the issues of it not going well gets messy. Having a good enough canter, being able to keep it, finding a reasonable takeoff—so much is dependent on the rider's skill making up for the horse's inexperience. It's a very challenging process. But that's what Young Horse competitions tend to do.

Some horses respond to the challenge of height by over-trying. A horse that over-jumps often makes people smile. But "giving it some air" or jumping exuberantly can be misleading. To jump 3 feet over a 2-foot fence feels great. It compels us to see what a 3-foot jump feels like. Now the horse tries to jump 4 feet high, and this is when he starts questioning his limits. Once there is a doubt in the horse's mind, it creates a marker of fear or hesitation, which is there for the future. This marker diminishes the horse's can-do attitude and puts a limit on his jump; something that will reappear later.

"Time is so important. I think each horse has a number of jumps in their life, and if you use them all when they are young, they will not have a lot left at the end."

—WILLY WIJEN, OWNER AND BREEDER OF EXPLOSION W, WINNER OF INDIVIDUAL
OLYMPIC GOLD IN SHOW JUMPING AT THE 2020 OLYMPICS IN TOKYO

To avoid this, keep jumps small until all of the many things going on in the horse's mind have become more familiar to him, until he learns the many issues that jumping throws at him, and until the arrival at the jump becomes something he willingly deals with, not just something organized by the rider. A slow start and deliberate progression will retain the can-do attitude for later, without a limiting marker being placed in the horse's mind.

Soon enough, the horse will learn that he does not need to jump a foot higher than the jump. As he discovers that he need jump only enough to clear a fence, then the 3-foot jump becomes a 3-foot-3-inch effort—much more comfortable for the horse.

Leaving the horse with a good feeling in the mind allows him to retain the can-do attitude as all the other issues of jumping become secure. This then allows the rider to build on the good and progress with the confidence that the horse hasn't installed any limits on his own potential. As time goes on, so the can-do attitude becomes more embedded in his mind, and his confidence in what he can do grows. No limits.

Long-term, a horse that believes in his own abilities is one that doesn't know failure or doubt. This is how you help a horse develop a good jumping conscience, an idea I will return to again later in this chapter. Start that attitude young and keep it.

Dealing with Overfacing

What if your horse already has a limiting marker in place? What should you do about it? Let's look at it from the horse's point of view.

The horse's choices are:

- "Jump, because I'm being pressed by my rider."
- "Jump, because I'm going too fast to stop."
- "Stop."
- "Look, assess, use my care and technique to prepare, and then jump."

The scars left in the mind of the horse from the first three options cannot always be seen but they are there.

- To do something because one is told, tends not to develop *partnership.*
- To do something because there is no other choice tends not to develop *commitment.*
- To doubt one's capabilities tends not to develop a *belief.*
- To stop tends to demonstrate an inability to *make a decision.*

But these four qualities—*partnership, commitment, belief,* and *sound decision-making*—are surely everything we want in a sport horse. Without them, ability alone is not enough.

The generosity of horses will often hide their anxieties. But just because they undertake a task doesn't mean they are comfortable with it. It's important for us to feel, read, and be aware of the signs of anxiety. And never be afraid to move down a level to rehabilitate the confidence in a horse's mind. It's a wise person who makes this move. It's a fool who doesn't heed the signs of overfacing.

Human athletes have the ability to think about their performance and analyze what they need to do better. There can be value in a lack of achievement as it can stimulate a rethinking of strategy and a deeper self-awareness. So for us, failure can be a powerful learning experience. It can motivate us to improve, build a resolve, an inner strength, a work ethic to do better next time, if handled the right way.

However, it is very different for horses. They do not have the ability to reason in this way. In most instances of a horse falling short, the human takes over, either to chastise or to intensify input. Neither of these responses is helpful. Instead, it begins to set limits in the horse's mind that affect how much the horse will try to help himself.

What can we do to facilitate the horse's learning? Find a start point and go back to the principles of progressive training. Start simply:

- Only jump from a gait that the horse is comfortable in. If cantering without a jump is challenging, then cantering with a jump will be even more so. So revert to trot.
- Only introduce canter when the obstacle is small enough that mistakes don't upset the horse. As the canter becomes more secure and adjustable, so the obstacle becomes more interesting. The horse will then focus on the jump and not worry about the canter.

- Retain the qualities of *forward, straight,* and *regular.*

- Allow some freedom of the rein to ensure the horse can use his neck when looking and jumping. (A neck strap can be helpful in allowing this freedom—see p. 84.)

- Ride interesting lines and include ground poles.

The riding in itself will improve the partnership. When you progress to more jumping:

- Make jumps small and interesting. Don't challenge ability but do challenge interest.

- Encourage curiosity and pleasure in achieving.

- Allow mistakes to happen, but let the horse make an effort to find a better solution.

- Keep in mind that a stop is more often from indecision than from bad behavior. So don't change the approach but do insist that the horse make a decision at the point of takeoff. You shouldn't mind if it is a bad decision, but no decision is unacceptable.

In jump training, we must do the same thing over and over again. The goal is to produce consistency in the approach, giving the horse the opportunity to find a comfortable method of negotiating the jump. The approach must be the same. The arrival may be slightly different as the horse learns to take greater ownership. The jump itself may also be different as the horse learns how to manage himself over the obstacle. The end result is that the horse will always expect a consistent approach and understand that it's his job to make the necessary adjustments to jump clean.

Avoid Scraping the Bottom of the Barrel

In the 1992 Barcelona Olympic Games, I went deeper into a horse's reserves than ever before or ever since. (He jumped clear with time faults in very hot conditions.) At the time I felt that, for the team, it was important to get home, over and above the feeling of what I was doing to my horse.

I have never felt so terrible about any equine relationship as I did after that. I had abused my horse's generosity. He had given his all, and I had asked for more. I remember to this day looking into his eyes and saying, "I'm sorry." To his eternal credit, he returned the look with a brightness of spirit that seemed to say, "It hurts, but it's okay." In an effort to make me feel better about my choice, the Irish team vet and a good friend said to me later, "He will be a better horse for it. He will understand where his limits are."

As it turned out, it was true with this horse. His look told me that his spirit was intact; he would be there again for me another day.

Unfortunately, there have also been many occasions when I have seen horses finish a competition and thought, "That's the last we'll see of that horse at this level." There is a look in the eye that reflects what's happening in the mind.

Sometimes going deep into the soul can strengthen the resolve to do better, as in the case of my Olympic ride. There are, however, plenty of times when it has the opposite

Horses Lack the Drive to Win

I am not alone in wondering what motivates horses to perform. Much has been written about this subject. Comparisons have been made between human and equine athletes. And many speculate about the limitations of humans and horses. In all sport we strive to push the boundaries. It is no different in equine sport.

Yet, if speed is an easily measurable yardstick for improvement, why has the speed of the Thoroughbred racehorse not improved over the last 60 to 100 years? Many studies have been done on this very subject. If we put aside the odd exception to the rule, it seems to come down to the fact that we have reached the end of what specialized breeding can do with the species.

However, I also believe that the horse's lack of cognition and lack of an attitude that asks, "What's in it for me?" also plays a part. As humans we understand what neural drive is: the function of the brain telling the body to "keep going." We know why we do it because we know the result we want to achieve. What drives the human to keep improving is the input of a cognitive brain. It gives us a reason to keep pushing through pain barriers and seek accomplishment—our own version of Olympic gold.

Horses have no comprehension of an outcome and so it has no meaning to them whether they succeed or fail. Their day is the same, win or lose. They do, however, have a different drive and it comes from herd instincts. They are competitive with each other. They are competitive to survive. They have developed skills accordingly, and we have been able to harness these attributes and direct them into equine sport. The horse has willingly taken on this task and does it with enthusiasm. But he does not have a cognitive thought process of the outcome or a means to measure performance.

effect, and it creates a "no-go area" where the horse's mind says to his body, "Let's stop before we get to my limit because it's not a pleasant place to be." This is getting to the "bottom of the barrel." Each time you have been near the bottom of the barrel, the next time you go there, you will find the bottom has moved up and your horse says "no" sooner. It's a really scary place to go, with a very uncertain long-term outcome. After Barcelona, I was lucky to avoid this place, thanks only to the resilience and can-do attitude of my horse.

Good training should avoid ever going there. We have a responsibility for the well-being of our horses. With that firmly in mind, let's solve specific jumping problems.

Jumping Problems and Solutions

1 PROBLEM: A LACK OF FORWARDNESS. _ _ _ _ _ _ _ _ _ _ _ _ _ _ _ _

2 WHY IS THE PROBLEM THERE? Remember the definition of forward? It's the horse "taking you," not you pushing him. Know your horse. Is his lack of forwardness a normal issue or has it suddenly appeared? If normal, then you must address it on the flat before you think about jumping. If it has suddenly appeared, is it something to do with the obstacle or question?

3 WHY DOES IT NEED SOLVING? Without the foundational quality of forward, nothing is likely to go well in the saddle, but that is especially true when going to a jump.

4 HOW DO YOU SOLVE THE PROBLEM? Work on the flat—no ground poles or jumps—is the first part of the solution. Before jumping, you need to be able to ride a canter worth at least a "6" or a "7" in a dressage test, consistently on a circle and a straight line. The canter must be adjustable in both directions—bigger and shorter—without the loss of its consistency. You should be able to change the shape of the line without losing the canter before introducing ground poles or jumps.

To go from a "7" to an "8" or a "9" in our scoring requires you to keep the same canter but have a little more useable energy (impulsion). Your leg aids are involved in asking the horse to produce a little more power without losing the regularity and the tempo that make up the consistency.

Now place a single pole along the chosen line. Ride the same canter and get used to taking the horse through the same exercise you started with. Then turn the pole into a small jump or jumps. You should not seek to "feel right" at the poles or jumps. You should not alter the canter in order to find this "right" feeling. Allow the horse to negotiate the poles and small jumps by himself out of that same canter, which you work at keeping consistently the same. This is the good canter that you might expect a "7" or "8" for. You will find a number of key things happening:

- The horse will begin to "allow" you to ride the canter, to influence the canter, and for the canter to become comfortably good.

- From the rideable, comfortable canter, the horse will begin to see the poles and small jumps but remain in the canter.

- From the rideable, comfortable canter, the horse will begin to measure where he needs to be in relation to the pole or jump to negotiate it with ease.

During this exercise, we should constantly ask ourselves:

- Is this a good canter?
- Does this canter have sufficient Impulsion to do the job?

These are questions to be asked every stride, not just once a day. I talk a lot about the word "forward" and it's meaning of "the horse taking you" and not "you pushing the horse." When jumping, grasping this distinction is especially critical. The horse should *allow himself to be ridden*. His intention must be to take you to the jump, only then will he have the tools necessary to negotiate the obstacle.

1 PROBLEM: RUSHING. _

2 WHY IS THE PROBLEM THERE? When the horse sees a jump and increases his speed toward it, he is rushing. There are many reasons why horses rush at jumps:

- There is often a misunderstanding in the early part of a young horse's training, when he is still coming to terms with what the leg aid means. As riders use their legs to keep the canter going, the horse can mistake this for an instruction to go faster. The distraction of the jump, to the young horse, can cause a loss of canter and a desire to trot, which produces a greater input from the rider, which in turn produces a faster canter from the horse. Now the horse believes that he is supposed to go faster toward the jump.

- On takeoff, riders might feel that they should "help" the horse and so a stronger leg is applied. The result is that the horse thinks he should have gone faster, when in fact the stronger leg was merely trying to support him on takeoff. Now the horse is distracted on takeoff, which interferes with the jump and landing. The confusion increases.

- It is tempting to try and jump from canter too soon with young horses. It is better to jump from trot and work on the canter without the distraction of the jump. Once the canter becomes reasonably established, then the two can be put together. (Re-read these sentences!)

There are other reasons that might cause an older horse to rush:

- A concern about how to negotiate the obstacle.
- A concern about his own ability.
- A misinterpretation of what the rider is asking.

3 WHY DOES IT NEED SOLVING? Rushing is a problem that has to be solved. The uncertainty that accompanies arrival at the point of takeoff in turn produces an uncertainty of the outcome of the jump itself, not only incurring faults, but also cause for concern from a safety point of view.

4 HOW DO YOU SOLVE THE PROBLEM? The solution sounds simple when written down: remove the cause of the problem and replace it with correct work. But in reality, when re-schooling the horse, this is not always easy to achieve. Rewiring the equine mind is slow and methodical work.

You should start by managing the gait so that you are able to create a degree of certainty in how you arrive at the fence. This certainty of the trot or canter provides the horse with the consistency of two parts of the jumping process: the approach and takeoff.

In trot, as the horse tries to rush, use the rein aids to restrain him, but at the same time keep a positive, secure, and supporting leg against his side. If the leg is removed as you try to restrain the horse from rushing, only part of the problem is solved. The horse must get used to the presence of the leg on his side and know that he should not run away from that presence. This may seem counterintuitive, but it is nevertheless important as it allows the rider to make the connection that leg does not mean "Go faster" but is related to a rebalance and communication.

The same will happen in canter. As the horse starts to rush toward the jump, it is counterintuitive to apply the leg aids, but it is necessary to do so. The leg aids are the first part of the rebalance aid and the horse must get used to this. (You may want to revisit the lengthier discussions of riding a rebalance on pp. 85 and 150.)

One of the best exercises to get the horse used to the leg aids being applied without allowing him to run away from them is to approach a small jump off a 10-meter circle. Start in trot and work up to canter. Increase the size of the circle to 15 meters. In doing so the horse won't see the jump and run, but has to wait for it to appear. At the same time he has to listen to the rider's leg and rein aids to stay on the requested line. This encourages patience from the horse and an understanding that the rider has an input on the approach.

The use of trot poles to regulate the speed can be helpful as well. Place them 8 to 9 feet from the jump, with 4 to 5 feet between poles. The horse should not speed up over these poles. If he does, then the poles are not working. (At canter, poles should be 10 to 12 feet apart, and the same distance for the last pole before the jump).

You could also try guide rails—flat rails used to create a funnel or channel toward the middle of the jump. They should be about 4 feet apart. They are a surprise to the horse and act as a distraction during the approach, which can slow the horse down. If using poles doesn't work, don't persist. Seek professional help.

The use of a stronger bit is not the solution. There may be a little more control, but this has not improved the problem. The tendency is for a horse to get used to the new bit and then start rushing again, for the rider to adopt an even stronger bit, and so on. It is a never-ending slide to becoming uncontrollable.

Remember that the horse must allow himself to be ridden from the leg aid and the result managed by the hand. When horses run away from the leg and the hands becomes the brakes, at some stage, the brakes will fail.

1 PROBLEM: RUNNING AWAY AFTER THE JUMP. _ _ _ _ _ _ _ _ _ _ _ _ _ _ _ _

2 WHY IS THE PROBLEM THERE? Does your horse land after a jump and immediately run away? This fault can have its roots in front of the jump. When leg pressure is applied on the approach and takeoff of a jump, some horses will react by landing and going! It's a way of releasing the pressure.

Sometimes, running away after a jump is a sign that the horse is nearing his limit of height and complexity. In this case, it's a warning sign. Or if a horse knocks a jump, it can increase his desire to "land and go."

3 WHY DOES IT NEED SOLVING? The landing and getaway from the jump are part of the approach to the next jump. These elements are, therefore, related. The course designer has thought of them as such. So the rider must also relate them. Whatever the cause of this habit, it is one that needs resolved to ensure a good ride.

4 HOW DO YOU SOLVE THE PROBLEM? Remove the cause. So firstly, you must pinpoint the cause. If the rider feels the horse is reluctant to go to the jump or is going to the jump with a quicker canter, these are signs to beware of. The remedy is to go back to a height of jump that the horse is comfortable with, where the approach and takeoff are calm and predictable. Build the confidence from there and reestablish the responsibilities.

On landing, the rider's upper body should come up and the rider's leg aids should be applied as part of the rider taking back ownership for the getaway. Immediately, the rider should guide the horse in a new direction, as this establishes proof of ownership. The horse should respond by rebalancing the canter and becoming rideable in the getaway canter. This process should be done over small jumps to confirm the habit.

Having re-established the approach, takeoff, the landing, and the getaway, the running away after the jump should improve. It is important to monitor this problem and know where the start point is so it's possible to go back and recover control of the situation.

1 PROBLEM: A LACK OF STRAIGHTNESS. _ _ _ _ _ _ _ _ _ _ _ _ _ _ _

2 WHY IS THE PROBLEM THERE? It is problematic when a horse deviates from the intended line toward a jump or loses straightness after a jump. It is important to understand why this happens:

- Remember, if you have a straightness issue on the flat it will transfer to jumping— or get worse when the distraction of a jump appears.
- If the flatwork is yet to be established, the horse cannot possibly be straight.
- When the jump is too high or complicated, uncertainty may lead to a loss of straightness.

3 WHY DOES IT NEED SOLVING? Course designers plan their courses to test the ability of riders to ride straight lines, while courses are measured on a designed line, so making the time is related to being able to ride that line (figs. 7.3 A & B).

The basic skill of being able to ride a straight line must never be underestimated in training. Time and effort must be spent to encourage the horse to buy into the need to be straight.

4 HOW DO YOU SOLVE THE PROBLEM? This issue is solved in the same way you deal with a lack of forwardness and rushing (see pp. 171 and 172). Basic flatwork requires that we be able to hold a line—be it straight, on a curve, or on a circle—and then manage a regular pace on that line. These fundamentals need to be brought with us when we jump.

A horse should follow the lead rein, allowing the rider to guide him on the required line, when jumping. Practice this by jumping off a circle and insisting the horse stay on the curving line. Change direction after the jump, asking the horse to follow the new direction.

Another exercise to try is to place guide rails on a slightly angled line and ask the horse to stay on that line to a jump and away from the jump. This develops the habit of following the rider's chosen line.

Horses tend to be predictable. A horse that drifts left will always tend to drift left. So know your horse. It may seem obvious, but practice the direction in which he

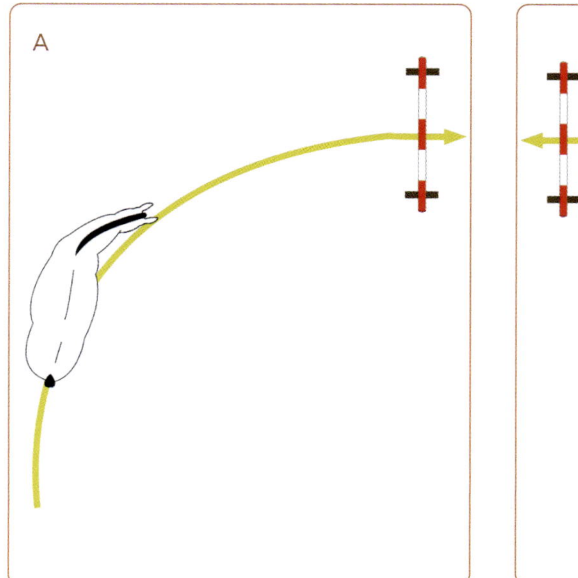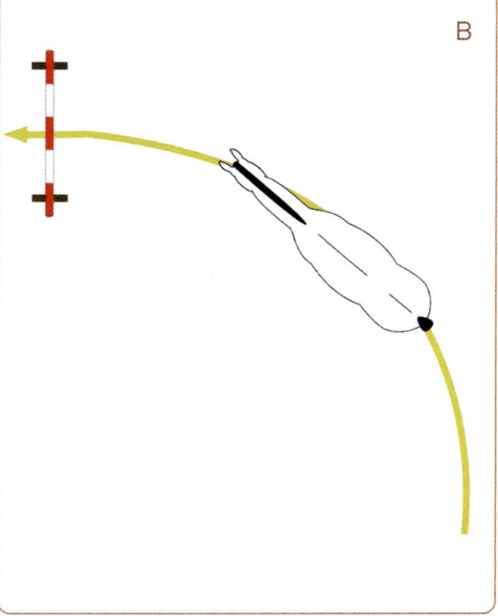

7.3 A & B Both horses are falling left, bringing different problems to the jump. Being straight is integral to jumping a course cleanly and making the time.

doesn't go well more than the other way. Encourage the horse to make correct turns and straight lines when jumping, as you do on the flat. Remember that *hindquarters follow forehand follows neck and head.*

If straightness in jumping is a problem for you, it's probably worth returning to chapter 3 (p. 50) to read the section on straightness again. Horses will revert to bad habits if the training of their weaknesses isn't continually pursued. So don't assume you have a problem solved for good. Keep at it.

1 PROBLEM: STOPPING. _

2 WHY IS THE PROBLEM THERE? There are many reasons why horses refuse to jump:

- A lack of forwardness.
- A lack of impulsion.

- A jump that is too big or wide.

- Uncertainty about takeoff.

- Rider uncertainty.

- Bad memories.

3 WHY DOES IT NEED SOLVING? We jump for the enjoyment of it so we would do well to eliminate this habit for both parties.

4 HOW DO YOU SOLVE THE PROBLEM? We've already discussed the topic of a lack of forwardness (p. 171). We must ensure a willingness on the horse's part to "join the party." This can also be related to not having enough impulsion or available energy to fulfil the task being asked.

He should exhibit a can-do attitude. To ensure that this can-do attitude is present and remains, the size of the jumps must remain within the capabilities of the partnership, including the rider's ability to get the horse to a predictable takeoff. Developing this skill to the point of consistency will give riders the confidence to feel that they also can do what is being asked. Essentially, the solution to stopping lies mostly in staying within the capabilities of the partnership, a topic discussed at length in the sections on overfacing (see pp. 3 and 164). Repetition of good experiences will reduce the likelihood of these problems happening.

Jumping Technique

Before getting into the next problem (hitting rails), I want to talk about technique, or how the horse uses his body to negotiate a jump. It is a subject that is widely debated. Whole books have been written it. Careers have been made from it and fortunes have been spent on buying technique.

But techniques in all sports evolve. For just one example, consider the "Fosbury Flop," the dominant style used in the track-and-field event of high jump. But it was not always so. The Flop was popularized and perfected by American athlete Dick Fosbury, whose gold medal in the 1968 Summer Olympics in Mexico City brought his signature technique to the world's attention.

Before Fosbury, most elite jumpers used the "Straddle Technique," "Western Roll," "Eastern Cut-Off," or "Scissors Jump" to clear the bar. Given that landing surfaces had previously been sandpits or low piles of matting, high jumpers of earlier years had to land on their feet or at least land carefully to prevent injury. With the advent of deep foam matting, high jumpers were able to be more adventurous in their landing styles and hence experiment with new styles of jumping.

In the equestrian world, economy of effort makes technique an important part of jumping (figs. 7.4 A & B). Using a technique that allows the center of gravity to travel as close to the highest point of the jump as possible makes for a maximum economy of effort. Poor technique means going higher to clear a jump, which is more effort expended!

Good technique is helpful, but it is not the only quality that makes for good jumping. A desire to leave poles up is probably more important. I refer to this as a jumping horse's "conscience." When teaching I am often asked, "Can I improve a horse's technique?" The simple answer is, "Not much." Horses are what they are. One can tweak things here and there, but when under pressure, the horse will always revert to his natural way of doing things.

We can influence a horse's desire to jump clean, however. And that is what we'll discuss next

Jumping Technique Problems and Solutions

1 PROBLEM: HITTING RAILS. _

2 WHY IS THE PROBLEM THERE? When horses have little regard for jumps and knock rails, I call it "careless jumping"—the desire to be careful isn't there. We are not talking about the odd pole down in the show jumping arena. I'm referring to the horse that habitually knocks down two, three, or more rails. This problem can be related to technique, but one shouldn't assume that good technique will mean you have a good jumper.

There are many reasons horses can be careless jumpers:

- Some horses are just careless. Very few, but they are out there.

7.4 A & B Two pictures of great horse and rider technique. I demonstrate in photo A, and Lizzel Winter in photo B. Both horses bascule over the jumps, meaning they arch their backs over the obstacles, stretching the neck forward and down, and jumping only the height they need to clear them. Both riders are sitting in the middle of their horses and remain in balance.

- A poor introduction to jumping.
- Poor guidance.
- Poor flatwork.
- Incorrect "help" from the rider.
- Incorrect bitting.
- Poor management of the horse's mental state.

3 WHY DOES IT NEED SOLVING? Careless jumpers are frustrating. We spend a lot of time and effort trying to make everything better in an effort to be more competitive, only to go in and knock poles. Finding a way to jump clean is important to improve our competitiveness and our enjoyment of the sport.

4 HOW DO YOU SOLVE THE PROBLEM? As the mind controls the body, we must first go and look at what's going on in the mind of the horse.

- Try to avoid looking at technique and drawing conclusions.
- Plan your training to minimize the influence of the rider, focusing instead on the horse being the responsible partner.
- Do not ride with a cluttered mind.

The aim is to encourage the horse to be responsible and to take ownership of the jump.

All too often the rider is encouraged to help the horse in the takeoff. But the more the rider does, the less the horse does! It can almost appear that the horse is blaming the rider for knocking the jump down! The real aim is for the rider to support and only help if the horse needs it.

Creating a Conscience in the Jumping Horse

As already mentioned, the approach to training the can-do attitude in jumping must be calm but also retain the constant qualities of forward, straight, and regular. With these qualities in place, the arrival is more likely to be predictable.

The Takeoff

Let's begin with the takeoff. The horse must initiate it; it is his responsibility. The rider's job is to support the horse's effort. If the horse makes no effort from a good approach, the rider must be quick to reprimand. A sharp smack behind the girth with jumping whip will awaken the horse. He may knock the jump down with surprise! This correction needs good timing. It must happen on takeoff as this is the moment when the horse has abdicated his responsibility.

Repeat the same process with a calm approach (as this is the rider's role) and be ready to use the jump whip again (hoping you won't need to). If the horse took anything in from the previous attempt, he will react on takeoff this time. Any reaction must be actively rewarded, even if the horse knocks the jump again. You are trying to stimulate the horse into making an effort to jump and not just go through the motions.

Educating the Response

Once the horse understands that the rider will insist that *he* do something on takeoff and that, for his efforts, he will be rewarded, he will start to buy in to the process.

Choose the Mind, Not the Technique

The very first horse my wife Sue and I owned together was a yearling called Spirit, by the famous eventing sire Master Spiritus. When I began her education as a rising four-year-old, my instincts at the time told me she couldn't jump because of poor technique. She didn't lift her shoulders and didn't seem very quick of mind. Or so I thought.

I duly sold her to a good friend of mine, the Irish show jumper Trevor Coyle. He proceeded to jump her successfully to the level of mini Grands Prix.

One day I asked him, "What did I miss?"

He replied, "She is so careful despite her technique. She would turn a somersault to avoid touching a fence."

It was a good lesson for me to learn: look at the mind, not the technique, and give a horse time to develop.

Now we can begin to think about educating the horse's response. But the rider or trainer must continue to feel that the horse is trying. The rider must also be careful not to get drawn into too much help. Support the horse's effort with a positive and secure leg aid, not a driving one—maintain a contact so the horse feels that you are there. This early stage of "giving a horse a conscience" should be conducted over small jumps (2' to 2'6"). At this point, I actually much prefer to take the horse to small cross-country logs. They don't knock down! The horse won't take long to realize this and begin to make some effort to jump *over* the obstacle. Now we have the horse being conscious that on takeoff and over the jump *he* must do something.

Technique is helpful, but a conscience is vital. Once we have opened the horse's mind to the idea of ownership and that it is in his interest to go *over* rather than through a jump, we have a great start point to begin improving the technique.

Gymnastic Jumping

Gymnastic jumping is not a cookie-cutter solution to improving jumping technique. Many clinicians use it for this purpose. Some horses do respond and become more careful; there are many others that just become confused. Grid work, done in the right way, is a personalized affair, tailored to the individual horse, with the distances and types of jumps specifically aimed to suit a horse's particular issues. Again, remind yourself of the purpose of the exercise: to help the horse find a conscience and exercise its use.

We want the horse to problem-solve. In doing so we should not set too difficult a question, but rather set questions that he can answer, as this will improve his can-do attitude as he becomes more athletic in his jumping ability. Here are some rules for productive grid work.

For horses with a long stride:

- Allow an extra foot on an 18-foot normal one-stride distance.
- Make a bounce a foot longer for a total of 9 to 10 feet.
- Don't challenge height; include nothing above 2 feet.
- Produce exercises to make the horses brain solve the question (cross-rail to a vertical to a cross-rail, for example).

Only when you feel the horse rebalance and shorten his stride should you revert to the normal distance. Then repeat the exercises and confirm the carefulness before asking anything more challenging.

For horses with a short stride:

- Canter poles set at 10 feet apart, opening out to 11 feet, are a good start. The canter will feel as if it is going too fast to start with, then it will become bigger.
- Make the canter poles into small jumps and encourage the horse to conform with the distances.
- Open the distance to a one-stride at 18 feet, and expect one nice stride.
- Then make the small jumps into a vertical and an oxer.
- When the horse opens his stride and stretches over the oxer, but remains careful, it is time to move on.

These are start point exercises to begin with to ensure the horse is paying attention to his job. With these done successfully, moving on to something more taxing for the horse's brain is possible.

The horse's technique will become quicker as long as his brain retains the desire to remain careful. This is a sign that he is buying into the process.

Do not expect the level of technique or carefulness demonstrated in the pictures earlier in this chapter (see p. 180), but you can expect results. The good of gymnastic jumping is that when done well, it can encourage a horse with not such good technique to understand what he needs to do to clear the jump. As the horse comes to understands what is being asked of him, the correct neurological pathways are formed.

"At three years old, put a rider on him, give him a couple of little fences under tack, then put him back in the field. Bring him back as a four-year-old, teach him the ropes a bit, go to a show or two, and put him back in the field. As a five-year-old, do a few more shows, then back in the field. At six you can do almost a whole year, and then at seven years old, you know what you have."

—Eric Lamaze, Canadian Olympic Gold Medalist in Show Jumping

The Rider's Role and the Wrong Kind of Help

Too much information and too many demands are placed on the rider when jumping. Confused messages being sent from rider to horse, and unclear partnership responsibilities being acted out, can contribute to the horse becoming careless.

If the rider can produce a canter worth a "7" or more (see p. 171), the horse is taking ownership of the jump, and you can hold a good and honest line to the jump, you have the very best chance for the horse to jump clean. Practice producing this canter over poles and small jumps will allow horse and rider to become confident and comfortable with their respective roles.

There is **NO** need to:

- "Set the horse up."
- "Get the horse engaged."
- "Bring the horse's back legs under him."
- "Get the horse off his forehand."
- "Get him onto his hocks."
- "Create more impulsion."
- "Use more leg."

These are all expressions said by coaches that ultimately confuse riders and horses (fig. 7.5). Horses are very capable of looking after themselves and jumping perfectly well without too much rider interference.

Good Mind Management

When I am presented with a long list of things that don't work on Day One of a clinic, I set about the problem-solving by returning to the things we *can* do, working on doing the simple things well, making roles and responsibilities clear, and showing some ways of improving skills.

I highlight the things riders can do and not what they find difficult. There is enough pressure on professional riders and amateur riders alike. To add to that pressure by teaching things that riders find difficult is insane. It merely creates gremlins that sit on your shoulder, whispering negatives into your ear—something all riders can do without (fig. 7.5).

The methodical process of placing the pieces of the jigsaw puzzle in their rightful places includes bringing flatwork with us to our jumping and understanding its place in how the horse negotiates the jumps in a way that leaves them up; knowing our role in the partnership; and avoiding complicated instructions and replacing them with something more rideable and simple for both horse and rider to understand. With this approach, problems quietly get better and may even disappear.

In my opinion, far too much emphasis is placed on telling riders what they should be doing while jumping. This misguided focus has consequences in all aspects of jumping, but especially cross-country, which we will discuss in the following chapter (p. 193).

Coaches tend to overestimate the influence riders have on their horses. There is little need for riders to busy themselves with a to-do list. In most cases the topics on this list become a distraction to the horse, so it is better not to think about them at all. It is far more

7.5 Sometimes you need to disregard "the voices" that whisper negatives in your ear and create doubt and confusion.

Don't Stop Yourself

Martina Navratilova was once asked, "How do you maintain your focus, physique, and sharp game even at the age of 43?"

She gave a humble reply: "The ball doesn't know how old I am."

You need to stop yourself from stopping yourself. Every game in life is actually played on the same ground—the 6 inches of space between your two ears. We don't live in bungalows, duplexes, or flats. We live in our minds. Life is great when things are sorted and uncluttered there. Keeping the mind messy with hatred growing on the table, regrets piling up in the corner, expectations boiling in the kitchen, secrets stuffed under the carpet, and worries littered everywhere, ruins this home.

The key factor to performing well in life and in every arena, including the equestrian arena, is the ability to control the quality and quantity of your internal dialogue. Performance is potential minus internal interference. Live in peace, not in pieces.

important to understand that the better the rider's conversation through the leg aids and the receipt of that energy through to the hands, the better the chance of the horse staying regular in his gait. Under these conditions, the horse can then focus on the jump, and there is a seamless handover of responsibility to the horse as the pair approaches the obstacle.

Don't Assume Bits are the Solution

Control of the jumping horse seems to have become more important than education. I have noticed that it is becoming increasingly rare for riders to ride in snaffles, from Pony Club to international competitions.

In the horse world we should ask ourselves: Why is this the case? My belief is that it comes from certain changes to our society. We are all in a hurry. We want quick fixes. Doing the job patiently, waiting for understanding before moving on, would produce a more lasting result and a more solid foundation. The building thereafter would have more meaning.

Why Counting Isn't Helpful

I was taught to count, "Three-two-one-jump!" How often do you still hear this taught? Far too often, I'm afraid. It still seems to be the go-to solution for seeing a stride. But more often than not, it turns into, "Three-two-one-jump—oh shoot!" and the fence comes down.

Counting is such a flawed technique of training that I cannot understand why it is still used by my profession. The issues as I see them are:

- If you knew when you started counting that you were going to be right, then why count?
- If you don't know where you are when you start counting, then why count, hoping to be lucky?
- If you don't know where you are just before you start counting and you add in a "set up," then you're really asking to win the lottery.
- If you do know where you are just before you start counting, then why set up, because now you're wrong!
- If you arrive at the "jump!" and the horse knows he is in the wrong place, it's going to be a bad outcome. Now he doesn't trust you; he waits to be told, rather than making decisions himself; or he is hoping the odds get better than fifty-fifty. (Not good odds for a clear round.)

My recommendation? DON'T COUNT. Horses can make good decisions for themselves, in their best interest, which is also in your best interest. They can shorten themselves; they can push off long by themselves. Make it in their interest to jump clean and they will do it by themselves. Your job is to support their efforts.

The use of a stronger bit, on the other hand, is seldom the solution. It may give the rider more control in the short-term, but it is a shortcut and will not improve the horse's understanding of the rider's rein or leg aids. Strong bits eventually lead to a much greater problem in jumping where the horse is encouraged to take the fence on and the rider controls the horse with brakes (the bit).

This approach leads to three main issues:

- The horse rushing.
- The bit losing its ability to get a response.
- Riders failing to understand the leg as the primary aid.

The implications of riding in stronger bits are becoming evident. More horses and ponies are being ridden with a hollow back, inverted neck, and an unsteady contact. Horses are being encouraged to go without impulsion that has been honestly created, and instead, they are going to a jump with speed, which is semi-controlled with a strong bit.

Remember, we are still tackling the subject of careless jumping. There is a relationship between bits and careless jumping, not only in show jumping but also in cross-country. When we invert a horse's spine (back and neck), we effectively lock its use. Many of the bits in common use today have an action that inverts the horse's spine. The spinal vertebrae are pushed closer together, which is less comfortable, while the ability of the horse to use his back is impaired. This happens at the very time we want the horse to use his very best athletic abilities to jump. It seems such a disconnect from what we do on the flat, where we are asking and rewarding our horses for using their backs, to then go jumping only to invert the back just when we need it most.

With a strong bit, we create:

- A poorer view of the jump.
- A poor rebalance with an inconsistent contact.
- Loss of energy due to a loss of connection.
- A greater dependence on the rein and less on the leg.
- Impaired use of the horse's neck on takeoff.
- Less freedom of the shoulders, which leads to a slower reaction time.
- A tighter back, which means less airtime and the potential for the horse to drag his back legs.
- A flatter jump with less bascule and a landing spot too far out.

And that's not to mention the issues particular to cross-country that we look at in chapter 8 (p. 193).

It is too simplistic to say, "Use a different, milder bit," as much as I would like to. There are, however, certain bits that should never see the light of day (I talk about this in some detail in my book *Two Brains, One Aim*). The most important thing is, having identified there is a problem, we relate flatwork to jumping to find a solution. We spend a lifetime asking the horse to work through the back from our leg to our rein contact and to be balanced and respond to the aids, only to forget these principles when we jump. It doesn't make sense.

Here is my advice on bits:

- Find and use bits with a direct contact, on the bars of the mouth.
- Avoid bits that invert horses, such as gags and elevators that apply lip-to-poll pressure.
- Re-focus on the roles in jumping: what the rider should "own" and what the horse should "own."
- Work on the rebalance, which should improve the horse's way of going, not merely slow it down.
- "Allow" the horse to jump.

Watch top riders like Michael Jung, Laura Kraut, Ben Maher, Billy Twomey, Scott Brash, Tim Price, and Peder Fredricson. They all have the above skills in abundance.

The Art of Appearing to Do Nothing

The more horses knock jumps the more we think we should be doing something to help the situation. But the more we do something, the more opportunity we give the horse to blame us for the poles coming down.

We need to have a mindset that is clear on responsibilities. It's not fair that the rider takes the blame when the horse doesn't do his job and vice versa. The rider must be busy keeping the canter up to a minimum that would achieve a "7" on a dressage test, and in return, the rider must feel that the horse is trying to oblige. The rider must also not distract the horse from his job, so sitting quietly (apparently doing nothing) is the rider's challenge.

Once the horse gets the hang of thinking for himself, making a plan, and measuring the jump, the whole process of jumping becomes easier. Horses will begin to measure where they are in relation to the jump and begin to rebalance themselves. This horse-initiated rebalance allows the rider to keep "riding" the canter. The rider supports the horse's effort by ensuring impulsion is retained and the speed is regulated. As the horse improves at measuring where the jump and takeoff are, so the rider learns to develop a better awareness of distance too. In time, the partnership works together to improve the arrival at the jump and achieve a positive outcome.

Good coaches don't tell you how, they show you.

CHAPTER 8

Cross-Country Jumping

THIS IS NOT AN EVENTING-SPECIFIC BOOK (SEEK OUT MY *Look...No Hands!* for more on the topic of cross-country riding, in particular), but it is necessary to show the link between subjects so we are not tempted to treat them in isolation. It is not necessary to be a specialist in every discipline, but an understanding of the common ground will allow for competence in all riding.

Much of what has already been discussed in the previous chapters is relevant to the most common issues met in cross-country riding. Skills that practice on the flat and in show jumping will come with us when we go cross-country. The qualities that the book is built around remain with us. The way I resolve problems on the cross-country course have their origins in the way problems have been dissected in the earlier chapters of this book. By the time we go cross-country, I would hope to have my horse *forward, straight,* and *regular.* I would expect to be able to go from 350 meters per minute to 575 meters per minute with a good *contact* and *connection* so we can display a *consistent* gallop throughout the course.

Cross-country issues that relate to these qualities get solved by going back to flatwork solutions that we've discussed in previous chapters. There are, however, a number of key concepts that we need firmly in hand to perform effectively when going cross country:

- Position and balance.
- Managing speed.
- Correct use of line and pace.
- Negotiating specific cross-country obstacles.

Let's look at each element in turn.

Position and Balance

There is no such thing as a "cross-country position"; rather, there are adjustments to the way we position ourselves that will enable us to go cross-country safely (figs. 8.1 A–C). Just as jockeys do, it is important to shorten the stirrup length first. The horse's center of gravity moves forward the longer his stride becomes, so for us to stay in balance, we need to be able to stay as near as we can to this center point. If we don't, it creates an imbalance that will affect communication, the horse's balance, and efficiency. (Dressage riders lengthen their stirrups also with the goal of remaining near the center of balance, which moves back

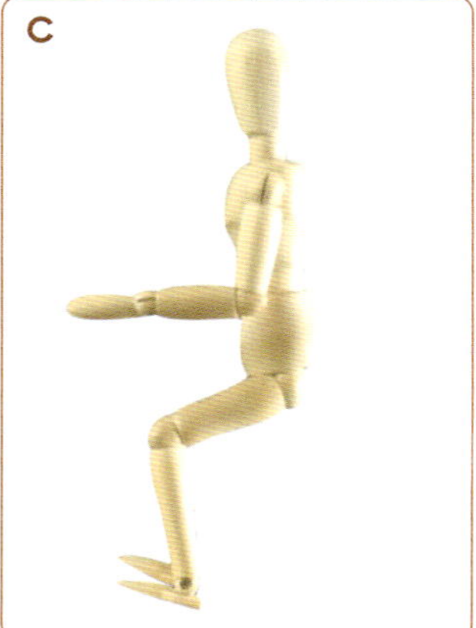

8.1 A–C The light seat gets used for three main functions when riding cross-country: the gallop (A—the rider's position does not interfere with the horse), the rebalance (B—note the legs slightly farther ahead and the back more active to "help" support the horse), and the drive (C—the rider straightens to "close" the seat and leg when "insistence" is necessary).

in the horse as collection is achieved.) By shortening the stirrups two or three holes, we change the way the rider's body has to function. It takes a little getting used to, and you should allow yourself time to adjust.

Here are a few good rules of thumb when adusting your stirrup length for cross-country: If your bottom is in the seat of the saddle and your knees are in the knee roll, you're riding too long. Instead, your knees should be in the knee roll and your bottom should sit on the back of the saddle. These are sound principles. (Read them again!) The logic behind this is that the knees in the knee roll provide security when the seat is not really needed in the saddle. The movement of body weight is much easier to manage as a result. This principle of "knees in the knee roll" is still sound even with close contact saddles. The support they provide is slightly more above the knee but nonetheless similar and important to the security of the rider.

When is this security required? In moments of imbalance, the knee closes against the knee roll, the lower leg goes forward, and the upper leg, from hip-to-knee, can now brace against these secure points. The result is that the body weight isn't as easily thrown forward. Being thrown forward too quickly in a moment of crisis on cross-country can result in a fall or in interfering in the horse's efforts at dealing with the crisis. It is possible to recover, without falling, but in order to do this, you need to teach your body how to react instinctively. This can be done by going cross-country schooling. Find small jumps that mimic the issues met in competition. As the horse negotiates these, the rider will feel the change in balance required to stay at one with the horse. The rider's body will come to recognize each step in the process as normal and so the balancing habit will be formed without any thought.

Position and Balance in the Takeoff

From the previous chapter, you are already familiar with the responsibilities of both horse and rider at various phases of jumping. In the moment of takeoff, the rider supports the efforts of the horse. It is a joint responsibility, but it also has a clear leader.

The horse's ownership of this lead is an important part of his training and is often misunderstood. The rider's position must be supportive. The rider must not take over but be there, giving encouragement as the horse makes decisions. As the rider closes the leg aids to the horse's sides in an act of support, the rider is also creating a position of security. I have continually stressed this relationship and the clarity of responsibility. It is more important for cross-country than any other type of jumping.

The unexpected should be anticipated. This is not negative riding but prudent riding. This mindset allows the rider's leg aids to be in exactly the right position to help the horse should support need to be increased to something stronger: an *insistence*!

The upper body, from the seat upward, requires an inner, core strength to fulfill a number of other functions, including maintaining the all-important balance. The rider must be careful not to let the upper body get *behind* the movement, as it is difficult to recover the proper balance from this position. The upper body also must not get *in front* of the movement, for fear of interfering with the horse's commitment to the jump. The body needs to stay central and ready to close the seat should there be a need for more help.

Managing Speed

Jumping cross-country obstacles at speed is as much of a skill as doing anything on the flat and needs just as much practice. To feel comfortable at speed and to know that control is still there takes work. For starters, the horse should practice at speed so he knows that it is not the same thing as "flight mode." The cross-country gallop should be every bit as measured, controlled, in balance, and in self-carriage as any other pace, and this requires practice. Bits and gadgets of control often indicate a lack of training in this department.

With speed comes a bigger and longer stride. This makes a difference to the relationship of the rebalance and the takeoff. This too needs practice to ensure both parties are comfortable with the cross-country way of going. Cross-country is not show jumping outside the arena! There are similarities between the two disciplines, but there are also differences. For example, in cross-country jumping, there is a time to change from "gallop mode" to "jump mode." This is a key moment for many reasons. To understand it will improve jump preparation, course speed, and overall competitiveness.

When is the right moment to make the adjustment? As I tell my students, you go from gallop to jump mode as early as you need and as late as you dare! Too early and you waste time, too late and you're not prepared to jump.

There is great skill involved in making the transition between the two speeds seamless. There should be as little physical adjustment and disruption to mental focus as possible. The aids used should be consistent with those the horse already knows and is used to.

Logic suggests that to rebalance from 600 meters per minute to 475 meters per minute will require the horse to manage his momentum. To do this, the hindquarters need to brace against the speed and take weight from the forehand. For this reason, the rider's leg aids—not the rein aids—should be the start of the rebalance. The rein aids applied almost at the same time reinforce the intention and they define the ultimate speed.

The timing of the aids depends on:

- How long it takes for the aids to have an effect.
- How much time the horse needs before the fence to focus and prepare.
- How competitive the rider feels.

When the horse doesn't answer the rider's request immediately, the partnership takes too much speed with them to the fence, often with a lack of focus. The result is an uncertain outcome to the jumping effort.

Practice will help you develop this very important skill. Here are some exercises to try.

Exercise 1: Practice a Basic Rebalance

Use open space to replicate as much as possible the feeling of going cross-country. Develop a feel for a good 500-meters-per-minute gallop, and allow the horse to do so as well. Then apply the leg aids, a stronger rein contact, and position your upper body more upright. The horse should feel these adjustments and respond by rebalancing to a slower pace.

Soften all the aids at the same time and the horse should recover the faster pace. There should be no need to push the horse forward again to the faster pace—he should go there the moment the rebalance aids are softened.

Exercise 2: Rebalance Off a Turn

Find a good gallop as you did in Exercise 1. This exercise is designed to practice the rebalance off a turn to replicate a course that is asking us to jump off the turn. Again, both leg aids are applied to advise the horse that the hindquarters are going to be needed. The inside leg's secondary function is to stop the horse falling in on the turn, so it will need to be applied accordingly. The inside rein indicates a direction requirement for the horse and the outside rein allows for the bend in the proper direction and manages the speed.

The rider's upper body is raised up as before to help the horse feel what's required. It sounds like a lot going on all at once, but it's important to break it down. Once both rider and horse understand the components of the rebalance on a turn, the mere movement of the rider and application of the aid will initiate it.

As the rebalance happens, so the focus changes to the line and jump. The rider's outside leg now encourages the horse in the direction the inside rein is guiding. The outside rein controls how much bend through the body is required to find and remain on the line to the jump.

This discussion between the aids and the horse is developed over time. It becomes more nuanced and less obvious the more it is practiced. The better it becomes, the less distracting it is and the more the partnership can focus on the jumps and being competitive.

The amount of rebalance can also depend on the impending jump. Some jumps will need more than others. Some horses will also need more rebalancing than others.

Negotiating Line and Pace

The topic of responsibility—or who in the partnership is responsible for which phases of jumping, the horse or rider—has occupied my thoughts and teaching for most of my coaching life. For me it has been one of the big topics in our sport that continues to be misunderstood and mis-taught.

I have already commented at length on my take on a horse and rider's respective roles in the previous chapter. As you recall, I argue that the rider's job is to manage the pace and line as the rider understands the task. The horse's job is to jump. It sounds so simple, and it should be kept simple in concept and application.

Line and *pace* are two words that appear in every aspect of riding. To spend some time watching cross-country is an interesting education. Focus on the lines people travel and the speeds people go and you will see a huge variety of both. There are many variables in our quest to go clear inside the allotted time. Each participant may have sound reasons for choosing a particular speed or line, but there is merit in looking a little deeper into at the issues that affect us all, with special consideration to the things within our control. What can we do to improve the efficiency of cross-country riding?

Remember, *the shortest distance between two points is a straight line*. So, in an ideal world, we could straighten out the whole course, making it more economical to ride. But that is not possible. We should, however, make every effort to smooth out the line and make it as near as we can to the shortest route so we save time.

Watching racing car drivers, you will see how they manage the line to maximize speed. We should look at their skills and think about where there is crossover to show jumping and cross-country riding. For instance, making a smooth curve instead of a turn allows us to keep an uninterrupted speed on an economical line. Think about it:

- If we can save 10 meters' distance on 15 to 20 jumps, that saves 150 to 200 meters per course.
- If we can make one or two fewer rebalances in front of 15 to 20 jumps, that will save 15 to 20 seconds overall.

Win-win. To do this requires all of the qualities already mentioned: quick thinking from the rider and horse, the ability to understand the task at each jump, quick decision-making, and understanding responsibilities.

Adjusting Line and Pace on Course

The first job for the rider and coach is to look at a course and determine, "What is the question I'm being asked by each jump?" Here are just a couple of examples.

VERTICALS

Course designers use verticals for different reasons at different places on the course. A true vertical will never be asked of the novice rider and horse from a galloping approach. But it may be asked of the advanced rider. The novice rider may get a vertical off a turn, the idea being that to negotiate a turn, the speed will have to be reduced and a better balance might be present as a result.

The rider should position the upper body toward the upright, with the seat closing to the saddle. You want the stride of the horse a little shorter and the balance more toward the back. The horse needs sufficient time to assess and understand the jump and the rider needs to ensure the horse gives the feeling of comprehension of the job in hand.

SPREADS

In novice courses, spreads are likely to appear in places where the horse and rider are able to be in a forward canter or gallop. This increases the likelihood of achieving a pace with some power. As we move toward the more advanced levels, the likelihood of spreads off corners and turns increases, testing the availability of energy (impulsion) on demand.

From a gallop, the change to a shorter stride length is important to allow options for takeoff to materialize. Too long a stride length reduces the options available to the horse while allowing insufficient time for the horse to assess the width of the spread.

Negotiating Cross-Country Obstacles

Having established the importance of understanding the horse's and the rider's responsibilities in the context of cross-country so the rider can maintain a balanced position, moderate speed, and manage the line at the maximum speed, let's move on to common issues encountered with various cross-country questions.

Cross-Country Obstacles Problems and Solutions

1 PROBLEM: DITCHES. _

2 WHY IS THE PROBLEM THERE? Horses can become "ditchy" for lots of reasons. A bad schooling session over a ditch may appear to be mended and then reappear at the first competition when the horse stops. How often have we heard this scenario? Now the problem has just increased exponentially—not just in the horse's mind but in the rider's as well. Overfacing the horse in the early part of his training can leave a bad experience that often doesn't go away.

3 WHY DOES IT NEED SOLVING? Having confidence that the horse has no worries about cross-country questions gives the rider great confidence in being competitive.

4 HOW DO YOU SOLVE THE PROBLEM? Plan every schooling session. Never be tempted to overface. Horses negotiate ditches in different ways. The ones that go lower and just get to the other side tend to do so because they are anxious, and they will be challenged as the question becomes wider, and even more so when the ditch becomes a trakehner. Horses that jump with a bascule (see figs. 7.4 A & B, p. 180) and give the ditch a little extra height tend to be better ditch jumpers. They will also find jumping trakehners easier.

Doing things the right way from the start leaves no baggage for the horse to carry around. If you have inherited baggage related to ditches, go back to the beginning and start again. Take time and rebuild the horse's confidence. Then in competition, try not to surprise your horse when you know a ditch is coming.

Ditches can appear anywhere on a cross-country course and should not be underestimated. The element of surprise may be used by the course designer, especially at the more advanced levels. Riders need to be very aware of how their horse responds to ditches when schooling because any hesitation or uncertainty is likely to be compounded in a competition scenario.

Line and pace are important when it comes to ditch jumping. Here are some things to keep in mind:

- The horse needs to be on the right line to have a good view and traveling at the right pace—which needs to be energetic and forward-thinking—to ensure commitment and resolve. Without these qualities horses tend to "look." Speed is not the answer to avoid this, as the faster you go the quicker the horse will stop!

- The ditch will encourage the horse to rebalance automatically, so while it is important to find the right pace, do not overdo the rebalance and lose vital energy. Ditches will create a natural way of jumping for the horse so too much interference should be avoided.

Take time between competitions to reconfirm confidence. Go back to smaller jumps and ditches that are not so wide as the ones in competition. Confidence is critical for all jumping.

1 Problem: Trakehners. _

2 Why is the problem there? The issues with trakehners are very similar to ditch issues. Once in the horse's mind, they are very difficult to erase. Overfacing, either when young, inexperienced, or not suitably warmed up is often to blame.

3 Why does it need solving? It's critical to introduce or reschool trakehners to build all-around jumping confidence.

4 How do you solve the problem? Most trakehner issues begin with seeds of doubt being sown in the horse's mind early on in jumping education—too many uncertainties presented all at once, which is part of overfacing the mind. Take note of how the horse looks at the jump and solves the question. The ditch-jumper that bascules is more likely to be a good trakehner jumper. And, by starting very small you can avoid sowing the seeds of doubt. Note:

- As with ditch jumping, make sure your upper body is more upright, your seat is close to the saddle, and your lower leg supports the horse's commitment.
- The rebalance mustn't be overdone as the jump itself will provide enough of a rebalance.
- Don't assume confidence. Retrace your steps and reschool over smaller jumps, as you do with ditches.

Once established, trakehners have a very helpful profile for horses with their clearly defined takeoff rail and horse-friendly profile.

1 Problem: Skinnies. _

2 Why is the problem there? The "skinny" jump tests whether the horse has developed an honesty to the chosen line. So, to begin with, if horses don't yet understand what we are asking when riding school movements, it's too early to ask them to jump skinnies. Other reasons for problems include:

- A natural tendency to drift.
- Being asked to jump too big or too narrow.

- Arriving at a bad spot.
- Having the wrong canter or trot.

3 WHY DOES IT NEED SOLVING? We know in our cross-country riding that the horse's honesty is going to be tested repeatedly. So, it's best to establish it early if we can, or reestablish it if we must.

4 HOW DO YOU SOLVE THE PROBLEM? If the horse habitually runs out or refuses, the first thing to puzzle out is why. Once you know the cause you can make a plan to tackle it.

The horse will normally give you a clue that he is going to be dishonest early on in the approach. Once he sees the jump and knows there is a skinny coming up, his negative thoughts come to the fore. He will lose forwardness, straightness, and attention. Most horses will have developed a one-sided escape strategy, which makes their behavior more predictable. This can all help in finding the solution.

- Create a scenario where all the cards are stacked in your favor. Start with a small skinny jump with big wings so the more attractive option for the horse is jumping the fence rather than running out.
- Manage the speed. A trot approach is easier to control and will allow for a good takeoff spot to be found.
- As the horse begins to think of drifting and running out, notice where his body is going and immediately correct him. Don't let the idea of running out dwell in his mind.
- Once the horse has jumped the skinny you should immediately reward him.
- Now repeat the process.
- Having achieved success 10 times, the negative outcomes are now outweighed by the positive outcomes.
- Then you can progress to approaching the skinny at canter off both reins. Use a shorter canter to begin with to ensure a close arrival to the jump, as this closes the "escape routes."
- Put a canter pole on the ground four strides in front of the jump, and build on the habit of jumping and holding the line.

- Make the four-stride distance a little longer and open out the canter. This will begin to ask the horse to trust a more open manner. This honesty to a line is the sign of good schooling when going cross-country.

It is a sign of good thinking and good cross-country riding to always be prepared for the horse to run out at skinnies. As I said, horses are normally predictable so you will have an idea of which way they will go. The course designer will offer an escape route. As riders we should always have the stick in the correct hand, ready to tap the horse's shoulder and close the escape route. Few people practice this obvious skill. Always anticipate the likely escape route and have the stick in that hand to "close the door." That means thinking ahead and being prepared to continually change your stick from hand to hand.

Never assume total honesty. Always be prepared to retrace one's steps and jump smaller and wider skinnies at a slower pace to confirm honesty.

1 PROBLEM: DROPS. _

2 WHY IS THE PROBLEM THERE? Problems with drops generally manifest in the horse stopping or launching themselves. They usually originate from the uncertainty of the outcome—from both horse and rider.

3 WHY DOES IT NEED SOLVING? Both horse and rider need to understand the mechanics of how to negotiate all types of cross-country jumps. Drops need confidence and technical understanding because they're going to be tested.

4 HOW DO YOU SOLVE THE PROBLEM? Horses tend to be uncertain when their near vision can't determine where they are going to land or what the footing is going to be. Riders have problems because they fear that momentum will take over at the expense of control.

Let's deal with the horse first. Trust is the first quality needed. The horse has to trust that the footing and where he is going to land is safe. Start small—1' to 1'6" is plenty big enough—to allow the horse to work out what to do with his feet. Begin in trot as it gives the horse time to think.

Rider balance and technique are key here. All too often, riders are told to lean back when negotiating a drop, but this is not something you should do. To remain in balance you need to adopt a position that is 90 degrees to flat ground. Then let the reins slip to allow the horse to drop away from you. This gives the horse freedom of the head and neck to find his own balance.

Gathering the reins after the drop is such an important skill to learn. It is something that can be practiced off the horse or while out for a hack. Once learned it will become second nature, and that will be invaluable later on. The left hand pulls both reins back and up to take up the slack and regain the contact. The right hand lets go and re-grabs both the reins farther down to regain the control. The left hand now

8.2 A & B Here I am at Badminton, one stride between the two photos, demonstrating the position and forwardness of thought needed to clear a massive drop. Note my reins slipped in A and gathered again in B.

drops the rein and regains a hold on the rein farther down, beside the right hand. Now both reins are the correct length for the next stride. This should happen in two strides (figs. 8.2 A & B).

Never assume total understanding in your horse—this is true for every skill we are discussing in this chapter, but it bears repeating. Always retrace and practice at a lower and less-demanding level. This continually confirms the confidence and honesty required for good cross-country riding.

1 PROBLEM: BLIND LANDINGS. _

2 WHY IS THE PROBLEM THERE? Unsurprisingly, it is the uncertainty of the outcome that causes problems with blind landings, such as a stop, poor technique, not making the height of the jump, or an uncomfortable jump.

When the horse is unsure of his footing or where he is likely to land, the horse's thinking process slows down, along with the front leg jumping action. The result can often be dramatic and sometimes dangerous. Horses can also develop a phobia about these kind of jumps (see the sections on overfacing, pp. 3 and 164).

3 WHY DOES IT NEED SOLVING? This is one of many cross-country tests that a horse and rider must demonstrate that they have acquired the skills to negotiate successfully and with consistency.

4 HOW DO YOU SOLVE THE PROBLEM? Dismantle the jumping process into trainable parts before reassembling them:

- The approach must be a good quality, with a short and energetic pace. This will allow the takeoff point to be close enough for the horse to see the landing and master his front-leg technique. The short, energetic canter allows the horse to be quicker with his front-leg action. A long and flat canter does the opposite and causes problems.

- The takeoff needs to be quick of thought and action. The front part of the horse must jump cleanly, and the back end will follow. Gymnastic jumping can help to improve reaction speed (see p. 183).

- The horse needs to use his neck to see where he is being asked to land, so it is important to enable this by offering some rein and not abandoning the horse by "throwing" the reins, but by following and allowing neck freedom.
- The rider's position needs to be slightly behind the horse on takeoff yet quick to go with the movement as the horse looks for support through the reins and seeks the right landing spot.

Practicing this type of question reinforces the speed of the technique. This is important for building confidence and an instinctive reaction.

1 PROBLEM: CORNERS. _

2 WHY IS THE PROBLEM THERE? Problems arise with corners when the horse questions the line the fence is to be jumped on. Corner jumps are there specifically to test the honesty of the horse and rider's line. Issues appear when the discipline of the line is not taught or understood by the horse early in his training. As jumps get higher and wider the honesty is challenged more, and horses deviate off the line as a means of escape.

3 WHY DOES IT NEED SOLVING? Corners are part of the cross-country test, so it is important that we demonstrate we have done our homework.

4 HOW DO YOU SOLVE THE PROBLEM? Every horse has a favored side or way of escaping. This should be remembered throughout all schooling. In moments of crisis horses will revert to type. It's our aim as riders to school the horse to be straight, symmetrical, and honest both ways as much as possible.

Cantering over a specific color on a pole is a good first test of the ability to hold a line. Do the same over a small oxer the other way. Then make a small corner with the colored poles (measure the width of the small oxer to 3 feet in from the point of the corner). That is the target line to jump over. Notice which way the horse drifts—toward the apex or into the wider part? To the right or the left? This will tell you which way he favors and will inform how you ride the jump in the future. As a trainer, it tells you what homework is to be done to correct the natural tendency.

- Know your horse's preferred escape route—to be forewarned is to be forearmed. It allows the rider to close the door before it opens!

- Make the corner into almost an oxer and focus on trotting over a particular part of the jump. Give yourself a target to aim for and insist that the horse holds exactly the line you want, with no deviation. Do this off both reins—they must become the same.

- Widening the corner angle will begin to focus the partnership on the available jumping options (normally about 3 feet from the point of the corner). If you keep it low, the horse will believe that it's easier to jump than not to and so build up the repetition of achievement.

- Again, the quality of the canter is important to develop. The better the canter and the more the canter can be ridden, the more consistent the arrival will be.

- Don't challenge scope or accuracy until the horse's mind has taken on a "Yes, I can do this!" attitude.

Repeat the corner schooling process over smaller jumps to reconfirm the honesty on both reins.

1 Problem: Combinations. _

2 Why is the problem there? Horses can become confused with the array of poles or elements involved in combinations, which are designed to test a horse's ability to solve a puzzle and the rider's understanding of the correct speed and line necessary for the partnership to be able to solve it.

Problems occur when this doesn't happen. There will be signs. They often appear as the horse approaches the combination: a change of canter, a drift to the right or left, a reluctance to go. The rider needs to recognize the signs as they indicate the nature of the anxiety. When a horse speeds up, it often means, "Let's get it over with," or "I don't know how to solve this but I'm going anyway." Slowing down can mean, "I just don't want to try and solve this," or "I'm not part of this party—you have to make me do it!" A drift off the line can be a warning that the horse is trying to find a way out. It can also indicate that the horse is making more space for himself. Either way, it is not helpful to solving the puzzle.

3 WHY DOES IT NEED SOLVING? Mental and physical agility are being tested when jumping. We must, therefore, ensure that our training enhances a horse's understanding that he needs to make decisions.

4 HOW DO YOU SOLVE THE PROBLEM? You need to go back to rebuilding and address your ability to present the horse to the jump on the appropriate line and in the correct canter. Then you can support the horse through the question knowing that you have done your homework and that it is within the capabilities of your horse.

School through grids and similar combinations to those that you are likely to meet in a competition, but again, avoid adding height to the equation initially. Height is the add-on when the partnership knows the answer to the puzzle. Combined, they become the ultimate test at the appropriate level.

What You Need

To sum up, the skills we need to cultivate to successfully pass the tests that cross-country throws at us include:

- The ability to hold a line.
- Facility with a variety of gaits and changing gears.
- A horse that thinks quickly and is happy to make decisions.
- Trust between horse and rider.
- Gameness to come back and try again after making a mistake.

This chapter shows how many qualities have come with us from the start of the book. Going at speed over big solid jumps with a horse that knows his job and is responsive to thought and action has been one of my greatest thrills. To have taught the horse from the beginning is an even greater thrill. The multitude of skills that have been learned, combined with the horse's recall and execution at speed, is truly satisfying as a trainer and a rider.

Too often the coach speaks to the adult, rather than to the child within, who is doing it for pleasure.

CHAPTER 9

Rider Issues

TO BE AN EFFECTIVE RIDER, YOUR POSITION IS VERY IMPORTANT. But that's not to say we all have to sit correctly to be effective. I think it is also important to acknowledge physiological individuality. Not everyone is able to sit in a supposedly correct position. Natural biomechanics or acquired ways of sitting means that we are destined to sit in our own way.

Many hours and vast amounts of money are spent on lessons and new saddles to enable us to sit better. Some of this spending is worthwhile, but a lot of it is wasted. The key to position and effectiveness in the saddle is *balance*. Correct balance does not always produce a perfect position no matter how much we might try. And sometimes by seeking perfection we lose balance, which then leaves us less effective.

When in balance, it is much easier for the rider to be effective. It is easier to use the aids independently of one another and to communicate with the horse rather than using the aids to hold on or to maintain a position. Balance also encourages connection, making it possible to allow the horse's back to work freely without interference. The independence of the aids enables us to test and explore further aspects of the education of the horse.

"We should improve your position, as you will ride better."

"A better position is better for your horse."

"A saddle that allows you to be deeper and more at one with your horse can only be good."

"Position right to go right and at the same time bring your left leg slightly behind the girth."

These are some of the many comments to be heard from trainers and coaches relating to riders' position and effectiveness. As trainers we are taught to begin making corrections to a partnership starting with the rider and then moving on to the horse, the basic principle being that better riding allows the horse to go better. Sounds good.

The frequent downside of this approach, however, is that the more we adjust riders, the less effective they tend become. At best, the horse doesn't get any worse and at worst, the horse does get worse as a result of the rider's adjustments. We just have to hope the problem is correctable!

Personally, I find it easier and more sensible to focus on the horse first. Then, as the horse goes better and becomes easier to ride, we can turn our attention to the rider. Having devoted the previous chapters to the horse, let's now deal with the rider. To begin with, I believe it is important to find your balance off a horse, and then take the feeling onto the horse. Understand how your body works and how you make adjustments to achieve balance without the distraction of the horse. That is not always what we are taught to do as trainers, but this approach has worked well for me over the years.

Where to Begin?

I'm stating the obvious when I point out that we are all different shapes and sizes and have different coordination abilities, different levels of understanding of the horse, and different expectations for our riding (fig. 9.1). In order to help people deal with these differences we need to find common ground and then build from there. So let's look at the most common issues that riders tend to face with their position and effectiveness.

Balance

Good balance is a fundamental requirement in all sports to be efficient, let alone good. Before hitting a golf ball, a tennis ball, a soccer ball, or even running, the balance of one's body is important to take into account. As a sport's demands increase, any imbalance causes us to work that much harder to do what the balanced athlete does with ease. We work against our natural biomechanics and use muscle power instead of coordination. The result is often diminished performance and an increased likelihood of injury. A good example of an extremely balanced athlete is the tennis player Roger Federer, who has remained uninjured for most of his career.

Many demands are placed on the rider to find a good position, but sometimes we fail to achieve balance. In our attempts to position riders correctly, which can often feel unnatural and restricting, it puts stresses and strain on the body, resulting in diminished efficiency.

9.1 Three "normal" riders.

The body will often resist positioning. In doing so it will revert to a comfortable position the moment it can. This resistance is the first thing to overcome before any long-term benefits can occur.

What if we try a different take on rider position? What if we used the body's natural desire to find its own balance? If we give the body a reason to find a position it can be more obliging in finding it by itself. The subconscious then takes over and we don't have to think about it so much. The conscious mind may have to remind the subconscious mind from time to time to avoid being lazy. But a good position can become a habit if there is a reason for it to be so.

The Balance Board Can Help

I designed a custom Balance Board many years ago specifically for riders (figs. 9.2 A–C). It has a unique feature that mimics the ideal stirrup position. It also develops muscle function to maintain lateral and longitudinal balance. It is good exercise and a fun thing to do with other riders in the tack room. It should be used on a surface like a carpet, not on concrete, which will damage the wood base. (In the photos ahead, you'll see that we used an old saddle pad on the ground to create an appropriate surface.) Ten minutes of playtime with the Board every day, if possible twice

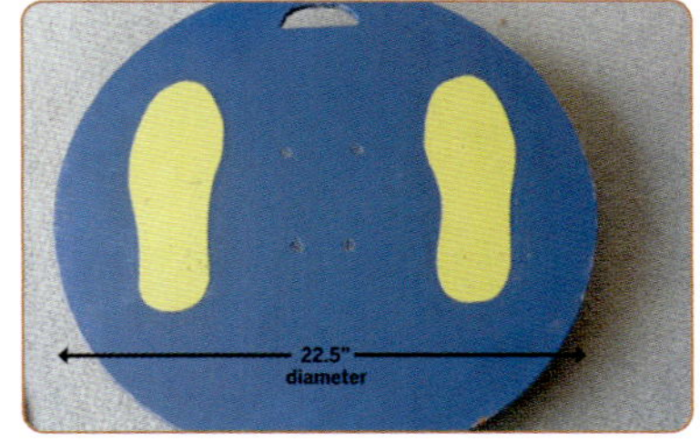

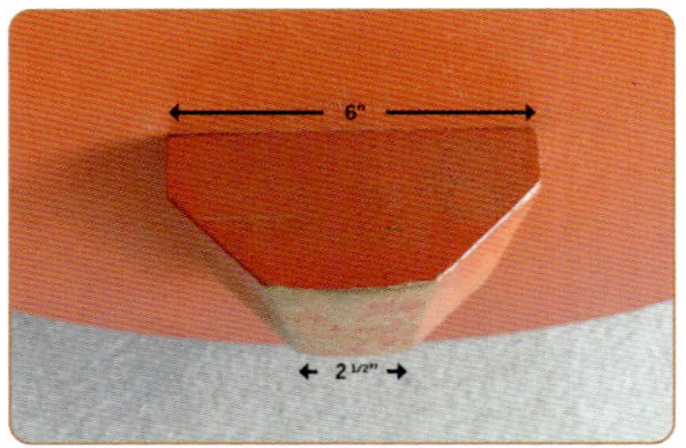

9.2 A–C My custom Balance Board. Note that my design is different from boards with a semi-sphere underneath, which you may have seen before. My Balance Board has been a great aid to help riders develop the feel for balance on a horse. It is not that difficult to make one, and I have included the dimensions in the photos.

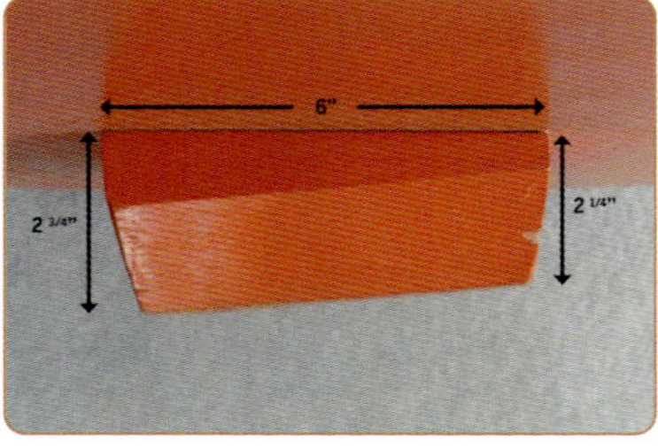

a day, will do wonders for subconscious control of your balance. The Board will help you find your own balance with little guidance.

This is not an "instructed position," this is a balanced position. Adopt a position looking in the direction you want to go and position your arms as if you were holding reins (figs. 9.3 A & B).

As you stand in this position, get to know your own body. Feel which parts have found it easy and not so easy to adopt this position. It is normal for certain parts of the body to feel the need to become accustomed to the position. A tendon or ligament needs slight stretching to get used to it, for instance. A muscle has to be told to hold a position. These are minor adjustments that the subconscious should be instructed to fix. Once you make the fixes deliberately a few times, your subconscious will begin to do it without being asked (a habit, or a *conditioned* reflex, is established).

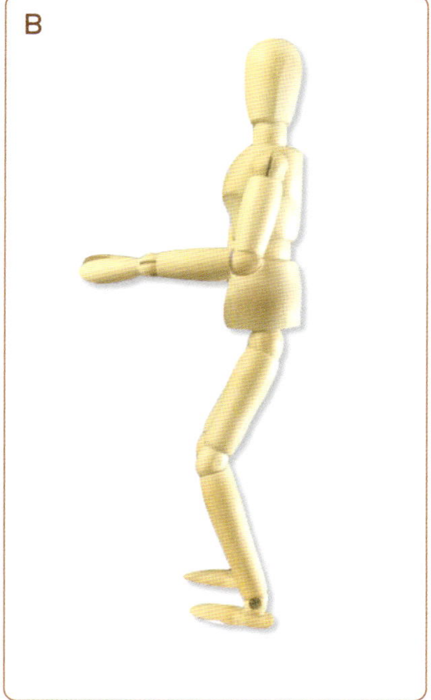

9.3 A & B A balanced position.

As you get used to finding your balance, you may find your muscles wobbling. Persevere. The wobbling is part of their method of finding out what you want them to do, and it will go away as they develop control.

Next, shorten the imaginary stirrup length and feel how the body reacts (fig. 9.4). Again, *know your own body*. Adjust the parts that didn't do what you wanted them to do automatically. Then do this a few more times, making corrections, to give the subconscious the idea of what you want. Looking in a long mirror as you do this exercise is helpful. This is all part of conditioning the mind to adopt what you would like it to tell the body to do. We do the same when teaching horses.

Shorten the stirrups again and practice jumping position and related movements (figs. 9.5 A & B). Go through the same process of correction, reward, and repetition. Each time you correct what you don't want, it must be done a few times in a very deliberate manner so the body gets the hang of what you do want (figs. 9.6 A–C). Habits are created this way. You need to *feel* yourself doing it correctly because once you're on a horse you will need to replicate the feeling.

Take your time in the saddle, with the horse at a halt, to rediscover the same feeling you gained on the Balance Board. Take note of which muscles you use to go from sitting

9.4 Adjusting your stance toward a shorter stirrup and jumping balance.

9.5 A & B Practicing a giving rein contact toward the horse's mouth (A) and a crest release (B) while in a jumping balance.

to posting to a light seat. Then ask the horse to walk and pay attention to the feeling of what the body has had to do to maintain the position. To be "at one" with a moving object requires movement on your part. Feel what part of your body has to move to enable you to keep your legs and arms from moving, as you want them to stay still to provide a reliable means of communication with the horse's sides and mouth.

You are likely to notice things, such as:

- The rider's shoulders allow the body to move while the arms, down to the hands, ensure the contact remains quiet and still.

- At the walk, the rider's seat follows the movement of the horse's back while the legs remain quietly at the sides of the horse.

- The rider's knee allows flexion as the body between the knee and the shoulders posts in rising trot, which allows the lower leg to remain quiet beside the horse's sides.

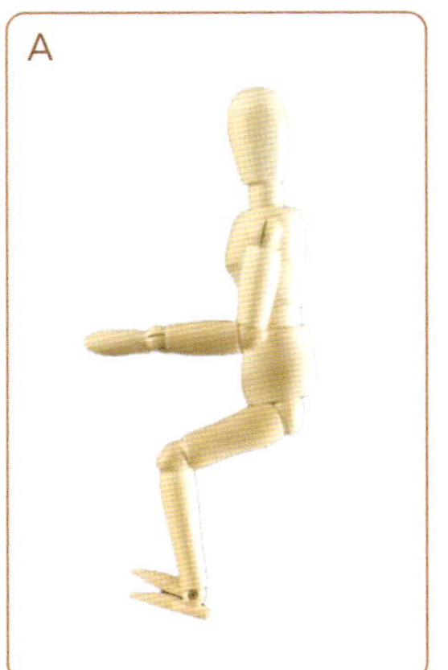

9.6 A–C The figure in A is too upright and needs to become more flexible through the ankles, knees, and hips. The idea is to be able to control each part without loss of balance going into the foot—not into the heel but over the whole foot. The figure in B is showing a common fault of being too far in front of the point of balance. A Balance Board will help to correct this fault. Practice adjusting the "stirrup length" so all the hip and knee angles open. The figure in C shows a loss of flexibility at the ankle, pushing the weight too deep in the heel. A Balance Board won't allow this to happen. The rider's weight should be over the ball of the foot.

Feel what is happening in your own body. Listen to the conversation between the conscious and the subconscious: the conscious guides and directs the correct responses to happen while the subconscious prepares itself to take over the controls.

For every movement the horse makes, the body has to define how it reacts and responds to enable the points of contact with the horse to remain consistent. This consistency of the points of contact is an important part of our communication with the horse. Finding the balance of our position is what allows it all to happen.

Coordination

The expression "having an independent seat" is used to describe the ability to move each aid independently of the others. Our communication with the horse requires us to use our aids independently. The aids must not be busy gripping to keep us secure if they are to be available as modes of communication.

To improve coordination, we should practice moving our body parts independently and improving our core stability, both on and off the horse. There are many exercises to help with this. Here are just a few examples:

- Go through the positions in the saddle without losing the balance over the foot.
- Add on some arm movements while doing the above.
- Ride with and without stirrups (or have someone longe you for this work).
- Cross your reins to help you remember to retain leg before hand.
- Riding with the reins in one hand.

The Value of Group Lessons

The value of lesson games and drill rides with other riders should not be underestimated. They are invaluable in improving;

- Rider coordination.
- Speed of reaction.
- Unselfish riding.
- Teamwork.

And they're fun!

A Word on Saddles

Balance is fundamental to our ability to communicate with our horse. Balance is certainly influenced by the saddle, although the saddle is not the only determining factor. As I've suggested earlier, an understanding of balance should come before placing ourselves into a saddle and trying to achieve balance there.

Marrying the saddle to the horse and rider is critical if balance and communication is to happen as we want it to. But this subject can be a minefield. Commercial interests raise their head the second the word "saddle" is spoken. They are very good at convincing us that the latest and greatest tack will solve all our position woes. But will it?

Let's take this question: Are dressage saddles really needed? Good dressage doesn't require a dressage saddle. It is a mistaken belief that a saddle will improve the rider's position and effectiveness. It may in some cases, but it can also have the opposite effect.

Furthermore, bad riding can often be attributed to a dressage saddle, although this can also be said of a jumping saddle. Problems with rider balance and the loss of effectiveness can lead to wrong choices being made: poles fall, horses stop, riders crash, horses have bad experiences. Problems in all disciplines can be attributed to a bad saddle, but just as often they can be attributed to poor riding or a poor fit between horse and rider. My advice is to avoid using the saddle as an excuse. You must ensure that you apply some thought to and seek good guidance on the subject.

It is worth noting that for over 40 years, I have had the same jump saddle. I have taken great care in its maintenance. It remains comfortable for me and my position. In all of my international competitions, I have also ridden in a general purpose saddle to do dressage. A fellow professional rider once said to me, "Balance and working with one's own body shape far outdoes trying to fix a position against one's natural body shape." I couldn't agree more. You should have a saddle that doesn't force you into an unnatural position but allows you to be comfortable and in balance. Remember *balance* is the goal, not position.

Saddles are expensive so don't be fooled into believing they are the one item that will make your riding better. The saddle must fit the horse comfortably and allow your own individual biomechanics to find a balance. With balance comes communication.

Jumping Position

When it comes to rider position in jumping, we know that minimal movement and a good balance support the efficiency of the partnership. So the two qualities we're after are balance and communication (fig. 9.7). Let's try and sort out some of the issues people have achieving these in their jumping position. These are issues most riders have and spend a lot of time and effort trying to correct. As you'll recall, it is difficult to deal with one issue in isolation. Most issues tend to be interrelated and need to be addressed as a package. The key is always to look for the core issue and work from there. It seldom works tinkering with the edges (or rearranging the deck chairs on the Titanic!).

Regardless of body shape and size, most people can stand on their feet. Therefore, their point of balance is the feet. Such an obvious statement, but it is often forgotten as soon as people get on a horse.

9.7 All you really need for jumping success is balance and communication.

Teaching beginners their very first lesson can be one of the most important lessons they will ever have. The muscle memory learned on day one stays with you. Done well it's a great start. If things start badly then the more the faults are practiced, the harder it is to change them. (I have said just the same earlier in the book about teaching horses!)

It's not that we will be able to "make a good position" on Day One, but you can start a bad one. What we should do is point people toward the road to finding good balance, highlighting how our body works and needs to work in order to find that balance, security, and communication that comes from a good position. Doing this at the very beginning we will identify muscles and tendons that need to be awakened and light up the neurological pathways that activate these muscles and tendons. This will help enormously in our journey.

I don't mean to make it sound very complicated, but each person has their own personal wiring. Sometimes this wiring suits the task we are doing and sometimes it doesn't. In order to readjust or readvise the brain how you want it to work, you have to be methodical in explaining what you want it to do. Conscious thought eventually leads to subconscious action.

Jumping Position Problems and Solutions

1 PROBLEM: LOWER LEG TOO FAR BACK. _ _ _ _ _ _ _ _ _ _ _ _ _ _ _ _ _

2 WHY IS THE PROBLEM THERE? A lower leg positioned too far back often goes with the upper body being too far forward.

3 WHY DOES IT NEED SOLVING? Don't try to reposition the leg because it won't stay where it's put. Go to the core issue: the function of the leg, which is to carry the rider's weight and communicate with the horse. Therefore, allow the leg to find a place underneath the rider and close to the horse.

4 HOW DO YOU SOLVE THE PROBLEM? We must separate each part of the body and find out how to manage the parts individually. Only then can we reassemble them correctly. Try this:

- Stand up in the saddle as if you were on the ground and the horse wasn't there. Don't let the heel drop more than 1 inch below the ball of the foot. To have the heel too low causes far too many problems. It locks the ankle, compromising joint flexibility, and it pushes the lower leg forward.

- Make your brain account for which muscles and tendons in the leg allow you to do this.

- Now sit down, relax, and do it again. Be conscious of how you stand up. Move the hips (the middle of your body) up and forward as you would in a rising or posting trot, keeping the lower leg still. Keep doing this and being correct. Each time your brain will have to instruct the body. This is the process of creating muscle memory.

1 PROBLEM: UPPER BODY TOO FAR FORWARD. _ _ _ _ _ _ _ _ _ _ _ _ _

2 WHY IS THE PROBLEM THERE? From the very earliest days of riding we are taught to "go forward" over a jump, sowing the seed of a terrible fault: being too far forward.

3 WHY DOES IT NEED SOLVING? There is only ever a need for the body to stay in balance over the ball of the foot and the hands to follow the contact. Nothing more.

It is difficult to retrain someone whose position is too far forward, so it's much better not to teach the mistake in the first place. The problems that can arise from an upper body position that is too far forward include:

- Excessive movement, which creates imbalance.
- Distraction of the horse.
- Knocking jumps.
- Delay of recovery after a jump, which can create knocking effects in the rest of the course.
- Safety issues on cross-country.

4 HOW DO YOU SOLVE THE PROBLEM? Stand on the ground and try to fold correctly (to stay with the horse). This action should not happen from the waist alone. There are a number of moving body parts involved. The knee and ankle joints bend, the seat goes back and down, the shoulders stay back with the head and neck looking up and forward. And you'll see that the upper body has no need to fold from the waist more than to stay over the knee.

The next action is key: Loosen at the shoulders and allow the arms to move with the contact, as the horse stretches his neck.

There are differing thoughts on the right way to release the reins over a jump, from a crest release to "toward the knees." All variables have the same intention: to allow the horse the freedom to use his head and neck while retaining a contact at the same time. This requires each part of the body to be moved with an awareness of what muscles and tendons are being used to do it correctly. It's only after a lot of slow, methodical, deliberate, and thoughtful repetition, that it will become easy and almost natural.

1 PROBLEM: BEING BEHIND THE MOVEMENT. _ _ _ _ _ _ _ _ _ _ _ _ _ _ _ _

2 WHY IS THE PROBLEM THERE? Being left behind occasionally as a result of an awkward takeoff is not a problem. It's the rider that does this every jump who needs help.

It all begins with the correct stirrup length. So let's start from there.

3 WHY DOES THE PROBLEM NEED SOLVING? Riding with too long a stirrup creates instability, which makes it difficult to stay with the movement of the horse. Riding with the lower leg pushed forward can also result in being behind the movement (fig. 9.8).

4 HOW DO YOU SOLVE THE PROBLEM? The start of the solution is to shorten your stirrups. The next step is to readjust the body's understanding of how it should react.

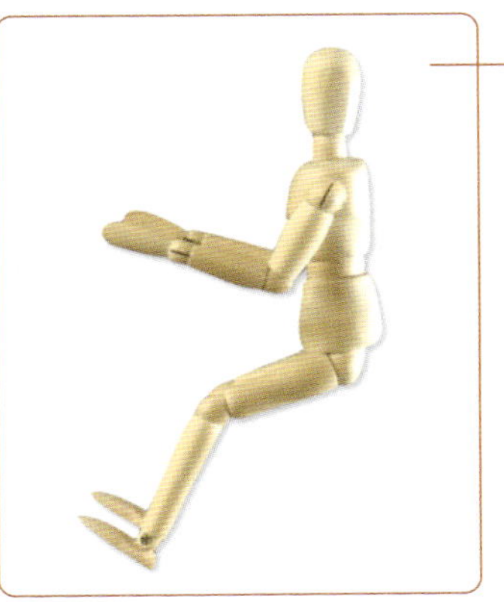

9.8 This model illustrates a position that is caught behind the movement of the horse.

Begin by shortening the stirrups one hole, later on, maybe two holes. Allow the body to find its balance while maintaining a good leg and upper body position (as described earlier in this chapter—see p. 212). Then repeat. It takes some thought to help the body conform.

1 PROBLEM: BEING IN FRONT OF THE MOVEMENT. _ _ _ _ _ _ _ _ _ _ _ _

2 WHY IS THE PROBLEM THERE? This is slightly different from the upper body being too far forward, although these problems can go hand in hand. Being in front of the movement is when the rider is ahead of the horse's actions and thoughts. It can be caused by anticipation, overthinking, or simply enthusiasm.

3 WHY DOES IT NEED SOLVING? In throwing your body into the process, you have gotten ahead of what's actually happening. I know that I have a tendency to do this.

4 HOW DO YOU SOLVE THE PROBLEM? The solution is to sit up, be patient, and trust the horse to do his job. Actively support the horse (with correct leg and upper body position and good balance) and trust in his education.

1 PROBLEM: KEEPING A CONTACT. _ _ _ _ _ _ _ _ _ _ _ _ _ _ _

2 WHY IS THE PROBLEM THERE? Being able to retain a good contact throughout the jumping process requires a balance that allows each part of the body to work independently of the other parts. This requires the correct neurological pathways to be established right from the start of learning to ride. Hands need to follow the moving part—the horse's head.

In walk it moves, in trot it stays "fairly" still, and then in canter it moves again. When jumping there can be quite a dramatic movement of the head and neck over a jump.

This movement is important for the horse in negotiating the jump clear.

3 WHY DOES IT NEED SOLVING? Dropping the contact and not following the contact can be dealt with together. They are either end of the same scale. Each is as bad as the other, although they may have different consequences.

9.9 These "wings" won't help your horse clear the jump—in fact, they can hinder his ability.

- Dropping the contact is a little like abandoning the horse, leaving him without support.
- Not to follow with the contact can restrict the movement of the horse's head and neck, thereby devaluing their use over a jump.

Hands that get "stuck" on the neck, elbows that "fly," and hands that "lift" can all be very restrictive to maintaining a good feel through the rein (fig. 9.9).

4 HOW DO YOU SOLVE THE PROBLEM? Alter the way the reins are held. Allow the reins to come through the thumb and forefinger directly from the bit. Keep the hands away from the horse's neck. It will feel strange, but you will find that the hands naturally will want to follow the head and neck movement over a jump.

For those who drop the contact, tie a knot in the reins so that they feel very short (or use reins that are very short). This will force you to take a contact farther down the reins with no space to "slip" them through your fingers. The result will be to encourage you to keep ahold of the contact.

1 PROBLEM: A HOLLOW BACK. _

2 WHY IS THE PROBLEM THERE? This is also known as the "hunter pose" (fig. 9.10). There are many who will say this cannot be listed under "positional problems." It is, after all, "only a style." I beg to differ.

3 WHY DOES IT NEED SOLVING? Just as with horses, a human body that is loose and free-moving is more athletic than one that inverts and locks. When the rider's back inverts into hunter pose, it is, firstly, an unnatural position for the human body, and secondly, it creates muscular tension in the back.

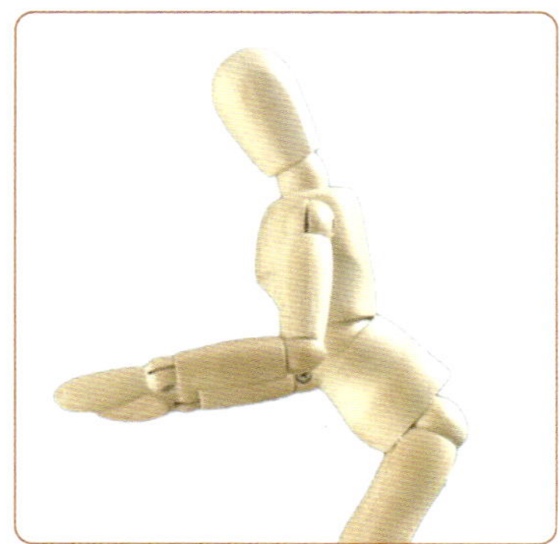

9.10 The arched back typical of the "hunter pose."

This tension can cause long-term back issues, but the position has no benefits to jumping. A "soft" back, on the other hand, does have benefits. It allows for an ease of movement of the hips and lower back as they seek to stay in balance.

4 HOW DO YOU SOLVE THE PROBLEM? Simply don't go there is too simplistic an answer, but it is a start. Don't copy trends. The good jumpers don't do it; that should tell you something.

Position problems like this often begin with how the rider sits in the middle part of the saddle. The two pelvic seat bones should be squarely on the seat of the saddle. The pelvis must not tilt forward, as this will hollow the lumber part of the spine. If the rider feels this happening, initiate this simple exercise: Sit and "rock" the pelvis backward and forward, more toward the back. Feel the lumbar region being pushed backward. Always end the exercise with it pushed back. You will feel like you are rounding your back, but you are not because your shoulders are still back. This will allow a much looser back over a jump.

1 PROBLEM: THE "CHAIR SEAT." _

2 WHY IS THE PROBLEM THERE? This is where it looks as if the rider is sitting in a chair (fig. 9.11). The weight is entirely on the rider's seat with an upright posture. The thighs are nearly horizontal, and the lower leg is forward. Riders can develop this position when they misinterpret the use of the seat.

3 WHY DOES IT NEED SOLVING? Too much *driving* from the seat is a misunderstanding of the aid.

9.11 A model depicting the "chair seat."

4 HOW DO YOU SOLVE THE PROBLEM? I tend to avoid talking about the use of the seat as an aid although I am acutely aware of its importance. I believe it is taught too soon and often erroneously ahead of the use of the leg. The seat is a subtle aid, an addition to the vocabulary in our *conversation* with the horse. It should NOT be confused with a driving thrust into the horse's back.

Is It Worth Trying to Correct Position?

Correcting positional faults can be hard, and it requires an enormous amount of focus. Better positions come from finding better balance. So we are not really striving to find better positions, per se, as that will happen by itself if we seek to achieve a better balance and communication. The benefits to doing so can be many.

There are athletes in many sports who have unique technique. In some cases, these athletes have reached the top of their profession, winning Olympic medals with the signature techniques they've developed. Nick Skelton and Michael Johnson are good examples: Both men had great balance and used their bodies efficiently (figs. 9.12 and 9.13).

While we should all try to improve our balance and communication, we should not do so to the detriment of our performance.

Watching athletes make it look easy is certainly one of my pleasures in life. It doesn't matter what sport I'm watching, I always admire the skill required to make something difficult seem effortless. Teaching it to happen is another thrill coaches get, sometimes not often enough.

In order to achieve this apparent ease of function, there is a need for core stability as well as an understanding of the damage done by unnecessary movement and loss of balance that results. Keeping unnecessary movement to a minimum requires mental and physical control. Sometimes we don't even know we are doing it, so when it is pointed out to us it

9.12 Nick Skelton, Olympic double gold medalist, and one of the greatest show jumpers of the last thirty years. He had a wonderful touch, feel, and balance, and was able to ride just about any horse with a unique style and position.

9.13 Michael Johnson was told on many occasions how unconventional his running technique was. It was stiff, upright, and his short steps defied the conventional wisdom that a high knee action was essential for maximum speed. As of 2012 Johnson held 13 of the top 100 times for the 200-meter and 27 of the top 100 times for the 400-meter.

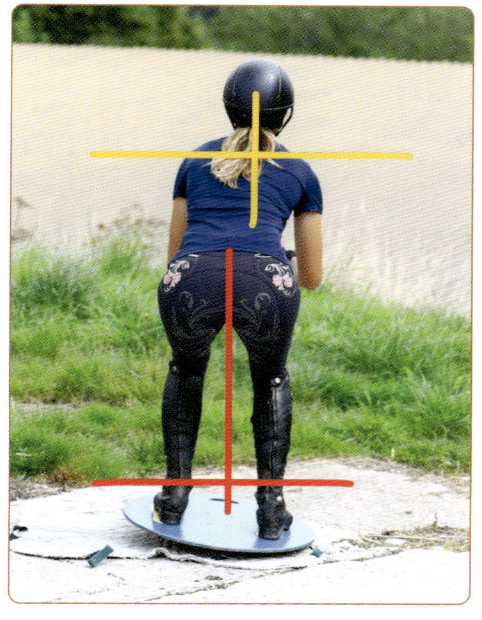

9.14 It doesn't take much sideways movement to alter a rider's balance.

can come as quite a shock (fig. 9.14). When we try and fix it, we can feel awkward and uncomfortable. We can sometimes feel less effective as riders—as if it's not even us riding the horse.

For my entire riding life I have struggled with positional issues. I know what they are and see them in pictures. I try to correct them in training, but ultimately, I find myself reverting to old habits unless I'm constantly reminding myself.

Removing unnecessary movement in our riding must in no way diminish our effectiveness. The goal is not to sit like stuffed dummies, but to awaken our body parts to move with the horse's movement. After all, we are encouraging the horse to do the same thing. A lot of the time, excess body movement comes from a belief that in some way we are helping the horse—we are not.

Good coaching ... facilitates learning.

Conclusion

T HE EXCITEMENT OF FEELING A HORSE PERFORM CANNOT BE overstated. It is truly wonderful. To have taught an animal that eats grass for a living how to perform a demi-pirouette, a shoulder-in, or even a square halt is something to savor. Equally exciting is the journey—knowing the steps and stages that need to be in place and methodically piecing them together is so rewarding.

To understand how to dismantle problems and fix them is a process we all come to appreciate as part of our journey to becoming horsemen.

A Methodical Approach

Progressive training is about the process of developing a solid base of education for a horse and building a well-reasoned series of skills and habits on that base. Each skill and habit needs to be taught patiently and with a plan of how it relates to the other pieces of the overall picture. It is much like doing a jigsaw puzzle where each piece links to the others and secures its neighboring pieces. The finished picture is a series of smaller components, in themselves important parts to be done correctly, as only with each part being constructed correctly can the whole picture be correct.

This methodical approach to the training of the horse is idealistic, I know. But we should strive to emulate the intention. At the same time I acknowledge that life doesn't always work that way. So as riders and coaches we need to know how and where each part of the picture fits and works so we are able to go back to where things stopped working (find a start point) and begin to rebuild in a better way.

I started this book to help people dismantle problems. Being able to look at and watch the horse and understand how he functions naturally, in his own world is a good place to start. We are, after all, only trying to reproduce these natural qualities in our work. Knowing where to start and where we want to go allows us to make a plan. This plan must have logic and make sense to both horse and rider, otherwise misunderstandings occur. My plan has been to take you through the route that we ride: Legs—hindquarters—back—poll—jaw—bit—hand. It's how we learn to put the horse between leg and hand with contact and connection to present a consistent picture. Knowing as we go along this road to produce the best outcome we can that we will make mistakes and inherit others, we should also keep in mind that we know how to correct them—because we have some idea where they came from and how to dismantle them before we move forward again.

All along we must use the appropriate language, not only for the horse, but with the humans involved. My profession is guilty of overcomplicating things, by assuming understanding, by attempting to sound knowledgeable, by trying to work above the level of the student. The security of our training base comes from true understanding and an ability to retrieve the information, to retrace our steps, correct what is wrong, and move on. Language must be clear to allow everyone to grasp our full meaning. I try very hard to be clear when I teach and worry over it when I write. There are some words that need to be used with care, thought, and precision or the message may get lost in translation. To alter these words or use them inaccurately perpetuates confusion among riders. This is not helpful when we are trying to communicate with an animal that needs a clarity of input and consistency of message to perform at his best.

Every coach has his own communication strengths. Coaches create interest and engagement with a variety of students by developing their own style. Sometimes, this allows students to hear a message in a new way that resonates with them and improves their uptake. But for the good of the partnership between horse and rider, the core message and words must never change.

*Enjoy the journey of
becoming a better horseman.*

Appendix

When I started thinking about this book, I asked a good friend of mine if he would like to make a contribution. To my delight, he said, "Yes." We discussed what I wanted him to write about (some veterinary comment on certain topics I have discussed in these pages), and off he went to have a think.

When he sent me what he had written I was absolutely overwhelmed and delighted with the result—way over and above what I had asked for or even needed.

I have decided to include it in its entirety because it is such an endorsement of all that I aspire to be in my equestrian life and have tried convey in my teaching.

—ERIC SMILEY

A Veternarian's Perspective

By John Killingbeck. BSc, BVM&S CertEP MRCVS

HORSE OWNERSHIP AND EQUESTRIAN SPORTS ARE UNDER EVER-increasing economic pressure because the financial rewards are not commensurate with the hard work necessary to produce young horses or to host equestrian competitions.

Without generous sponsors and owners and an army of hardworking volunteers, it is doubtful if there would be a viable industry.

The domino effect for the young horse is the understandable tendency to rush to sale or to compete very young horses to recover production costs.

To understand how this might adversely affect a young horse, it is important to understand how the horse has arrived in the twenty-first century.

The earliest known ancestor of the horse, *Eohippus* ("The Dawn Horse"), is believed to have existed 55 million years ago. This was a small, free-roaming, gregarious animal who lived in mixed herds with males fighting for mating rights and herd dynamics controlled by dominant females. Man's influence on this timescale is minimal. At the most it is only 6,000 years since man hunted horses for food or tamed wild horses for transport. The significance of this statistic is that 6,000 years is too little time to change what evolution has created. The modern horse is, therefore, physiologically, metabolically, psychologically, and in many ways, anatomically unchanged from its early ancestors hundreds of thousands of years ago. The influence that man has been able to affect is selecting for size, speed, and athleticism to create the "modern horse" for transport, for war, and now, for sport. But at what cost?

It is well known that racing speeds and race times have changed little if any in several generations.

Similarly, conception rates are little changed other than we can now breed from mares and stallions that have such low fertility that without significant veterinary input they would not be able to produce foals. Are we perpetuating extreme athleticism and infertility for commercial gain but weakening the natural evolved qualities of the horse? Are we improving what evolution has created or are we testing it to destruction?

Management

The question I often ask young riders is: "How much time do you spend riding your horse each day?" An average answer is one hour. The next question is, "How much of your interest, effort, and acquisition of knowledge is targeted at the remaining 23 hours of each day?" The common answer? "Very little. My groom does all that."

To a naturally gregarious, free-roaming animal, a stable might be compared to solitary confinement for a human being. The stable environment can have an enormous influence on the horse's mental well-being and general health. The air quality, bed hygiene, feeding regimens, and the ability to move freely are influential. Would you like to eat, drink, and sleep in your lavatory? If stabled, your horse does for 23 out of every 24 hours!

Success starts in the stable, like a racing driver whose success starts, not on the racetrack, but in the garage. A successful racing driver needs to understand how his car works. The more you know the better able you are to take care of your horse and the better prepared your young horse will be to compete and to stay healthy and sound.

It is a sad truth that many horse owners derive much of their knowledge from those who are selling them services, feedstuffs, drugs, and equipment.

If you do not understand how your horse's digestive system works, how can you know that you are feeding correctly? Do wild horses suffer from colic, azoturia, and laminitis? These are management diseases that threaten performance and life itself.

If you do not understand how the equine respiratory system works, it is difficult to know if the environment in which you keep your horse compromises his health.

If you have no knowledge of anatomy and mechanics, you are less likely to recognize if your training methods might jeopardize your horse's soundness. It will also be more diffi-cult to recognize minor injuries, and you might then compete too soon and exacerbate a minor injury into a more serious problem.

Basic Training

In my experience, there are many problems for which a veterinary solution is sought which are, in reality, "production problems," and to understand the source of many of these prob-lems, we need to examine the early management of the young horse.

Horses are slow maturing and do not achieve full maturity and strength until eight or even nine years of age, but many are competing regularly from the age of four years, the only qualification being they are of the "appropriate age."

Stressing immature bones and joints compromises long-term soundness and jeopardizes a competition career. (Similar problems are well-recognized in young human athletes, such as gymnasts.) Achieving skeletal maturity is critical to maintaining long-term soundness. The growth plates in the neck vertebrae, for example, do not close until eight years of age, but these are stressed long before maturity. The neck is crucial to performance. (I will talk about this again later.)

Young horses are like young people: They develop at different rates, but even the slow developers have the potential to achieve the same level of performance as the precocious ones, given *time*. Time, however, is a factor that is often in short supply, and many horses fail to perform to expectation or potential because they are rushed. Temperament issues and resistance to training can be and often are due to the young horse lacking the necessary core strength and balance to respond to the rider's demands. Along with this difficulty is the concurrent risk of repetitive strain injury, usually to tendons and ligaments. Once these structures are damaged, they never return to full normality.

It is now widely recognized in human academic circles that short lectures and short presentations are better assimilated by students than the traditional long lectures. Horses are no different. Schooling and drilling young horses until they are submissive is little more than bullying. Traditional hacking or trail riding outside the arena encourages young horses to go forward and face the unknown bravely. While, there are good reasons why hacking is less practical, and in some cases, impossible, in the modern world, trudging round and around a riding ring rarely achieves the same benefits, and in my experience, encourages injury.

It is not widely recognized that young horses learn while on vacation. By that I mean giving a young horse a break from training—and it need only be a few days—often allows them to assimilate what the rider is trying to achieve. Sadly, many believe it is a mistake to give a young horse a break because it will result in the horse "going backward." In my experience, such thinking is outdated and untrue.

The All-Weather Surface

Many competitive owners and riders now have all-weather surfaces for training purposes because it facilitates training during inclement weather or when the local road or trail conditions are unsafe for riding. In some cases, the all-weather surface may be the only safe place for exercise and training, but this often leads to overuse, which I have found has the potential to cause soft tissue injuries. Many such injuries were unknown 20 years ago but are now commonplace. Another potential risk to exclusive exercise on an all-weather arena is that it fails to encourage the young horse to go forward as bravely as other exercise scenarios might and occasionally leads to temperament issues, particularly in the older horse who has become bored with constantly turning around corners.

To understand why overuse of an artificial surface risks injury, it is necessary to consider the mechanics of the lower limbs. I stress the *lower limbs* because most soft tissue injuries—in fact, most common lameness—occurs in the lower limbs, and particularly the lower forelimbs. Soft tissues such as tendons, ligaments, and muscles function by stretch and elastic recoil, rather like a rubber band. Similarly, the weight-bearing hoof compresses and recoils. These actions can be likened to a bouncing ball. When a ball strikes a hard surface, such as the ground or a racket, it compresses before bouncing back under natural recoil. However, if you bounce your tennis ball on your all-weather arena, it does not bounce. In the same way the natural function of the horse's lower limb and hoof can be compromised on the all-weather surface. Blood circulation through the hoof relies on this compression and relaxation, and it may also be compromised if the only surface the horse works on is artificial.

It must be stressed that I am referring to exclusive and overuse of all-weather services. However, many coaches and course builders have told me over the years that even after just one day working on an all-weather surface, their legs are more tired than when doing the same job on a grass surface. And many types of horses—from racehorses to show jumpers—perform better on grass than on artificial surfaces if they are carrying old lower limb ligament injuries.

Conformation, the Hoof, and Farriery

Conformation is often overlooked when purchasing or training the young horse. Ability, technique, and movement take priority, but if conformation is weak, injury is always on the horizon. If one recognizes these weaknesses and allows the horse to mature physically before he is put under pressure, these weaknesses in conformation become less of a risk. Good conformation is simply the proportion of long bones and angles of joints that experience has proved to be more often associated with long-term soundness and athleticism. It is an important component of horsemanship and is not difficult to master.

A common mistake is to believe that a novice seven-year-old has little commercial value because the horse has too little experience in the competition world.

Better a sound, confident, inexperienced seven-year-old than an eight- or nine-year-old that needs his joints medicated every six months.

Low-grade bilateral hoof pain is a common cause of impaired performance and unrecognized lameness. Such horses may not look overtly lame because it is not possible for a horse to limp on two limbs in the same stride. Many forelimb lamenesses are misdiagnosed as hindlimb lamenesses because the hindlimbs adopt an abnormal swing phase to avoid over-reaching onto the forelimbs, which have a shortened stride length because of discomfort.

This unrecognized lameness may be due to less-than-ideal farriery, a weak hoof capsule, flat soles, or under-run and collapsed heels. Such poor hoof conformation is often permanent and has its origins in the neglect of the young horse's feet.

It is very common to see young horses with neglected and untrimmed hooves. This may not be a problem if the horse has strong, perfectly conformed hooves, but few are born perfect. Not trimming the young hoof and failing to maintain a good shape will often build up problems for the farrier in later life and may never be corrected. If the hoof becomes misshapen because the heels have collapsed and are under-run, you will never restore that hoof to normal conformation.

Many horses with less-than-perfect feet are sound and comfortable in a straight line, but when turning, torque is added to the loading stresses, and they can become uncomfortable if not obviously lame. "My horse goes better one way than the other," is a common complaint. Check his feet: Are they well-balanced? Are the walls flared? Are the heels weak? That may be the source of your training problem.

Most riders entrust hoof care solely to the farrier and have no real interest in developing their own knowledge. This is, I believe, a serious mistake. If you are not familiar with "normal" it will be more difficult to recognize developing problems, and you will be less able to avoid potential soundness issues.

Correction of a misshaped hoof is a slow process because the hoof must grow to a better shape; that takes time and there are no shortcuts. Many horses with bad feet are perfectly sound, but if something happens to compromise soundness, that same horse might be lame for many weeks.

Understanding good and normal hoof anatomy is fundamental to proper horsemanship. Remember, success starts at home in the stable. Remember also that the majority of such problems have their origin in the neglect of the young, unshod horse.

Few understand why the front and hind feet are a different shape. Hoof horn grows from the coronet and from the surface of the laminae, which are attached to the periphery of the coffin (pedal) bones. The coffin bones—and to a certain extent, the coronets—act as templates for hoof shape, and the front and hind coffin bones are a different shape.

However deformed the hoof might be, the coffin bone remains unchanged so the template is still normal, and therefore, many flared and deformed hoof capsules can be restored to normal. Unfortunately, the coffin bones do not extend into the heels so once they are deformed or collapsed, you will not be able to effect much change. It is important to appreciate that major blood vessels, ligaments, and tendons are located in the heels, and if these structures, particularly the arteries, are crushed, blood supply is impaired and the health of the whole hoof might be compromised. "No hoof, no horse" is still a truism.

A worthwhile exercise when your farrier is present is to trot your horse on a good level hard surface and assess the horse's gait, then repeat after removing the shoes.

At least 75 percent of all horses, if they have reasonably good feet, will move appreciably more freely barefoot than when shod, even a dishing action is often reduced. You should ask yourself, "Why?"

Fitness and Conditioning

"Fit and strong" is a concept that is rarely understood, particularly among event horses. Because eventing is a multi-discipline sport, it does not demand the ultimate athleticism and ability demanded by a single discipline.

Eventing does, however, impose huge demands on the horse's soundness, his training, and his willingness to compete. The biggest scariest cross-country jump requires modest athleticism compared to jumping 1.60-meter show jumps or galloping down to Becher's Brook (a famous fence in The Grand National race). This results in many riders and horses, particularly at the lower levels, competing successfully with poorly prepared horses.

Many riders believe that a fit horse is a lean horse, and in many ways it can be, but if that horse is fully fit with better muscular development, he will be better prepared to compete, particularly at the higher levels when in eventing, the horse has to show jump after a strenuous cross-country effort. No one would expect a runner in the Cheltenham Gold Cup to come out at the next day and pass a veterinary inspection and go show jumping.

Strength comes with maturity, and as maturity is not achieved until eight or nine years of age, strength is often lacking in the younger horses, even if they are fit.

With this maturity comes the necessary strength to maintain balance. Without balance, fatigue becomes a greater risk, and with fatigue comes the potential for injury. This risk is greatest in the big-moving horses that are often unable to maintain extravagant movement until they are mature.

Which part of the horse becomes tired first when the horse is working hard?

The neck.

Not the legs or the back, and not the hindquarters (but maybe the rider!).

The horse's head is a heavy weight at the end of a long lever. Most importantly, the young horse needs to move his neck in order to maintain balance, much like a man on a tightrope uses a pole.

A common mistake is made when riders fix the horse into an outline to place the head and neck in the "ideal position" with draw-reins or side-reins, and then work the horse into that outline. Such an approach is rarely beneficial and often negatively affects the horse's ability to build strength and flexibility. Horses that have been worked in this way are often easily identified by the lack of muscle at the base of the neck and behind the saddle. Such horses often suffer sore backs because they lack adequate muscle development and have restricted movement.

A new "modern" disease is kissing spines where adjacent dorsal spinous processes impinge one on another. Inappropriate training, poor muscle development, and restricting the horse's natural movement commonly lead to a horse requiring back surgery that might otherwise have been avoided.

Many espouse the opinion that too much muscle development creates excess weight for the horse to carry. This argument loses credibility when one understands what happens as the horse becomes fitter. With time and training, heart muscle and skeletal muscles enlarge, but more importantly, they become more efficient. The metabolic processes that produce energy for work and remove waste products also do so more efficiently with increasing fitness.

This increased efficiency occurs at a cellular level, which allows muscles to work more efficiently and recover more quickly. Within reasonable limits, therefore, the more muscle one has the easier work is performed and the quicker muscles will recover. Lungs, on the other hand, show very little adaptation—they do not increase in size or capacity. Any increase in efficiency of oxygen consumption and utilization occurs mainly in muscle cells.

A fit horse will produce energy by aerobic metabolism, which essentially only produces carbon dioxide and water as waste products, but the unfit or tired horse is likely to produce more complex waste products, such as lactic acid, and these are more difficult to remove from the muscles and so cause the muscles to fatigue more quickly. This can be critical in eventing when the horse show jumps after cross-country. In that scenario, the horse may appear sound and comfortable, but muscle function and elasticity will be compromised and show jumping faults are likely to be higher.

Feed and Nutrition

Feeding and nutrition is a massive subject often poorly understood by owners who may be vulnerable to the advertising of endorsed products. Endorsement by a leading rider may simply mean that the rider has been given free samples and not necessarily that their own research has led them to using these products. The horse's digestive system is simple and unchanged in hundreds of thousands of years. The small intestine, where complex food stuffs are broken down and absorbed, is short and only comprises about 25 percent of the digestive tract. The large intestine, on the other hand, comprises about 65 percent of the system, and this is where the bulk of digestion by bacterial fermentation is undertaken. This fermentation processes produce many essential nutrients from the simplest fiber ingredients, such as hay or grass. The early days of training and even light competition can be accomplished on a simple fiber-based diet. Feeding complex foods, such as proteins, sugars, and starches are often an unnecessary waste of money and a potential for digestive upsets.

If too many complex nutrients pass undigested from the acid environment of the small intestine into the alkaline environment of the large intestine the natural balance of the digesting bacteria in the large intestine become disturbed. This disturbance is often the starting point for colic, laminitis, azoturia, and other life-threatening problems. Many owners believe or are advised by their feed merchant that a "feed balancer" is necessary when feeding a simple fiber-based diet. What are they balancing? If a balancer is necessary, something by definition must be unbalanced. I remain to be convinced. The bacteria in the large intestine will produce many of the essential nutrients not found in simple fiber products.

Feeding practices can and do influence temperament and excitability. Too much soluble carbohydrate in the diet can lead to an excitable temperament, and I have experienced horses fed preserved grass products that became very excitable, and I always likened it to feeding small children too many fizzy drinks and too much chocolate. There are extremely good reasons for feeding such products, but if your horse has an excitable temperament to start, you may be better to stick with traditional hay.

Equine gastric ulceration syndrome (EGUS) is now widely recognized as a performance-limiting problem, but in most cases, the primary cause is inappropriate feeding practices and management. The evolved digestive tract expects a continuous input of a high fiber diet for 16 to 17 hours each day.

Stress is the underlying cause of EGUS, and this comes in many forms, a number of which are normal management practices. Even traveling from home to a competition may precipitate an episode, and it is good practice to treat a nervous horse with an acid suppressant when he is going to travel away from home for several days.

Veterinary Treatments

The most experienced and knowledgeable veterinarian is unable to improve what evolution has created. Evolution and natural selection have a significant head start: Weak and unsound individuals fell victim to predators, leaving only the strong and sound to produce the next generation. In many ways, modern breeding selects for unsoundness, and we all know of mares who retire to stud following injury. If injury was preceded by a long and illustrious career, all well and good, but this is not often the case.

Prevention rather than treatment should be the objective when producing the young horse. If a tendon or joint surface is damaged it may heal and the horse may return to the previous level of athletic performance, but the effected structure will not return to pre-injury normal. Soft tissues repair by laying down scar tissue, which has reduced elasticity, reduced mechanical strength, and reduced blood supply compared to normal tissue.

Joint treatments have become extremely fashionable, even for horses that have not reached physical maturity under the very misguided mantra, "I need to maintain his joints." Even more reprehensible is the fact that many such treatments are given without any diagnostic investigation. Joint treatment essentially suppresses the inflammatory process that injury has caused, but they do not effect a true cure. Except for problems such as osteochondrosis (OCD), few horses are born with defective joints. They may be born with weak conformation that predisposes to injury, but in most cases, it is the over-stressing of immature joints that must be recognized and avoided.

There are many treatments available to the veterinarian, but with the exception of corticosteroids, many have now been abandoned by human orthopedic specialists, who one might reasonably conclude have more reliable feedback from their patients than we do from horses.

Corticosteroid use is never without the risk of inducing laminitis. There are now several high-profile and eye-wateringly expensive legal cases involving the treatment of horses that foundered after administration of corticosteroids. In most cases the legal challenge arose because treatment was not preceded by any diagnostic investigation. In some European countries, it is illegal to treat animal's joints without the appropriate investigation.

Prevention should be the aim when producing young horses, particularly when one recognizes that most treatments are a "patch up," not a cure, and many treatments carry a high risk of disastrous side effects.

Conclusion

Knowledge is key, and an understanding of basic conformation and function is fundamental to good horsemanship. Evolution has created an equine athlete that man has been unable to improve without compromising what time has created. Prevention is always better than an imperfect cure because sound horses invariably outperform patched-up horses. There are no risk-free shortcuts, and many of those in common use can compromise welfare.

JOHN KILLINGBECK has more than 46 years experience in equine practice. He holds the RCVS certificate in Equine Practice and has a particular interest in competition horses, with a special emphasis on orthopedics and lameness. He has traveled extensively around the world with a number of national event teams to four Olympic Games and several European and World Championships, winning over 20 gold medals between them, and was the Official Veterinary Surgeon to the British Three-Day Event Team from 1992 to 1997.

John now acts as an FEI Veterinary Delegate at several international competitions each year. His knowledge and experience of lameness diagnosis, and in particular, foot problems, is widely recognized. John is an examiner for the Worshipful Company of Farriers and has also acted as an examiner for the RCVS. He lectures on a regular basis at the Royal Agricultural College in Cirencester and contributes to various equestrian publications.

Eric Smiley on Enterprise by Carrie Green

Acknowledgments

This will go down as one of the many "COVID books," written when in lockdown with an active mind and keen to put it to some use. As always, I am grateful to Martha Cook and Rebecca Didier at Trafalgar Square Books for giving me the confidence to "go again" in the airing of my thoughts.

To Kate Adams who stuck with me through the editing process—thank you for your patience.

And thank you to the many friends on both sides of the Atlantic and in Denmark who have supported me as my journey with horses continues to evolve.

Thank you also to:

My riders.

Emily, who yet again put life in my diagrams.

Penelope Daukes, for making me smile with all her cartoons.

Katja Schumann, for allowing me to delve into another world of training horses.

Susanne Colloredo-Mansfeld and Annie Penfield. The debt of gratitude to this family is simply beyond measure.

Lynnleigh Farm: To Robin and Darcy Sundeen for introducing me to their life.

Carrie Green: a gifted artist who brought life to a picture of me riding Enterprise on the facing page.

Thank you to Joanna Dillon of Equipe Saddles.

Diagrams by:
  Emily Secrett-Hill
Cartoons by:
  Penelope Daukes

Photography by:
  Maria Sage
  Irina Kuzmina
  Orla Murphy LaScola
  Aimi Clark
  Janeric Dahlin
  Chris Dundee
  Horse & Hound Magazine
  Venkat Narayanan

Riders:
  Layla Felgate
  Sarah Gillard
  David Taylor
  Camilla Albery
  Lizzel Winter

Index